An American Trade Strategy

An American Trade Strategy

Options for the 1990s

ROBERT Z. LAWRENCE

CHARLES L. SCHULTZE

editors

The Brookings Institution
Washington, D.C.

Copyright © 1990 by

THE BROOKINGS INSTITUTION

1775 Massachusetts Avenue, N.W., Washington, D.C. 20036

Library of Congress Cataloging-in-Publication data

An American trade strategy : options for the 1990s / Robert Z.
  Lawrence and Charles L. Schultze, editors.
     p.   cm.
  Includes bibliographical references and index.
     ISBN 0-8157-5180-X (alk. paper) : — ISBN 0-8157-5179-6
  (pbk. : alk. paper) :
     1. United States—Commercial policy.   2. Free trade—United
  States.   3. Protectionism—United States.   I. Lawrence,
  Robert Z.   II. Schultze, Charles L.
  HF1455.A72   1990
382'.3'0973—dc20   90-42576
                                                            CIP

9 8 7 6 5 4 3 2 1

Foreword

FOR THE FOUR DECADES after the Second World War, the United States took the lead in promoting a liberalization of world trade and the negotiation of multilateral agreements establishing the 'rules of the game' for that trade. Industries subject to stiff foreign competition sometimes managed to secure trade protection of one kind or another, but political leaders and academics widely accepted multilateral free trade as the basic principle of American policy.

Recently that principle has come under increasing attack, and not just from representatives of older industries trying to ward off low-wage competition from abroad. The large American trade deficits of the 1980s, the inroads into domestic and third world markets by Japan and other industrial countries, and fears for the future competitiveness of American high-technology industries have produced mounting pressure in Congress for a more aggressive government policy to promote American trade and retaliate against countries whose practices are termed unfair. On the academic scene, many economists have developed new theories or refined existing ones that explain how, at least in concept, a nation can enrich itself by using activist trade policies to expand the market share of its high-technology industries. In addition, the United States has concluded bilateral free trade agreements with Israel and Canada and is actively considering others.

Defenders of the traditional approach have not been silent, however. The Reagan and Bush administrations and many professional economists have repeatedly warned of the economic costs and political dangers likely to ensue if multilateral negotiations and free trade principles are abandoned in favor of aggressive, bilateral, and highly interventionist trade policies.

Given this ferment in the public debate about the future direction of American trade policy, the Brookings Institution, in September 1989, held a research conference entitled An American Trade Strategy: Options for the 1990s. Three principal papers were presented at the conference, each defending an alternative policy approach: multilateral free trade, aggressive bilateralism, and managed trade. This book contains revised versions of these three papers, together with the remarks of the official commentators on each paper and the comments of a panel of three experts who, in the final session of the conference, reflected on the discussion and its implications for American policy. The book also includes two introductory chapters in which the editors, Robert Z. Lawrence, senior fellow in the Brookings Economic Studies program, and Charles L. Schultze, director of the program, evaluate the alternative strategies and summarize the papers and the discussion.

The editors are grateful to Jagdish N. Bhagwati, Paul R. Krugman, and Sylvia Ostry for valuable comments. Theresa B. Walker edited the manuscript, Pamela Plehn verified it, and Susan L. Woollen prepared it for typesetting. Brookings gratefully acknowledges financial assistance for this project from the Alfred P. Sloan Foundation and the Alex C. Walker Educational and Charitable Foundation.

The views expressed here are those of the authors and should not be attributed to the trustees, officers, or other staff members of the Brookings Institution.

BRUCE K. MAC LAURY
President

July 1990
Washington, D.C.

Contents

An American Trade Strategy

Evaluating the Options

Robert Z. Lawrence
and Charles L. Schultze

DURING THE FIRST four decades after the Second World War, the U.S. government and a clear working majority of both political parties espoused an international economic policy whose principal component was the promotion of a regime of multilateral free trade. It was widely agreed that trade among sovereign nations should be conducted with the minimum of tariff or other economic barriers and that the rules of the game should be developed in an international forum, the General Agreement on Tariffs and Trade (GATT). Practice did not always live up to principle. Industries beleaguered by stiff foreign competition sometimes managed to secure protection of one kind or another; and governments were not above providing subsidies or other aids to favored export industries. Nevertheless, through most of the period, practice was as close to principle as it was in other areas of public life.

Over the years, periodic rounds of multilateral negotiations succeeded in greatly reducing the protection inherited from earlier periods. Importantly, in the United States there was fairly broad agreement not only that the principle of multilateral free trade was a desirable one but that it was also at least approximately achievable in practice. The legislative battles were waged over securing exceptions to the principle rather than over its legitimacy. In economic theory, agreement that a regime of multilateral free trade was the best approach for promoting economic welfare was so universal as to be almost a prerequisite for membership in the association of professional economists.[1]

---

1. Of course, during this period international trade economists were developing theorems and arguments about the possible conditions under which a nation's welfare might, or might not, be improved by infant industry protection, by optimal tariffs, by regional customs unions, and the like. Nevertheless, on a broad combination of theoretical, practical, and political grounds, most Western economists strongly advocated a system of multilateral free trade as the most desirable overall regime for international trade, certainly among developed countries.

1

No longer. Times have changed. An increasing number of politicians, especially Democratic members of Congress, numerous business executives, and even some former trade officials of the Reagan administration, while still giving lip service to the potential advantages of multilateral free trade in an ideal world, have come to view the real world as one in which the machinations of other governments, or the particular economic structure of some countries (read, Japan), have rendered the principle unachievable in practice. Further, it is argued, continued pursuit of that unachievable ideal by the United States harms its economic interests and, in particular, leaves some of the most essential and dynamic U.S. industries vulnerable to erosion and incursion by foreign firms whose societies do not play by the rules of free trade.

Simultaneously, back in academe, some highly respected economists have been developing new concepts of international trade that provide a possible, theoretical rationale for active intervention by government to pursue a "strategic trade policy," benefiting its own citizens at the expense of other countries. Unlike classical trade analysis, these theories apply to a world in which there are sometimes large gains from "getting there fustest with the mostest," especially with specialized, high-technology products. If one or a few firms can gain a foothold in a new market, through protection at home and favorable credit terms or subsidies for expansion, they may then be able to take advantage of economies of large-scale production and gain a sizable share of the world market. They can, for a significant period of time, exploit the market to earn high incomes to be split among workers and owners.

In a related vein, some other academics have argued that the electronics and other strategic, high-technology industries produce knowledge and technological advance critical to the expansion of technology and productivity in this country. The expansion of those industries should be promoted by the federal government, and they should be protected against the policies of other countries who are seeking the dominance of their own strategic industries in world markets.

The Sources of Dissatisfaction
with Free Trade

Traditionally, the main political threats to free trade have arisen because of a fear of loss of jobs. The infamous Smoot-Hawley tariff was passed during the early stages of the Great Depression. And in the first truly deep recession of the postwar years, 1974–75, the Organization for

Economic Cooperation Development (OECD) felt it urgent to get a pledge of no new trade restrictions from its member governments. Fears of job loss in weak and declining industries threatened with increased competition from abroad have long been the main source of selective pressures for protection during periods of prosperity. But while today's currents of dissatisfaction with a policy of multilateral free trade have many roots, they now seem to stem from new sources and to call for types of government intervention different from the older forms of protection.

For more than seven years now, job growth in the United States has been good, and the unemployment rate has been steadily pushed down to low levels. Today's dissatisfactions arise not so much from fear of unemployment as from a growing concern about the stagnant growth of real wages and incomes in the United States, the availability of "good jobs at good wages," and an identification of that problem largely with international pressures on the U.S. economy. Correspondingly, the pressure on government has been not only to protect older, declining industries but to push aggressively for a wider opening of foreign markets to American exports and to insulate newer, high-technology, U.S. industries from real or alleged predatory practices of industries in other countries.

American productivity growth slowed sharply after 1973 and recovered only a little of that loss in subsequent years. The slowdown in productivity growth together with a sharp run-up in oil prices—which in real terms are still well above their pre-1973 levels—virtually halted the growth in the real wage of the average American worker over the past fifteen years. Moreover, the slowdown was not evenly distributed. In particular, younger, adult, male workers with a high school education or less have done especially poorly; their real wage in recent years has been well below what it was in the early 1970s. In earlier decades these principally blue-collar workers benefited from relatively high wages in the tradable-goods manufacturing industries. Recent research has shown that much of the decline in the relative wages of unskilled or semiskilled workers was not because of the disappearance of high-paying manufacturing jobs and their replacement with low-paying service jobs, but rather because of an almost universal decline in the relative wages of unskilled and semiskilled workers in all industries. Nevertheless, the widespread belief persists that the problem of lagging real wages, especially among blue-collar workers, is because of the disappearance of "good" manufacturing jobs.

Coincident with the developments that produced a stagnation of real wage growth were several other developments that tended to single out the international trade sector of the economy as the problem area. With the overseas value of the dollar rising sharply after 1982, the United States began to run a large and mounting trade deficit; imports swelled and exports stagnated. Although the dollar reached a peak in 1985 and the trade deficit, after some delay, declined, that deficit remains huge by earlier standards. And within that overall picture the bilateral trade deficit of the United States with Japan stands out sharply. In 1989 the trade deficit with Japan was $49 billion, and even that deficit was held down by the U.S. surplus of agricultural trade; in manufacturing the trade deficit with Japan stood at $66 billion, virtually undiminished from its peak in 1987. Partly because of this fact, partly because Japan has been so successful at displacing highly visible American goods—in traditional industries such as automobiles and consumer electronics and in the newer industries such as semiconductors—and partly because Japan imports a smaller share of manufactured goods consumption than any other advanced country, it has become a particular focus of the dissatisfaction.

At a popular level, concern began to grow that American goods were being frozen out of many foreign markets. At a more analytic level even some academic economists became fearful that barriers to imports in other countries, especially Japan, would require the United States to undergo an excessive depreciation of the dollar and a consequent unwarranted lowering of living standards in order to balance its international accounts. A more desirable outcome, involving a smaller depreciation of the dollar, would be a wider opening of Japanese markets to imported goods.

Another trend, parallel with these developments, reinforced the feeling among a number of influential people that U.S. trade policy needed serious changes. In the earlier postwar decades the United States was the unchallenged technological leader of the world. But as the countries of Europe and Japan, and later the dynamic smaller countries around the Asian rim, began to close the technological gap—most of them devoting large shares of their national income to gap-closing investments in modern plant and equipment—the technological edge began to narrow, and in many sectors to disappear. Never mind that the recovery of Europe and Japan, and the rapid growth of other smaller countries had long been a prime objective of farsighted American policy. The hard fact was that many Americans began to sense a big slippage in

American competitiveness and to believe the nation needed a more activist government policy to compete successfully in the world market and more generally to keep American industry from falling behind in the creation and adoption of modern technology.

While all of this ferment was going on, the defenders of traditional trade policy were not silent. The Reagan administration yielded on several occasions to political pressures for protection, usually of the traditional kind to help older industries such as steel or autos, but occasionally of the newer variety to protect high-technology industries such as semiconductors. And some members of the Reagan and Bush administrations made it clear they had joined the camp of those calling for more fundamental changes in trade policy. Nevertheless, despite the slips and the intramural debates, the two administrations tried hard to hew to the traditional American policy of multilateral free trade and vigorously fought against congressional efforts during the last several years to impose a shift in the trade policy stance.

Academic defenders of multilateral free trade have not been wanting in numbers or in articles critical of the new strategic trade theories. The criticisms did not so much dispute the theoretical possibility that carefully calibrated government trade intervention might, in certain circumstance, bring gains to the United States, but principally argued that the potential gains were small; that intervening in a productive way would pose impossible information requirements; and that political pressures would convert an initially well-meaning intervention policy into a boondoggle for special interests.

These political, economic, and intellectual developments have combined to bring national trade policy to the political forefront in a way it has not been for many years. The legislative result of this ferment was the Omnibus Trade Act of 1988, a compromise among the many viewpoints. Its most noted innovation, Super 301, straddles the issue. It provides a mechanism through which U.S. trade negotiators can threaten the eventual imposition of special surcharges on a country's imports if that country does not agree to modify its "unfair" trade practices (as unilaterally defined by the United States), but gives the president great flexibility in determining whether or how far to apply the sanctions. Enactment of this legislation has not settled the issue. If the growth of American productivity and real wages remains low, and, as is likely, the U.S. trade deficit and bilateral deficit with Japan remain high, trade policy will continue to be at the forefront of the political dialogue.

The papers and discussion in this volume represent an effort to organize and present, in a relatively brief and accessible form, the main economic and political arguments about American trade policy. Each of the three main papers sets forth and defends one of the three main lines of thinking that can be distinguished in the current debate. Anne O. Krueger presents the case that the United States should continue to espouse a policy of multilateral free trade. She argues that the United States should deal with the problems and shortcomings of the current world trading system not by abandoning it for something new but through a vigorous campaign to open markets further in the ongoing multilateral negotiations under the GATT.

Rudiger W. Dornbusch describes and defends a policy of aggressive bilateralism. He diagnoses America's trade problems as stemming principally from formal and informal barriers to American imports in several foreign countries, especially Japan, the consequence of which is to force down the value of the dollar and depress American real wages and living standards. He proposes to meet this problem in two ways: set numerical targets for American imports into Japan (or any other country with unreasonably low imports), using sanctions like those provided in Super 301 as a threat to induce the offending country to meet the targets; and negotiate free trade areas with other countries, as the United States has done recently with Israel and Canada.

Laura D'Andrea Tyson offers quite a different version of a new U.S. approach to international trade. Essentially she argues that the United States needs a government policy that, in contrast to current laissez-faire attitudes, actively promotes the development of high-technology industries. The rapid development of those industries sets in motion, she believes, forces that indirectly strongly benefit the rest of the American economy. Especially because other governments actively support their high-technology industries in carving out a share in world markets, the United States cannot afford to leave their development to market forces alone. As part of a broader effort to foster development of its high-technology industries, the United States needs a new policy of managed trade that would recognize this imperative. Among other elements, her proposals envisage the negotiation of a series of international agreements recognizing that governments do subsidize, protect, and otherwise support their high-technology industries and codifying rules of the game for such intervention. If such agreements cannot be reached, Tyson argues that the United States should then set numerical targets for foreign exports to the United States or U.S. exports to other countries (applied to certain industries rather than globally as Dornbusch proposes) and use the threat of various sanctions to enforce those outcomes.

At a Brookings conference in September 1989 each paper was discussed first by a designated critic, then by a panel of experts drawn from business, government, and universities, and finally by a broader audience. The next chapter provides a summary of the papers and the surrounding discussion. Each of the three following chapters includes one of the three main papers, the critique of the designated discussant, and a capsule summary of the conference discussion of the paper. In the final chapter, a three-person panel evaluates the papers and the debate. The remainder of this chapter presents the editors' evaluations of the three alternatives and then offers a set of recommendations for American trade policy.

What a National Trade Policy Can and Cannot Accomplish

It is widely believed that, whatever their other consequences, protectionist measures to restrict imports can increase domestic employment. Under most circumstances, that belief is wrong. The United States has for some years been operating at or near full employment, and the Federal Reserve consistently takes action to try to ensure that the United States does not seriously deviate from this path with either too much or too little spending for goods and services. Imposing a wide range of protectionist measures may indeed increase employment in the protected industries as a larger fraction of demand is satisfied from domestic production rather than from imports. But with the economy already at or near full employment, the new surge in the demand on the nation's capacity will threaten inflation, and the Federal Reserve will have to step in with higher interest rates to restrict economic activity elsewhere in the economy to prevent overheating. Job gains in the newly protected industries will be offset by job losses in the industries depressed by the higher interest rates, chiefly construction, machinery and equipment, and exports. In brief, trade restrictions can change the composition but not the overall level of national employment.

Similarly, a country cannot, except in the very short run, change its trade balance—the excess of exports over imports—by changing its trade policy. Whether a country runs a trade deficit or a trade surplus, and how large, is determined by its saving and investment propensities not its trade policies. If, for example, a country insists on saving less than it wants to invest domestically, it will set in motion a train of events that will cause it to run a current account deficit. The best illustration is what happened in the United States during the 1980s. The national saving rate fell substantially. Both private households and the government increased their spending relative to their incomes; indeed, the federal government began to run an unprecedentedly large budget deficit, simultaneously reducing its income with tax cuts and increasing its spending for defense.

To prevent the surge of spending from leading to an overheated boom and renewed inflation, the Federal Reserve permitted and actively helped engineer a sharp rise in real interest rates. The high interest rates did somewhat reduce domestic investment spending, but another important effect was to attract a lot of foreign funds into the United States to take advantage of the high returns. The "normal" foreign demand for dollars to buy U.S. exports was supplemented by the demand from foreigners wanting dollars with which to buy American securities and otherwise invest in this country. This rise in the foreign demand for dollars drove up its overseas value sharply and made exports very expensive for foreigners to buy while lowering the price of foreign imports for American buyers. As a result the United States began to run a large trade deficit, and a net inflow of goods and services into the United States was created to match the net inflow of foreign investment funds. In short, a country like the United States with a basically good credit rating can spend more than it produces by importing more than it exports and setting interest rates high enough to attract sufficient foreign funds to finance the resulting trade deficit. The converse is true of a country like Japan. It saves a good bit more than enough to finance its domestic investment opportunities. The excess of domestic saving drives down interest rates, Japanese funds flow abroad seeking the higher returns available there, the yen falls, and Japan runs a balance-of-payments surplus. It is the relationship between saving and investment in Japan and the United States, not trade policies or practices, that is responsible for balance-of-payments surpluses or deficits.

As another illustration of the inability of trade policy to have serious effects on the balance of payments, consider what would happen if, by whatever means, Japan greatly increased its propensity to buy imported (let's say American) goods, while neither Japan nor the United States changed its domestic saving and investment habits (leaving interest rates in the two countries unchanged). The demand for American exports by Japanese buyers would surge, leaving fewer surplus dollars potentially available for Japanese investors. But with interest rates in the United States remaining higher than in Japan, Japanese investors would continue to be interested in purchasing U.S. assets. The potential scarcity of American dollars relative to Japanese yen would lead to an appreciation of the dollar and a depreciation of the yen. The demand for American exports to Japan would fall back somewhat, and Japanese exports to the United States would rise, until the American trade deficit and the supply of dollars available to Japanese investors was restored to more or less its original level.[2] But notice that in the process Americans would be better off. U.S. currency would appreciate and terms of trade improve; that is, the United States would be buying more Japanese imports at lower prices (while the trade deficit would be no worse than it was before). The buying power of American wages would be greater and living standards consequently higher.[3] And, of course, if the United States simultaneously succeeded in getting the Japanese to open their markets wider and raised its own national saving rate, the nation could have both a lower trade deficit and a higher living standard.

Clearly, there is wide agreement that the choice among alternative trade strategies has nothing to do with how best to lower the American trade deficit or to increase American output and employment. Trade policy cannot achieve either of those goals.

Although economists generally agree that trade policy measures cannot alter employment, an increasing number of people have been arguing that trade policy can and should do two other things. First, to the extent American trade policy can induce other countries to increase their demand for American-made goods, the United States can improve its terms of trade, that is, it can exchange its exports for other countries' goods on more favorable terms. Each hour of American labor spent in producing exports will buy more imports, thus improving American living standards. Dornbusch's paper is built upon this theme,

2. Indeed, the temporary export boom would force the Federal Reserve to raise U.S. interest rates, which would would make dollar investments even more attractive and hasten the transition back to the "old," higher trade deficit.

3. The consequences for Japan might go either way. If the original barriers to trade had indeed been keeping the Japanese consumers from exercising their basic preferences, then the more open access to imports would improve their well-being. But they would have suffered a loss in their terms of trade—they would be paying more for the old level of imports. Another way of saying the same thing is that to the extent that Japan has artificial barriers to imports, those barriers are both helping and hurting its citizens and it is impossible to say, in the abstract, what the net balance is.

especially as it applies to Japan. Second, even if trade policy cannot raise American output and employment, it can change their composition, favoring some industries at the expense of others. None of the authors in this volume, and few economists anywhere, favor traditional protectionist measures that seek to preserve jobs and output in declining American industries that face successful foreign competition in domestic markets. Virtually all agree that in the long run, such protectionist policies reduce American living standards. But lately, some business executives, former trade policy officials, and economists have argued that governmental trade measures can and should be used to improve the fortunes of America's high-technology, high-profit, and high-wage industries and defend those industries against the predatory policies of other governments—Japan is usually named as chief culprit—thereby raising American productivity and incomes. This is the basic thrust of Tyson's paper.

At its core, therefore, the modern trade debate is not about jobs but about incomes.

The Axes of Debate

Though the modern debate about trade distinguishes itself from earlier controversy because of its concentration on wages and living standards rather than jobs, the simplicity of characterization ends there. An examination of the papers and discussion in this book, and a more general review of recent proposals for changes in American trade policy together with their rationales, reveals three different dimensions or axes along which the protagonists divide themselves. Any particular set of proposals may differ from any other set not just by one differentiating characteristic, but by three.

First, as noted earlier, proposals differ according to which of two principal goals they seek: improving America's terms of trade, a traditional objective of an activist trade policy; or the more novel and controversial proposals for a strategic trade policy, designed to aid industries considered essential to the advance of technology.

Second, proposals may be distinguished by the means or tools they would use to achieve their goals. There are several alternatives. Some proposals would abandon or modify America's postwar reliance on multilateral arrangements and substitute bilateral deals and the establishment of free trade zones with one or more trading partners. Other proposals are grounded in the view that in some countries—usually

Japan is held out as the chief offender—there exist strong barriers to trade, as well as other trade practices inimical to U.S. interests. Such obstacles are not amenable to being fixed by agreements about governmentally determined rules of trade, and hence agreements that stipulate quantitative outcomes for sectoral or even aggregate import or export flows among countries are needed.

Finally, the various trade proposals can be differentiated by whether their rationale is, or is alleged to be, essentially offensive or defensive in nature. Thus, Dornbusch would threaten Japan with a tariff on its imports as a device to widen its markets for American goods because, he argues, the barriers to imports that exist tilt the terms of trade between the United States and Japan unfairly in favor of Japan. His policy proposals are urged as defense against the consequences to the United States of Japanese customs and market structures.[4] Tyson would favor certain strategic U.S. industries, principally the high-technology electronic and communications industries, both on positive grounds, because she believes their expansion will confer special productivity-improving advantages on the U.S. economy, and on defensive grounds to avoid what she believes would be a shrinkage in their markets under the onslaught of the aggressive trade practices of other countries (again, Japan).

The current public debate about these issues has been confused because the various protagonists often use the term "managed trade" to describe different kinds of trade policy whose only common feature is some form or other of governmental intervention in international trade flows. Before proceeding, it will be useful to try to clear up the confusion.

The term managed trade has at least three different meanings as used in this book. Some authors use the term to denote results-oriented measures—the establishment of quantitative targets for imports or exports, along the lines just described. In this definition managed trade policies are contrasted with rules-oriented policies, under which governments establish the rules of the trading game, whether they be protectionist or free trade in spirit, and then let the market determine the outcome. In this use of the term, Dornbusch's proposal to establish quantitative targets for American exports into Japan represents a managed trade policy.

4. Interestingly enough, his argument implies that the effective prices of Japanese goods to U.S. consumers are too high and that the United States does not import enough from Japan, given the overall saving and investment position of the two countries.

Tyson uses the term managed trade in a different manner, namely, to describe her strategic trade policies that, in turn, are a subset of a broader national industrial policy designed to promote the high-technology industries. She would have the U.S. government use both results-oriented and rules-oriented trade measures to help achieve this end.

More loosely, the term managed trade is sometimes used simply to describe an overall trade policy characterized by frequent and specific governmental intervention in trade flows, through tariffs, import quotas, quantitative targets for American exports into specific countries, the active use of antidumping laws, and so forth.

In view of this confusion, we will not use the term managed trade in the remainder of this chapter. Rather we will describe Tyson's overall approach as strategic trade policy and denote measures that would establish quantitative targets of various kinds as results-oriented policies.

In evaluating the various arguments and proposals for a new American trade policy we first evaluate the two chief objectives—improvement in the terms of trade and strategic industrial policy—and then turn to the various means suggested for their attainment. When relevant, we will identify the offensive or defensive nature of the proposals and what that implies for their validity.

Objective 1: Terms of Trade

As Krueger elaborates, traditional economic analysis suggests that free trade is the best approach to raise global welfare. But this traditional analysis has long recognized that a country like the United States, with the world's largest market, could try to exploit its monopoly power by using the threat of taxing imports or exports to extract from other countries agreements that would expand American exports (or limit imports) so as to improve U.S. terms of trade, and thus the United Status would do better than under free trade. This so-called optimal tariff policy could backfire, however, if other countries retaliated with tariffs of their own.[5] Indeed, given the importance of the United States in the global economy, U.S. actions are likely to have systemic consequences. Protectionist policies by the United States will inevitably lead other countries into defensive actions or even into policies that outdo the

5. See Harry G. Johnson, *International Trade and Economic Growth* (Harvard University Press, 1967), pp. 31–55.

United States with yet more aggressive measures. In the long run, therefore, a protectionist United States would leave all countries, including the United States, worse off.

Although it would be risky for the United States to try to exploit its monopoly power, the same logic suggests it could be foolhardy to ignore the protectionist actions of others. Foreign protection or export subsidies can reduce the U.S. terms of trade. If, for example, foreigners subsidize aircraft exports, U.S. exporters have to charge lower prices to match the competition. Similarly, if foreigners erect barriers against some U.S. exports, then to achieve a given U.S. export level, more exports of other products will be required. To induce greater sales of those exports, they will have to be more attractively priced. As long as other nations help companies that produce goods the United States imports, the United States gains. But if countries subsidize their exports to third markets or protect domestic firms against U.S. exports, they can lower U.S. living standards.

As already noted, Dornbusch believes that the informal, mainly nongovernmental, barriers to manufactured imports into Japan have biased the terms of trade against the United States. He seeks to increase aggregate U.S. manufactured exports to Japan because that would improve the terms of trade. Similarly, he argues that the negotiation of additional free trade areas with other U.S. trading partners would do likewise and might have the additional advantage of putting extra pressure on Japan to agree to trade concessions in the form of increasing its imports of U.S. goods. (If the United States entered into a number of free trade agreements with countries who were Japan's export competitors, the Japanese might lose some of their U.S. markets.) But Dornbusch is not explicitly concerned about the specific composition of U.S. exports; one dollar's worth of exports is as good for the United States as any other dollar's worth. In particular he does not argue that priority be given to high-technology or any other strategic group of industries. Thus, when he proposes the negotiation of numerical targets for the expansion of imports into Japan, he envisages an aggregate target for manufactured goods and sees no reason to look beneath the total.

Objective 2: Promoting Strategic Industries

Tyson is concerned about high-technology products. She and other proponents of industrial policies argue that some industries are more important than others. They voice two concerns: that market forces left to their own devices will not channel sufficient resources into the critical high-technology industries; and that the trade and industrial policies of other countries will drive U.S. producers out of these key sectors and thus lower U.S. living standards.[6] But why do the proponents of industrial policy and managed trade believe that all industries are not created equal? What special characteristics do these high-technology industries have that warrant the government favoring them at the expense of others? If market forces were operating well, they would automatically arrange matters so that the last (that is, the marginal) dollar of resources allocated to each industry yielded the same benefit to the economy. The next dollar invested in making hamburgers would yield both the same economic returns and the same social benefits as the next dollar invested in computers. Otherwise, firms could increase profits simply by shifting resources from the low-yield to the high-yield use with national living standards being improved in the process. And the same reasoning applies to world trade; in world markets operating well, the marginal dollar of imports or exports would yield the same benefit in every line of business.

According to the advocates of managed trade and industrial policy, however, there are three principal kinds of departures from the world of efficiently functioning markets that make some industries "more equal than others" and that warrant interventionist policies.[7] One, because of the nature of their products and production processes, some markets are necessarily imperfectly competitive and can generate, for a limited number of firms in the world market, surplus profits (rents)—profits higher than necessary to induce investment in the sector. If a country can somehow secure a place for its firms in such markets, it can earn surplus profits—its capital investments would earn more than could be earned in other uses. Two, some industries pay workers surplus (premium) wages, more than their experience and skills could earn elsewhere in the economy. Expansion of those industries will increase real wages and living standards. Three, the production of certain goods produces

---

6. Even if other countries were not promoting the expansion of their high-technology industries in world markets, Tyson and other supporters of industrial policies, who believe that high-technology industries are critical to economic growth, would presumably favor government policies that especially promoted the expansion of those industries. But in that case, the relevant policies need not be oriented to foreign trade (although they would surely have effects on trade).

7. The emphasis given each of the three departures differs among the various theories underlying proposals for managed trade.

"spillover" benefits for the rest of the economy; that is, the benefits to the economy from the production of the goods in question are greater than the revenues earned by the producers, so that private incentives alone will not call forth as much output of those kinds of goods as it would be beneficial for society to have. It is argued, for example, that high-technology firms do an unusually large amount of research and development (R&D), many of whose benefits cannot be kept within the originating firm through patents and secrecy. These and related benefits spill over from high-technology industries into the rest of the economy in the form of free knowledge and faster technological advance.

Let us consider each of these three market imperfections in turn. How important are they, and to what extent do they warrant special governmental intervention, either at home or in foreign trade flows, to correct the resource allocation of the marketplace?

Surplus Profits

In recent years the analysis of trade has moved beyond the assumption that competition is perfect, to take account of the existence of economies of scale (that is, the tendency of average production costs to fall as the scale of production rises) and of the widespread reality of imperfect competition.[8] In industries that produce very specialized products, and in which the fixed costs of research and development, investment, and market development are high, the world market may have room for only a limited number of firms producing at low unit costs. The high fixed costs, and perhaps a long period of learning, may make it possible for the firms in the industry to go on for some time earning surplus profits. The new trade theories suggest that in such imperfectly competitive situations a country may be able to use government intervention strategically, to enrich itself at the expense of other nations. In particular, a direct export subsidy or one provided indirectly through protection in the home market could discourage foreign competitors and shift profits toward domestic producers.[9]

8. For excellent introductions, see Elhanan Helpman and Paul R. Krugman, *Market Structure and Foreign Trade: Increasing Returns, Imperfect Competition, and the International Economy* (MIT Press, 1985), and *Trade Policy and Market Structure* (MIT Press, 1989).

9. Barbara J. Spencer and James A. Brander, "International R&D Rivalry and Industrial Strategy," *Review of Economic Studies,* vol. 50 (October 1983), pp. 707–22. See also Paul R. Krugman, "Import Protection as Export Promotion," *Monopolistic*

Though theoretically interesting, however, the circumstances under which these monopoly-promoting policies might pay off are extremely difficult to detect in practice. They depend crucially on behavioral features in the market, the degree to which other countries retaliate, and the supply responses of other firms to the government intervention.[10] Moreover, it is not enough for government to know the consequences of its policies on the favored firms. It must also know the full consequences in the industries from which the resources are drawn. Redirecting scarce scientific and engineering resources into a particular sector could create losses elsewhere in the economy that outweigh the gains in the sector being promoted.[11] The literature has also shown how fairly minor modifications in various elements of the problem can radically change the nature of the optimal policy, for example, from subsidizing trade to taxing trade.[12] Thus Avinash Dixit studied the U.S. automobile industry and concluded the optimal policy for the United States was a tariff on imports and a subsidy to domestic production.[13] But Kala Krishna, Kathleen Hogan, and Phillip Swagel demonstrated that with relatively minor changes in specifying the industry demand curve, the optimal policy changed to a subsidy on both imports and domestic production.[14]

Since economists' ability to estimate demand and costs' curves with

Competition and International Trade, Henryk Kierzkowski, ed. (Clarendon Press, 1984); and Paul Krugman, "Is Free Trade Passe?" *Journal of Economic Perspectives,* vol. 1 (Fall 1987), pp. 131–44.

10. Subsidies may drive foreigners out of the market, but they could also induce entry by domestic firms. The added competition, as Horstmann and Markusen have emphasized, could ultimately dissipate the potential rents into the pockets of foreign consumers through lower prices. See Ignatius J. Horstmann and James R. Markusen, "Up the Average Cost Curve: Inefficient Entry and the New Protectionism," *Journal of International Economics,* vol. 20 (May 1986), pp. 225–48.

11. See Avinash K. Dixit and Gene M. Grossman, "Targeted Export Promotion with Several Oligopolistic Industries," *Journal of International Economics,* vol. 21 (November 1986), pp. 233–50.

12. Thus Eaton and Grossman have shown that in the same duopoly model used by Brander and Spencer, if firms react to prices rather than quantities, the optimal policy is taxing rather than subsidizing exports. See Jonathan Eaton and Gene M. Grossman, "Optimal Trade Policy under Oligopoly," *Quarterly Journal of Economics,* vol. 51 (May 1986), pp. 383–406.

13. Avinash Dixit, "Optimal Trade and Industrial Policy for the U.S. Automobile Industry," in Robert C. Feenstra, ed., *Empirical Methods for International Trade* (MIT Press, 1988), pp. 141–65.

14. Kala Krishna, Kathleen Hogan, and Phillip Swagel, "The Non-Optimality of Optimal Trade Policies: The U.S. Automobile Revisited, 1979–1985," Working Paper 3118 (Cambridge, Mass.: National Bureau of Economic Research, September 1989).

precision is very low, to predict the response of other firms to the market changes induced by government intervention is lower still, and to calculate the general equilibrium effects from the drawdown of resources elsewhere in the economy "is virtually nil," there is very little chance that government could know in advance whether any particular beggar-my-neighbor policy of subsidy or protection will add to or subtract from national income. In any case, profits are usually a relatively small share of overall value added. And the evidence suggests that in industry, rents in the form of surplus profits usually range from small to nonexistent.[15] Wages, however, are another story. They are a larger share of value added, and rents in the form of premium wages are potentially a larger source of benefits.

Surplus or Premium Wages

Several recent studies of the U.S. wage structure suggest that some industries systematically pay premium wages (rents)—wages that are higher than workers with the same skills and other easily observable characteristics could earn in other industries.[16] Unionization may be one reason for the premium, but the studies suggest that there may be other "efficiency wage" reasons for the premiums. In some industries— importantly those with high capital intensity—it is very costly to firms if employees have a high absenteeism rate or shirk on the job. Such firms pay premium wages as a means of maintaining productivity at high levels, giving employees an incentive to keep absences and shirking at a minimum—get caught and you lose your premium wage job. But many workers with the requisite skills and other characteristics who are working in low-wage industries could be equally productive at such jobs if only the output for the premium wage industry could be expanded.[17]

Some have advocated using trade policies to enhance employment in

15. Katz and Summers have found, for example, that "shareholders in American firms receive only very small monopoly rents. The weak, available evidence suggests the same for Japan." Lawrence F. Katz and Lawrence H. Summers, "Industry Rents: Evidence and Implications," in *Brookings Papers on Economic Activity, Microeconomics 1989*, p. 269.

16. See, for example, Katz and Summers, "Industry Rents."

17. Market forces alone won't generate enough output for these industries, since payment of the premium wage keeps the price of the output high. A subsidy could lower prices and expand output; the industries that would be displaced would have lower productivity and lower wages, so the economy would gain from the transfer.

sectors with premium wages.[18] One study argues that American export industries tend to be high-wage industries and that export promotion would raise national productivity and real wages.[19] But there are problems with this analysis and the associated trade policies. Statistically, it is difficult to distinguish between wage rents and payments that reflect skills, abilities, and attitudes of workers and characteristics of the job such as the disutility of certain types of labor. One critique has noted that the studies may be overestimating the size of the premium.[20] If what appear to be rents are in fact payments for skills, abilities, or other characteristics of workers or jobs, a governmental policy that subsidized the expansion of these industries could have damaging consequences. And policies that supported high-wage industries would encourage unions to claim even higher wages, while the distributional impact of such policies could be perverse.[21] Also, many high-wage industries— autos, steel, primary nonferrous metals, oil refining, glass, cans, paper and pulp mills, coal mining, tobacco—are not high-technology industries. On the other hand, several of the most prominent high-technology industries—computers and electronic components and accessories— while paying at or a little above the manufacturing average, are not at the top end of the wage scale. A policy of supporting the highest-wage industries would not be fully congruent with a policy of supporting high-technology industries. Finally, the distributional impact of using taxes to support high-wage sectors is regressive.

Spillover Benefits

The view that some industries, usually the high-technology ones, provide productivity-enhancing spillover effects to the rest of the U.S. economy lies at the heart of the arguments of many proponents of policies for managed trade. Tyson is among this group. Her paper recognizes the difficulties and dangers a country faces in trying to manipulate trade policy to capture surplus profits in imperfectly competitive industries.

18. See William T. Dickens and Kevin Lang, "Why It Matters What We Trade: A Case for Active Policy," in Laura D'Andrea Tyson, William T. Dickens, and John Zysman, eds., *The Dynamics of Trade and Employment* (Ballinger, 1988), pp. 87–122; and Katz and Summers, "Industry Rents."

19. Katz and Summers, "Industry Rents."

20. See Charles L. Schultze, "Comment" on Katz and Summers, "Industry Rents."

21. See, for example, the report on Victor Norman and his paper, "Imperfect Competition and General Equilibrium Aspects of Trade," in Centre for Economic Policy Research Bulletin (London, October 1989), pp. 5–6.

And she does not rely on the existence of premium wages as the mainstay of her arguments for favoring certain industries. But the existence of spillover benefits from one set of U.S. industries to other ones is critical to her conclusions.

It is not sufficient for the argument that certain goods or activities generate spillover benefits—the spillovers must be of more benefit to the country in which they originate than to the world at large. Otherwise the United States (or any other country) could sit back and gain the full advantage of other countries' spillover-generating activities—one wouldn't need to worry about where the world's high-technology production was located. And though some spillovers may be confined to one location or one country, most are not. Innovations by U.S. companies allow foreigners to improve their technology through reverse engineering. Similarly, foreign consumers could benefit from intensified competition.

The power and the wide diffusion of spillovers affecting consumers in a single economy is well known. It is striking, for example, that the wages of workers in high-technology industries rise little if any faster than the wages of workers in the rest of the economy. The real buying power of barbers, whose productivity has shown almost no improvement, will rise at the same rate as that of people producing semiconductor chips because the benefits of innovation in chips are passed on to all consumers through lower prices. What matters for living standards is the overall rate of innovation, not the rate in the sector in which a worker is employed.

Spillovers diffuse not only within a country, but across its borders especially in the modern world where information, goods, and capital move so much more freely than they did in earlier eras. The chief explanation for the convergence in incomes among developed economies in the world economy during the postwar period is precisely that U.S. innovations spilled over to the rest of the world. Moreover, the fact that incomes in small countries (such as Switzerland, Sweden, Austria, Denmark), which have highly incomplete industrial structures, are no lower than incomes in large countries suggests that global spillovers are powerful. What matters for living standards, therefore, is not only what a country produces but also the access it has to the innovations and products of others.[22]

---

22. Indeed, because of spillovers, a particular country (and the world) could be better off if it does less innovation and allows other countries with a comparative advantage in innovation to do more. See Gene M. Grossman and Elhanan Helpmann,

Nonetheless, not all spillovers are fully diffused outside a country's borders. The tendency of companies from the same industry to locate near one another, for example, Silicon Valley, does suggest some role for geographically confined spillovers. In principle, the existence of geographically confined spillovers could deprive a country of important benefits because market forces would not generate the appropriate amount of output from the spillover-creating industries. But even then it does not follow straightforwardly that government policies to promote these industries are called for. As Paul Krugman has pointed out, even where there are external economies (that is, spillovers), "If additional resources of labor and capital are supplied elastically to the industry, the external benefits of larger production will not be confined to the promoting country. Instead they will be passed on to the consumers around the world."[23]

Even granted that specific industries do generate spillover, and that some of those spillovers are not diffused on a global basis, how are those industries to be identified and favored? Industries in Washington are like children in Lake Wobegon—they are all above average. If no consistent set of principles exists to determine which industries the government should support, who will decide? An industry committee with a vested interest in cheap financing is scarcely the appropriate arbiter of how society's scarce resources should be spent. To choose among claims, the government would need a consistent and defensible set of principles on which to base its choices; adequate information to determine if claims are justified; and adequate restraint to avoid political pressures to provide aid where it is not justified.

Proponents of an industrial policy, for example, have advocated support for sectors that are high technology, pay high wages, have high value added per worker, are intensive in research and development, have strong links to other industries, or show rapid growth in productivity. Indeed, Tyson generally talks of high-technology sectors rather than specifying the ones meeting the precise conditions required to warrant government intervention. But almost any industry can make a claim under one or another of these headings. Basically, proponents of industrial policy and strategic trade intervention ignore the principle that intervention and the associated costs are worthwhile only if those

Comparative Advantage and Long-Run Growth, Working Paper 2809 (Cambridge, Mass.: National Bureau of Economic Research, January 1989).
    23. Krugman, "Is Free Trade Passe?" p. 140.

measures yield a higher return than would other uses of the same resources; people often forget that in a fully employed economy, resources redirected by the government into high-definition television or steel or any other favored industry will reduce output elsewhere in the economy. Nor is there any reason to think government officials can predict market outcomes better than private businesses can.

In theory, economists may agree that market failures exist, resulting in rents and spillovers, which may justify government intervention. In the real world of scarce information, uncertainty, and pervasive rent seeking, policymakers will inevitably miss the crucial and subtle distinctions between profits that are high because of rents and those that are high because of risk; between wages that are high because of rents, and those that are high because of skills; and between sectors that provide inputs, and those that result in spillover externalities. Moreover, policymakers would find it extremely difficult to identify appropriate sectors and confine public largesse to sectors meeting such criteria.

Although these considerations suggest that the benefits to the United States from such strategic trade policies are likely to be highly uncertain, it does not follow that the costs to the United States from its trading partners who pursue such policies are negligible. Even though the United States might benefit little from its own strategic policies, it is possible that the strategic policies of others could seriously hurt the United States—however misguided such policies may be in the interest of those other countries. To be sure, foreign policies to induce innovation or subsidize exports are not necessarily bad for the United States, but they can be. Those directed at lowering the costs of goods the United States can import will raise American living standards. But those directed at U.S. export industries could hurt. Foreign targeting must be taken more seriously as foreign economies become more competitive with the United States. Similarly, as long as the U.S. market was much larger than those abroad, the scale economies provided to foreign firms from domestic protection could be ignored. But as foreign markets have expanded, these considerations have become more significant. Before discussing appropriate defensive strategies against potentially harmful trade measures of other countries, however, consider first the various means or instruments of trade policy.

The Means and Instruments of Policy

Krueger stresses the advantages of the traditional U.S. strategy of negotiating multilateral (as opposed to bilateral) rules-based procedures (as opposed to quantitative targets) as the vehicle for accomplishing American trade objectives. But increasingly this view is being challenged. Indeed, while the proponents of a change in American trade policy would add some new policy objectives to the traditional ones, the big disagreements in this volume turn more on differences over means than on differences over ends.

One thrust of the challenge to traditional policy comes from those who maintain multilateralism is too weak and should be replaced or supplemented with unilateral and bilateral approaches. This view is stressed by Dornbusch. U.S. trade policy has already shifted in this direction. In the 1980s the United States concluded bilateral free trade agreements with Israel and Canada. In 1990 it entered into serious negotiations for a free trade area with Mexico and stated a long-term goal of a free trade area with Latin America. In 1988 the United States enacted legislation containing the famous Super 301 clause, which uses the threat of denying access to the U.S. market to back up the U.S. position in bilateral negotiations aimed at removing or modifying foreign trade practices the United States deems inappropriate.[24]

A second challenge comes from those who question the feasibility of securing through multilateral negotiations and multilateral rules the enlarged objectives they propose for American trade policy. Thus many proponents of a more interventionist U.S. trade policy, while tipping their hat in the direction of the desirability of multilateral rules for trade behavior, argue that in a world in which most major countries pursue industrial policies, it will sometimes be necessary to influence trade flows through the establishment of numerical targets for trade outcomes. This is essentially the position taken by Tyson; multilateral rules to manage competing industrial policies would be the best result, but until all the chief players become genuinely committed to free trade, multilateral rules probably cannot be successfully negotiated. Thus, quantitative targets will often be a necessary fallback.

Of course, bilateralism and results-oriented agreements are not mutually exclusive. Indeed, Dornbusch combines bilateralism with quantitative targets, while Tyson advocates a more multilateral approach to the establishment of such targets. Nonetheless, it is useful to discuss these notions separately.

24. For an extensive discussion, see Jagdish N. Bhagwati and Hugh Patrick, eds., *Aggressive Unilateralism* (University of Michigan Press, 1990).

Bilateralism

It is tempting for the United States to try to solve its trade problems with particular trading partners on a bilateral basis. As the world's largest economy, the United States appears in a particularly strong position when it confronts smaller and weaker economies one-on-one. Bilateralism allows the United States to press its case forcefully.[25]

But bilateralism has numerous disadvantages. It may be costly politically. In many countries the notion of submitting to American economic influence is not popular. U.S. actions under section 301 have sparked Koreans to burn the U.S. flag and a Thai cabinet to resign. Bilateral approaches may also increase friction with excluded third parties. The improvements in trade with some countries could come at the expense of broader relations with others.

Bilateralism also may not lead to the best economic results. Multilateralism can increase the number of potentially liberalizing deals. To take a simple case, the United States might make a concession that favors Germany, who agrees to something that is particularly important to South Korea, who in turn liberalizes in an area of special importance to the United States. Indeed, in an interdependent global economy many problems simply cannot be solved bilaterally. A multilateral deal brings all interested parties to the table simultaneously. This is a great simplifying device compared with piecemeal discussions that occur under much greater uncertainty when several bilateral negotiations are implemented. Concessions made in one bilateral deal may undermine concessions made to another trading partner in an earlier deal. A sequence of bilateral deals may not be readily transformed into a multilateral system. There is the important danger that proceeding piecemeal will result in a complex, crazy-quilt system in which U.S. trade with different partners is subject to different regulatory regimes.

Bilateral arrangements in the form of free trade areas are sometimes beneficial, but their proliferation could pose serious problems. In particular, free trade agreements, like the recent U.S. one with Canada, usually do not solve the really sticky problems, such as U.S. antidumping practices, partly because the absence of other negotiating countries ruled out the multicornered bargains necessary to make progress in reducing such long-standing barriers. In the case of Canada these

25. For a more complete treatment see Robert Z. Lawrence's discussion of Dornbusch in this volume.

problems were left to be dealt with by a special Canadian-U.S. commission. This might be fine for one or two free trade agreements, but their multiplication could introduce a frightening array of separate trade barriers, each with its own administrative committee, rules, and temptation to give in to special pleaders.

These problems with bilateral approaches suggest the United States should give its highest priority to multilateral arrangements. The GATT should be used whenever possible to settle bilateral disputes and to negotiate new trade rules.

Bilateralism that is used to gain concessions only for the United States should be distinguished from bilateralism to achieve most-favored-nation (MFN) concessions for all members of the GATT. For the most part the United States has used bilateral negotiations to demand MFN concessions. Thus while the semiconductor agreement was negotiated between the United States and Japan, it set targets for purchases of semiconductors from foreign- and not just U.S.-owned firms. Similarly, the United States negotiated a more open Japanese market for imports of beef and citrus from all producing countries.

Indeed, bilateral approaches need not always undermine GATT processes and rules. The GATT allows the suspension of the MFN principle in the case of free trade areas that lower barriers across a broad range of products among participants. As long as the United States conforms to GATT laws, seeks MFN concessions, and objects to practices that violate international agreements, bilateral approaches may have some merit. Indeed if the United States is able to conclude a free trade agreement with Mexico, it would be well worth pursuing. But it is always tempting to use these bilateral approaches to gain special advantages for the United States. It is also tempting to withdraw concessions granted under the GATT to persuade countries to agree to practices not covered by the GATT. An egregious example was the raising of tariffs bound under the GATT against Brazil in a 301 case on intellectual property rights.[26] And finally, as enshrined in the Super 301 legislation, it is tempting to use bilateral responses not only with countries who have violated commitments made in international agreements (unjustifiable practices) but also those who engage in practices that the United States unilaterally deems unreasonable.

It is one thing to use carefully articulated bilateral initiatives to

---

26. For a critical view of Super 301, see Jagdish N. Bhagwati, "U.S. Trade Policy at Crossroads," *World Economy*, vol. 12 (December 1989), pp. 439–79.

reenforce MFN and GATT rules. But it is quite another to pursue aggressively short-term national advantages that are counter to the letter and the spirit of a multilateral trading system. If the United States were indeed to declare that the "GATT is dead," the consequences for the global trading order could be disastrous.

On a broader scale, a regional Western Hemisphere free trade area, as recently proposed by President George Bush, could be a trade-liberalizing component of the GATT if it incorporated several essential characteristics. First, it should be negotiated simultaneously among all, or at least most, of the countries in the hemisphere—piecemeal negotiations would be much less likely to achieve substantial liberalization, and early signatories might well resist the loss of preferences they would suffer as others sought entry. Second, it should provide, for all the members, a substantial phased-in reduction of the high tariffs and nontariff trade barriers among the Latin American countries and a significant liberalization of the United States' principal selective barriers, such as quotas on steel, textiles, and sugar and U.S. use of the anti-dumping laws. Third, those countries that entered the agreement with especially high trade barriers against outside GATT members should reduce them, thus tending to ensure that the formation of the regional free trade area was consistent with GATT's article XXIV and did not end up injuring the rest of the trading world.[27] It is not obvious that such an agreement could be negotiated, but if it should prove possible, it could be a pathbreaking complement to the GATT system by demonstrating the scope for multilateral liberlization between developed and developing countries.

Results-Oriented Trade Policy; Quantitative Targets

U.S. trade policy has generally been directed at improving the rules that govern trade. This has been true both in negotiations at the GATT and in bilateral negotiations with trading partners.

Increasingly, however, there are calls for the United States to shift its demands from equal opportunity—a level playing field—to affirmative action. Some argue that Asian countries such as Japan and Korea will

---

27. This third point is a suggestion made by Jagdish Bhagwati, "Multilateralism at Risk," The Harry Johnson Memorial Lecture, London, July 11, 1990. See p. 24 for a discussion of the role of regional free trade associations within a GATT framework.

never play by Western rules.[28] Indeed, given the outstanding performance of the Japanese economy, the outside world has no right to demand that Japan change some of its internal practices that have served it so well; long-term stable relationships between industrial firms and their suppliers are an example. Instead of trying to change these countries, the outside world should simply negotiate quantitative import targets and allow their governments, which best understand their economic system, to ensure these targets are attained. The new slogan is, therefore, "results rather than rules."

But exactly what kind of outcome should the United States be seeking? One key principle of economic policymaking is that policy instruments should be precisely targeted to policy goals. A serious difficulty in designing and negotiating results-oriented trade measures is that there must be a precise agreement on goals so that the quantitative results are appropriately specified. Indeed, because advocates of such measures do not share the same goals, they differ over the countries they would include in their arrangements and the numerical targets they would define.

The list of goals sought by the various proponents of results-oriented trade policy includes avoiding needless frictions that arise from detailed discussions about institutional differences; improving the U.S. terms of trade; increasing U.S. domestic production; increasing production by U.S.-owned multinational companies; improving the U.S. defense industrial base; obtaining spillovers for the U.S. economy; maintaining the technological capacity of U.S.-owned firms; avoiding unfair trade practices; and saving jobs.

Because their goals differ, there are noteworthy differences in the outcomes that advocates of results-oriented trade policy would like to ensure. Targets include aggregate trade balances, bilateral trade balances, aggregate exports, aggregate imports, exports of specific products, and imports of specific products. Some would confine their approaches to countries, usually Japan and sometimes other Asian nations such as Korea, whose economic systems are seen as operating by rules that are too different from the United States.[29] Others advocate global, sectoral, quantitative arrangements, patterned, for example, after the

---

28. See the writings of Pat Choate, Clyde Prestowitz, James Fallows, and Karl von Wolferen.

29. See, for example, Pat Choate and J. K. Linger, *The High-Flex Society: Shaping America's Economic Future* (Alfred A. Knopf, 1986), pp. 63–77.

Multifiber Arrangement.[30] Some would set bilateral numerical targets (for example, imports from the United States), others multilateral targets (imports from the world), some would allow only purchases from U.S.-owned firms to qualify, others would include foreign-owned firms. Finally, there are differences in the number of parameters proponents would like to have negotiated, for example, simple dollar value or quantitative targets or more complex sharing agreements encompassing sales volumes, prices, and other relevant competitive parameters. Clyde Prestowitz, for instance, believes international trade generally should be managed like IAATA—the international airline cartel.[31]

But setting numerical targets is rarely an effective mechanism for achieving specific goals. Consider two examples from the papers in this volume.

AGGREGATE EXPORT TARGETS. Dornbusch is concerned that protection of the Japanese market by nontariff and invisible barriers restricts U.S. exports to Japan. Accordingly, he seeks to increase the quantity and price of U.S. exports and to raise U.S. living standards by demanding that Japan increase the volume of manufactured goods it imports from the United States by 15 percent a year for the next decade. In the absence of such a response, Dornbusch advocates the imposition of a tariff on Japanese exports to the United States.

The advantage of this approach is that it would avoid the dollar devaluation that would otherwise be necessary to induce Japan to buy more U.S. products. Dornbusch argues that what is important from a U.S. perspective is "good jobs at good wages."

This proposal cannot be faulted on logical grounds. Forcing Japan to buy more products produced in the United States would have a favorable impact on employment and profits in U.S. export-producing firms. It should be stressed, however, that it would have several other, deleterious effects.

In the absence of a shift in saving and investment behavior, more imports into Japan would entail more exports from Japan. Indeed the motive behind the approach is to achieve a weaker yen. It would imply increased competition for American industries who compete with the Japanese here at home or in third markets abroad. Moreover, as

30. See Robert Kuttner, *Managed Trade and Economic Sovereignty* (Washington: Economic Policy Institute, 1989).
31. Clyde V. Prestowitz, *Trading Places: How We Allowed Japan to Take the Lead* (Basic Books, 1988), p. 324.

advocated by Dornbusch, the approach would entail trade diversion from other countries. Dornbusch's target is for imports from the United States and this would sharply increase frictions with other countries.

Dornbusch argues it is irrelevant whether an American or a Japanese firm in the United States produces the exports for the Japanese market. An increased demand by Japan for imports from the United States raises the demand for American labor. However, if, as is the current practice, most of the imports are brought in by Japanese firms, the official and private practices that limit the degree to which newcomers can contest the Japanese market could continue. Although the Japanese market might have more imported products, these could still be priced to maximize the profits of Japanese firms with monopoly power. Japanese consumers would not necessarily enjoy the full benefits of access to cheaper imported products.

Although such a results-oriented approach might raise the volume of Japanese trade, it could actually lead to a market with more rather than less government and corporate control. Import targets can only be enforced if the Ministry of Trade and Industry (MITI) is powerful enough to guide Japanese firm behavior in great detail. MITI would be forced to organize and monitor numerous buying cartels. Firms would be forced to collude on how imported products are to be handled. Instead of encouraging Japan in the liberal direction urged in its own official Maekawa report, the policies would be driving it back toward precisely the system the world finds so difficult in the first place. Such an approach gives up on the idea that the Japanese economy will ever be genuinely open. It settles for making sure that at least Japan buys a certain amount of imports as a quid pro quo for its exports. By insisting Japan implement such a system, the United States would severely limit Japan's ability to become a genuinely liberal economy, and slow or halt the current movement in that direction. Although these arrangements are sometimes justified as an interim step toward a more liberal trading system, they represent a movement in the opposite direction.

Even acting in good faith, the Japanese government could not carve up many of its markets for U.S. goods. And when it did succeed, it could be counterproductive. Forcing the Japanese to buy goods by government edict is scarcely the way to enhance the reputation and the long-term future of American products in Japan.

HIGH-TECHNOLOGY COMPETITION. Tyson is particularly concerned about the fate of high-technology U.S. industries. Accordingly she supports the use of so-called voluntary import expansions to boost the sales of U.S. high-technology firms in Japan.[32]

In principle, Tyson believes in a rules-based international regime for high-technology trade, but in the short run she defends results-oriented trade measures such as the Semiconductor Trade Agreement (STA), which set minimum prices for Japanese chip exports and required Japan to boost purchases of foreign chips. Tyson argues that without such interim, results-oriented measures, the U.S. economy will lose strategic key sectors. She points out that in some industries knowledge does not easily spill over across national borders. Such knowledge accumulates in firms in the form of skilled workers, proprietary technology, and difficult to copy know-how. "The goal of intervention, therefore, is not simply to improve the trade balance or to address external barriers abroad, but to secure a share of world production and employment in such industries with the local knowledge, skills, and spillover benefits that they generate."[33] While the promotion of beneficial spillovers within the U.S. economy may be Tyson's goal, it is far from clear that the STA helped produce these advantages. Indeed, having sharply raised the price of semiconductor chips to most U.S. computer manufacturers, it may have discouraged some production from some industries that presumably have beneficial spillovers. It is a good example of the weaknesses both of the general proposition that trade policy should be managed to favor specific industries and of the use of quantitative targets as a mechanism to achieve that goal.

It is striking that the sideletter to the semiconductor agreement, which was negotiated between the United States and Japan, called for the products of non-Japanese companies to achieve 20 percent of domestic sales in Japan by 1991. It reflects concerns for the interests of U.S.-owned companies rather than for U.S. domestic production. The semiconductors that Texas Instruments produces in Japan or Korea, with Japanese or Korean labor and spillovers benefiting those countries, qualify for this quota, while the semiconductors that NEC or Fujitsu produce in the United States with U.S. labor and spillovers, do not. As it has been implemented, therefore, this initiative certainly does not

32. The Advisory Committee for Trade Policy and Negotiations (ACTPN) also suggested that U.S. Trade Representative Carla Hills should set sector-specific targets for Japanese imports. But it advised choosing sectors in which the United States was competitive rather than simply those that were high technology.

33. See Tyson's "Managed Trade Is the Best Trade: Making the Best of the Second Best," in this volume.

encourage spillover effects on the domestic structure of production in the United States.

Japanese semiconductor firms, it is argued, gain a strategic advantage because their home market is protected. This enables them to enjoy rents not available to U.S. firms. The semiconductor agreement settles for giving foreign-owned firms 20 percent of that business, but it does not fundamentally undermine the basis of the rents. Indeed, because the semiconductor agreement has actually cartelized the global market for DRAMs (dynamic random access memory), it has dramatically increased the profitability of Japanese chip firms while raising the price of chips and the cost of production to U.S. computer manufacturers and other high-technology chip users. The agreement has done much more to boost the profits of Japanese firms who dominate world production than those of its U.S. competitors.

Tyson argues that mandatory shares for foreign firms will liberalize the Japanese market. But they are more likely to institutionalize a cartelized distribution system for semiconductors in Japan.[34] Moreover, the agreement has thus far not been successful in raising the share of foreign chips in Japanese consumption close to its target. Thus Japanese firms continue to enjoy the scale economies from their strong domestic position.

One of the key problems with sector-specific, managed trade solutions is that they will be dominated by industry participants whose interests do not necessarily coincide with those of the United States as a whole. This is particularly true in a key linkage sector such as semiconductors. The cartelization of the global market for DRAMs is certainly not in the interests of those U.S. computer firms who are not vertically integrated. Indeed this is a critical weakness of the whole concept of strategic industry trade measures like the Semiconductor Trade Agreement. Since a large fraction of so-called high-technology products serve as parts and components in other high-technology products, the United States can easily undermine itself by propping up the prices and restricting the production of items whose cheap availability is a boon to U.S. high-technology industries. Instead of favoring so-called linkage industries

---

34. Tyson argues that such a quota pressures Japanese semiconductor users to design sophisticated foreign chips into their products. Perhaps, but the global shortage of DRAMs (dynamic random access memory) has also enabled Japanese DRAM producers to insist on the purchase of their more sophisticated chips as a condition for obtaining DRAM supplies.

for these cartellike arrangements, the United States should be particularly reluctant to include them.

In sum, the semiconductor agreement is a clear demonstration of the pitfalls of the managed trade approach to strategically important sectors.[35] The precise specification of its goals reflects a capture of public policy by a subset of U.S. firms whose interests are not coincident with those of the U.S. economy as a whole. The semiconductor agreement affords more financial benefits to U.S. competitors than it does to U.S. firms. It has established, in the name of saving the U.S. consumer from foreign price gouging, a cartel that can gouge its customers. As David Mowery and Nathan Rosenberg have noted, if the Semiconductor Trade Agreement is an example of successful strategic industry trade policy, it is hard to know how one would define failure.[36]

CONCLUSION. Strategic industry trade policy is simply a bad approach, and results-oriented trade measures are poor tools to employ. They replace competition among firms with competition among bureaucrats. Conceivably, in the Japanese political system, the choices of which industries to favor, which to let decline, and what means to use in pursuing those goals might be made on the basis of cold economic logic and calculations of what is best for the national economy. But the division of powers in the U.S. political system is ill-suited to managing the details of the economy. In the United States any attempt to divide the pie would be based not on strategic economic and trade criteria, but on political trade-offs that would reflect lobbying skills and masquerade under the rubric of "fair shares."

As I. M. Destler points out in his commentary for this volume, U.S. trade policy for most of the past fifty years has been amazingly successful not only defensively in fending off special interests, but offensively in achieving round after round of trade liberalization. One of the keys to this success—which flies in the face of cynical interpretations of democratic politics—was precisely the fact that the United States adopted a doctrine of adherence to a regime of multilateral free trade, a "standard to which honest men could repair." The numerous special pleaders

35. For further discussion see Kenneth Flamm, "Policy and Politics in the International Semiconductor Industry," paper presented at the SEMI ISS Seminar, January 1989; and Flamm, "Semiconductors," in Gary Clyde Hufbauer, ed., *Europe 1992: An American Perspective* (Brookings, 1990), pp. 225–92.

36. David C. Mowery and Nathan Rosenberg, "New Developments in U.S. Technology Policy: Implications for Competitiveness and International Trade Policy," *California Management Review*, vol. 32 (Fall 1989), pp. 107–24.

could be told that however heartrending their problem, their plea for protection was completely inconsistent with basic and longstanding U.S. policy. It didn't always work, but it was successful far more often than not. Under a regime of managed trade, however, where the name of the game is precisely to use trade policy to foster the interests of particular industries, and where any lobbyist can buy a study attesting to the dynamism, technological potential, and strategic character of his or her client, the barrier against special interests would crumble rapidly. It is not that the U.S. political system is necessarily a patsy for special interests. There are many examples to the contrary. But the United States does have to be careful in designing policy instruments that have serious economic effects to make sure that they are shaped with the special nature of U.S. political institutions in mind. A policy of strategic trade intervention and results-oriented agreements does not meet that test.

When results are being managed, clearly the devil lies in the details. Unless there is a clear rationale for the policy, the specifics could make the results disappointing. For some purposes, for example, enhancing the welfare of U.S. workers, it may suffice to emphasize greater import volumes; for other purposes, for example, enhancing the profits of U.S. firms, it may suffice to seek increased participation by U.S. firms in Japan. But these approaches should not be confused with policies that aim at increasing global welfare by achieving a market that is open in the most fundamental sense, that is, a market that can be readily contested by new firms, both foreign and domestic, who chose to supply products made at home and abroad.

Finally, sector-specific agreements are always justified as transitional measures. But their history suggests that once established, they expand, become institutionalized, and extremely difficult to eliminate. Thus the voluntary export restraint in cotton textile exports from Japan to the United States in 1955 became the Multilateral Short-Term Arrangement in cotton textiles in 1960, then the Long-Term Cotton Arrangement in 1962, and eventually the Multifiber Arrangement in 1973, which has been renewed and tightened and is still in force today.[37] Today, many developing countries who objected to its establishment have acquired a vested interest in its perpetuation.

By the same token, those U.S. firms who are given guaranteed access

---

37. See William R. Cline, *The Future of World Trade in Textiles and Apparel* (Washington: Institute for International Economics, 1987), chap. 6.

to a market will be unwilling to give up those guaranteed market shares. Though a results-oriented trade arrangement may make the numbers look better in the short run, it is likely to be a step away from, rather than toward, the open, free trade regime the United States would like to see established.

Trade Policies for the 1990s

We have outlined some of the problems associated with bilateralism, strategic industrial policy, and results-oriented agreements. But that does not mean that the issues raised by advocates of these measures can be ignored. The United States needs policies to counter foreign practices that worsen its terms of trade. It also needs responses to policies of foreign governments that promote favored industries at the expense of otherwise competitive U.S. industries. In this section, we outline briefly what we believe are appropriate U.S. policies to deal with these questions.[38]

Open Markets

U.S. companies need open global markets. The United States has seldom used trade policies to protect its high-technology products, and it should continue this restraint. But as long as the United States provides foreigners with the ability to profit from sales here, it is justified in demanding similar access for its own firms and its own exports to markets abroad. Because scale economies are critical in the development of many high-technology products, a protected home market can give domestic firms an unfair advantage. A protected home market like Japan can also provide domestic firms with surplus profits they can use to accelerate their technological development.[39] The United States must

38. We do not discuss programs to deal with the trade deficit because we believe these should be dealt with through macroeconomic measures. Nor do we discuss the problems of the domestic dislocation owing to foreign competition. For more complete treatments of these questions, see Robert E. Litan, Robert Z. Lawrence, and Charles L. Schultze, *American Living Standards: Threats and Challenges* (Brookings, 1988); and Robert Z. Lawrence, "Protection: Is There a Better Way?" *American Economic Review*, vol. 79 (May 1989, *Papers and Proceedings*, 1988), pp. 118–22.

39. Especially for newer industries, capital markets are far from perfect. Access to large amounts of internally generated funds does provide an important advantage for expansion and technological gains.

insist that mature industrial economies not adopt infant industry approaches. This would mean establishing several trade policies.

First, with respect to firms operating abroad, the United States should demand that all countries treat high-technology companies of all nations identically. If programs for research and development are organized in the European Community, Japan, or the United States, foreign-owned firms should be allowed to participate. The United States should make participation by the firms of other countries in U.S. government-funded research programs and institutions contingent on the granting of "national treatment" to U.S. firms operating abroad, that is, they should be given equal treatment with domestic firms.

Second, if foreigners protect high-technology sectors with barriers against imports, the United States should impose tariffs on the sale of products developed that way. The key lies in putting foreign countries on notice during the development phase of such programs, rather than in waiting until U.S. importers have become dependent on such products as was the case with Japanese semiconductors. Carrying out such a policy will require the use of actions under section 301 of the Trade Act of 1974, which are directed at targeted programs in their initial stages.

Two changes need to be made in U.S. antidumping policy. First, it needs to be retargeted. The current emphasis on preventing firms from selling below "full costs" is normally an unwarranted interference with normal business practices and needlessly costly to American consumers.[40] The definitions of predatory pricing for foreigners should conform to those for domestic firms.[41] Emphasis should be shifted to preventing classical price discrimination, that is, selling abroad at lower prices than are charged in the home market, which is universally recognized as an unfair trade practice. But second, the retargeted antidumping laws should be promptly and strictly enforced. As Michael Borrus has argued, antidumping laws have no "teeth" since the remedy

40. There are exceptions, however; see the discussion in the following pages on antitrust policy.

41. As Ostry has noted, "Logically the principle of national treatment under domestic competition policy should replace antidumping regulation. The same definition of undesirable pricing behavior that is applied to domestic firms should apply to foreign firms entering into the domestic market." See Sylvia Ostry, *Governments and Corporations in a Shrinking World* (New York: Council on Foreign Relations, 1990), p. 91.

is only to restore a fair market value.[42] A more severe penalty for discriminatory dumping should be applied.

The United States should not succumb to the temptation to negotiate a market share for its firms. This approach will not solve the essential problem, which stems from the fact that the foreign market is not open. Indeed, it is likely to reinforce foreign monopoly powers. How then should the United States deal with the well-established fact that the Japanese market effectively restricts the volume of imports?[43] Japan continues to import an unusually small percentage of manufactured goods from all countries; it has an extremely small amount of intraindustry trade.[44] Japanese firms abroad account for unusually high shares of Japanese imports; a large share of U.S. exports to Japan, for example, pass through the hands of the ubiquitous Japanese trading firms. The prices of imported products are much higher in Japan than elsewhere, and foreign investment levels are unusually low. Japanese producers abroad show strong preferences for buying Japanese materials, parts, and components.[45] While some of these characteristics may be partially explained by fundamental economic factors such as Japan's poor natural resource endowments and its distance from its trading partners, a variety of official and unofficial barriers also play a role. Other barriers reflect particular Japanese business practices that have been successful in raising Japanese industrial efficiency—the close and long-term relationships between particular producers and their suppliers is a key example. Nevertheless, if Japan is to play the leading role it sees for itself in the world economic community, and, more to the point, if it is to continue as a principal world exporter, it must be prepared to modify those practices and institutions that keep out imports.

Unfortunately, there is no simple solution to removing the barriers to imports and foreign investment in Japan. Neither simple numerical targets nor free trade agreements will do the trick. Detailed sector-specific negotiations to change the rules are inevitable.

While the United States has pursued sector-specific goals, it put too

---

42. Michael G. Borrus, *Competing for Control: America's Stake in Microelectronics* (Ballinger, 1988), p. 247.

43. See Robert Z. Lawrence, "How Open Is Japan?" paper prepared for NBER Conference on "The United States and Japan: Trade and Investment," October 1989.

44. See Edward J. Lincoln, *Japan's Unequal Trade* (Brookings, 1990).

45. Mordechai E. Kreinin, "How Closed Is Japan's Market? Additional Evidence," *World Economy*, vol. 11 (December 1988), pp. 529–42.

much emphasis on unilateral threats and bilateral negotiations. Japan is able to divert attention from legitimate complaints when they are made under U.S. Super 301 by arguing those complaints simply reflect U.S. "unilaterialism." When Japan is criticized by the United States alone, it rebuts the argument by pointing to internationally recognized U.S. weaknesses, fiscal policy, the poor state of productivity growth, and the low level of saving and investment. But these are not the point. The case for a more open Japan can be made most compellingly and convincingly precisely when it is made at the multilateral level. Indeed the agreements opening the markets for beef and citrus have come precisely when Japan found the GATT was going against it. Instead of using 301 as a first resort and multilateralism second, the United States should have recourse to multilateral channels first, whenever they are available.

Although most Americans would in principle favor the use of multi-lateral pressures and reliance on market-oriented trade measures, the number of voices calling for the abandonment of those remedies has been increasing. The so-called revisionists claim that such measures will not work in relation to Japan, that Japanese trade is not responsive to macroeconomic adjustment pressures through exchange rates, and that Japanese markets are not made more open through rules-oriented negotiations. But neither of these claims is correct. In the three years after 1985, as the dollar weakened against the yen, U.S. exports to Japan increased by almost 70 percent, from $22.6 billion to $37.7 billion. Similarly, U.S. exports of manufactured goods increased from $12.3 billion to $22 billion—a rise of almost 80 percent in a period of relative price stability.[46] During this same period, the volume of Japanese imports from all countries increased by 39.4 percent, and the overall volume of Japanese imports of manufactured goods increased by 78.3 percent. By the first quarter of 1989, Japan was importing twice the volume of manufactured goods it had in 1985. Those who claim exchange rates do not change Japanese buying patterns have simply not examined the data.

This is not to say that all reliance should be placed on exchange rate adjustments. Negotiations for market opening are still necessary. But here also the traditional methods have paid off. Particularly rapid growth in U.S. exports has occurred in those sectors in which negotiations to change the rules have been concluded. Ironically, the widely cited report of the Advisory Committee for Trade Policy and Negotiations (ACTPN),

---

46. Department of Commerce, *United States Trade Performance in 1988* (September 1989), pp. 83–84.

which made headlines with its advocacy of sectoral import targets, also documented the success of the traditional negotiations. Thus, after ten years of pressure, virtually all barriers to the importation of tobacco into Japan have fallen.[47] The four sectors that were singled out for negotiation under the maligned Market-Opening, Sector-Specific (MOSS) talks in the mid-1980s have shown impressive growth in Japanese imports. According to the report, from 1985 to 1987, U.S. exports to Japan in the four product categories combined increased by 46.5 percent, well above the 24.8 percent increase in total U.S. exports to Japan over the same two-year period. The report dismisses this performance because the total increase in exports of the products (of $1.3 billion) was small relative to the entire bilateral trade imbalance. But no one expected negotiations in a few sectors to turn the entire imbalance around. The problem may not be the approach, that is, emphasizing rules and concentrating on certain import-limiting practices, but the limited resources and narrow focus of the number of sectors brought into consideration. The United States needs not only tough, persistent, sectoral negotiations but enough patience to let the results begin to build.

Trade Policy as Antitrust Policy

Unlike the situation in the first three decades after the Second World War, the United States is no longer the overwhelming source of technological advance and industrial innovation in the world. Quite naturally, indeed partly because of successful, U.S. postwar policies, other countries have joined the United States at the frontier of technology. As long as the United States remains a vigorous economy, the fact that the nation now has more nearly equal partners is a healthy, and, in any event, inevitable development. One consequence is that the United States cannot expect to be a chief player in every new industrial and technological specialty. And so, the United States is likely to become dependent on foreign supplies for some important high-technology products. Foreign countries also face a changed climate in world competitiveness. In earlier decades, when the United States was the technological leader in virtually all fields, the competitive environment in U.S. industries ensured that dependence on a foreign source of supply for a technologically advanced product would not subject them to monopolistic exploi-

47. Advisory Committee for Trade Policy and Negotiations, "Analysis of the U.S.-Japan Trade Problem," Report to Carla Hills, Washington, February 1989.

tation. An effective U.S. antitrust policy offered substantial, de facto protection to the rest of the world against monopoly in any sector of traded goods. That is no longer true. These changed circumstances have important implications for both trade and antitrust policy, here and abroad.

Especially in the United States, but also abroad, it will be tempting to subsidize domestic production on the grounds that dependence on foreign suppliers (and owners) renders the country vulnerable to foreign pressures, political and economic. Occasionally this argument will be compelling. But not all dependence is bad, while the policies that would seek to avoid all instances of dependence would be. If foreign suppliers are geographically diverse and compete vigorously, countries have little to fear from dependence on foreign ownership or supplies. Or, to put it more precisely, in the United States and abroad, the problem of the relationship between foreign suppliers should be viewed from the standpoint of antitrust policy. All countries are potentially harmed if takeovers threaten undue concentration of the global market. Indeed, whatever the route by which one or a few firms come to dominate an important global market, all countries should be concerned. And so, both the United States and other industrial countries have an interest in beginning to negotiate a set of internationally applicable antitrust rules. But even if ultimately successful, this task will be thorny and protracted. In the meantime the Unites States may have no option but to use its antitrust laws to deal with economic threats from global monopolies and cartels.

When foreign takeovers threaten undue concentration of the global market, they should be stopped. Similarly, antitrust authorities must be vigilant if the United States relies on a few foreign suppliers for a vital input. Antitrust policies should be used to ensure the rapid diffusion of foreign products to the United States. If, for example, a few foreign firms in control of the market for DRAM semiconductors were to engage in monopolistic practices that denied access to U.S. users, or if they engaged in price fixing, U.S. antitrust policies should be invoked. Those damaged by these practices should be entitled to the normal treble-damages compensation.[48] This is also the context in which one should view foreign suppliers who sell in the United States at prices well below

---

48. For an application of the antitrust principles to the issue of foreign inputs for defense, see Theodore A. Moran, "The Globalization of America's Defense Industry: What is the Threat? How Can It Be Managed?" in *Industrial Organization* (forthcoming).

costs. If the world industry is reasonably competitive the United States should not use its antidumping laws to deprive American buyers of low prices. But if it is a foreign monopoly or cartel doing the selling, driving out U.S. producers in the process, then the United States should treat it just as it might predatory practices in the United States that might bring about a monopoly.

Like any set of antitrust policies, carrying these recommendations out in practice will involve many sticky questions and much argument over how the principles apply in particular cases. Moreover there will always be a temptation to be much more aggressive in applying the antitrust approach against foreign firms than against domestic ones. Nevertheless, formulating U.S. trade policies on the basis of such principles offers the best hope of walking the appropriate line between seeking the advantages of free trade and protecting the U.S. economy against real—as contrasted with trumped-up—dangers from unfair foreign trade practices.

Global Harmonization

In the early postwar period, tariffs and quotas obstructed trade, and capital movements were severely restricted. When economic interdependence was limited, trade policy needed to deal only with policies, such as tariffs and quotas, that directly affected trade in goods.

Economic interdependence has now expanded so much that serious differences and inconsistencies among government policies in much broader areas can no longer be readily tolerated. As border barriers have been eliminated, national differences in such areas as antitrust, regulation, tax, financial, and technology policy can now seriously distort trade and investment flows. Critics are correct, therefore, when they argue the GATT must extend its purview beyond tariffs and quotas. Indeed, the agenda of the current GATT negotiations, which includes areas such as services, agriculture, intellectual property rights, trade-related investment measures, and subsidies, indicates that the majority of GATT members feel the need for improvements in the global rules on these issues. Improved mechanisms for surveillance and dispute settlement are also needed.

In 1990, in particular, with negotiations reaching a critical point, U.S. trade policy should place its highest priority in achieving progress through GATT reform. Unilateral policy measures that might conflict with this goal should be studiously avoided. However, subagreements within the GATT that promote trade, combined with conditional MFN treatment in their application, may well be appropriate when a significant bloc of countries refuses to participate in agreements that would be beneficial to a large number of other countries.

Over the medium term, U.S. trade policy should strive for an open, global trading system governed by common rules. This regime should be implemented through a vastly strengthened and extended GATT apparatus.

Once the GATT negotiations are concluded and the mechanisms for creating a single internal European market are achieved in 1992, the next step should be a multilateral effort to achieve a single OECD market for goods, services, and capital by the year 2010.[49] The approach should use the example of the initiative for Europe 1992. The European governments decided they needed to complete the internal European market by removing all remaining obstacles to the free movement of goods, labor, and capital within the Community by 1992. In a 1985 White Paper they laid out the 300 measures required to achieve this goal. The OECD should similarly be given the task of formulating measures to create an integrated market for goods, services, and capital.

Of course, it would be impossible and undesirable to obtain identical practices across all nations. But this should not be necessary. Indeed, some competition among regulatory regimes could be beneficial. The difficult task will be to determine those issues on which harmonization will be essential, and those in which principles such as national treatment and mutual recognition of technical standards will suffice.

Participating countries would agree to procedures for handling allegations of unfair trade as well as measures to provide safeguards. Ideally, they could go further and establish a multinational tribunal to rule on whether allegations of unfair trade practices were supportable. As an interim approach, the findings of the tribunal would prevail unless explicitly overruled by the chief executive of the complaining country. Participating countries would also agree to rules to encourage innovation. These would include provisions for nondiscriminatory government procurement and national treatment for foreign firms. Similarly, an international entity would supplement national antitrust policies.

---

49. For similar proposals see Gary Clyde Hufbauer, *The Free Trade Debate*, background paper for a report of The Twentieth Century Fund Task Force on the Future of American Trade Policy (New York: Priority Press, 1989); and Ostry, *Governments and Corporations*.

It is striking that most proponents of bilateralism and managed trade still believe that ultimately a single world market with a rules-based regime should be established. They advocate their approaches as more effective means for achieving these objectives. Sometimes it is necessary to take one step backward to take two steps forward. But in this case, the steps toward bilateralism and managed trade are steps in the wrong direction.

Summary

Robert Z. Lawrence
and Charles L. Schultze

IN THIS CHAPTER , we summarize the papers by Anne O. Krueger, Rudiger W. Dornbusch, and Laura D'Andrea Tyson. Their discussants, Robert Kuttner, Robert Z. Lawrence, and Avinash Dixit, respectively, are also summarized. Finally, we present the commentators: Robert E. Baldwin, I. M. Destler, and Robert E. Reich.

The Free Trade Alternative
by Anne O. Krueger

Krueger defends two principal propositions. One, on the positive side, the case for adopting a relatively uncompromising free-trade approach to international trade policy is even stronger than suggested by the classic textbook arguments that economists have long been using, principally because of the benefits that accrue as trade inflows help impose competitive pressures on domestic industries. Two, on the negative side, all of the serious alternatives to free trade suffer from several theoretical, informational, and political shortcomings. Though she acknowledges some serious flaws in the current world trading system that violate its objectives of multilateral free trade, Krueger argues that the appropriate response is not the abandonment of the system but an aggressive move within the current Uruguay round for a large-scale dismantling of most, if not all, of the current nontariff barriers to trade and an elimination of the remaining tariffs in the developed countries.

The Traditional Case for Free Trade

On the positive side, the case in favor of free trade is even stronger than set forth in the classic textbook arguments. The "comparative advantage" argument for free trade in a competitive world environment is too familiar to require elaborate exposition. Unless a country has

42

monopoly power in trade, it will always be able to attain a higher level of welfare if it permits trade at international prices. A theoretical case can be made for an optimum tariff when a country has some monopoly power. But even then, the tariff must be limited in size to prevent a welfare loss. In any event, the current controversy about the appropriate direction for U.S. trade policy does not include optimal tariff arguments, and so there is no need to pursue the point further.

The traditional argument for free trade is greatly sharpened by the usefulness of free trade as a means of strengthening a competitive environment within countries. The benefits for a country from the existence of international competition have almost surely been increased by recent developments in technology. Increasingly, trade and production are concentrated on highly specialized goods and services, which adapt advanced technology to closely defined and specialized purposes— in the fields of information generation and processing, communications, roboticized production processes, biotechnology, and the like. Even in a large country, the internal market may only be able to support a limited number of firms producing a particular product or service at a scale large enough to achieve minimum costs and support the research and development necessary for further improvement. Free international trade sharply expands the number of actual or potential competitors and confers on all countries the benefits of the lower costs and prices thereby achievable.

Free trade, argues Krueger, can best flourish in an environment of multilateral rules and negotiations. Primary reliance on bilateral bargaining between countries, or, as some prominent people have recently urged, between large trading blocs, would be inferior. In particular, bilateral bargaining is likely to be accompanied by the frequent issuance of threats, the creation of bargaining chips that inevitably are protectionist (à la Super 301). Moving to such a world would create a fertile breeding ground within each country for special interests and narrow, parochial, political alliances to press successfully for either protection or mutual cartelization in important world industries (for example, the U.S.-Japan Semiconductor Trade Agreement).

The Case against the Other Alternatives

The advocates of free trade are often put in the impossible position of having to defend their position against every conceivable theoretical possibility brought forward in opposition to free trade, often including hypothetical possibilities containing little empirical content. To deal with this problem, Krueger formulates three generic arguments against the most common approaches that have recently been proposed as alternatives to multilateral free trade. One, on the basis of standard welfare calculations, the chief instances of traditional protectionism now extant in the United States turn out to be extremely costly. Two, the "new" sectoral trade strategies, which typically include a combination of rent seeking, the fostering of external economies, and infant industry protection in imperfectly competitive industries, are based on extremely fragile assumptions and pose impossibly demanding information requirements, which in no instance have yet been met. Three, in democratic countries, perhaps especially in the United States, adherence, even if sometimes imperfect, to a system of multilateral free trade is an important safeguard against political intervention in the marketplace in favor of special interests.

THE COSTS OF EXISTING PROTECTIONIST MEASURES. When one examines the chief sectors in which the United States has adopted protectionist policies during the past several decades, one finds it difficult to point to a single instance of great economic gains—large welfare losses are the rule. Consider, for example, protection of textiles (and apparel) and steel.

In 1984 U.S. adherence to the Multifiber Arrangement was estimated to have been the equivalent of placing a 30 percent tariff on the protected imports. It cost American consumers some $27 billion annually, about $11,000 per textile and apparel job protected, an average cost of about $270 a household, the same magnitude for the average family as a 5 percent increase in the federal income taxes it paid.

Steel was given something akin to a minimum price umbrella through trigger pricing arrangements in the late 1970s and early 1980s. In 1984 and 1985, the United States, using the threat of action against dumping, secured "voluntary" export restraints on forty different steel products with twenty-nine steel-producing countries. It has been estimated that the cost to steel users in higher steel prices amounts to some $22,000 per steel job saved through the protection of domestic steel production. More important, while textiles, through their use in apparel, are chiefly consumer goods, steel is a widely used intermediate product. A 1987 study by the U.S. International Trade Commission estimated that the voluntary export restrictions, while saving 17,000 steel jobs, probably cost about 52,000 lost jobs in steel-using industries.

NEW SECTORAL TRADE STRATEGIES. The modern, sophisticated arguments for protection urge that certain infant industries, producing specialized products under conditions of imperfect competition, be given protection for one or both of two reasons. One, they are subject to decreasing costs because of big, fixed costs of investment, research and development, worker training, or market development; and strategic protection or subsidy can secure substantial rents for the protecting country. Two, production of many high-technology products generates important spillover benefits for the country in which they are located. These benefits to society from the output of a firm are not captured in the revenues of the firm; too little of this activity will therefore be undertaken. Protection and promotion of those industries are critical for advanced economies if a country is to stay at the technological frontier and improve productivity.

According to Krueger, the proposals to pursue strategic trade policies are long on assumptions and short on empirical content. Even if political forces allowed purely economic factors to dictate policy, many criteria have to be surmounted before it can be shown that protection is warranted. How are the claimed spillover benefits to be identified and their magnitudes assessed? Such benefits, for example, have to be of sufficient size so that later gains, after removal of protection, would pay the welfare costs incurred in the initial protection. How can one distinguish, in this respect, among the many high-technology industries and subindustries—semiconductors, specialized chips, high-definition television, biotechnology, fiber optics, pharmaceuticals, robotics, cryogenics, telecommunications, new chemical products, and so on down the list? (How can one know that the capital and the skilled engineers, designers, and craftspersons shifted into the favored industries would not have been more productive where they now are?) When reasonably objective estimates do become available, for example, the recent Congressional Budget Office study of high-definition television, they tend to show that the claimed spillover benefits are vastly overstated.

In the case of rent-seeking strategies for decreasing cost industries, the declining cost curve must be steep enough compared with the size of the market, and the protected producers must be efficient enough relative to potential entrants, that the rents secured by protection last long enough to warrant the initial costs to society of subsidy or protection. When the anecdote-filled arguments for protection of one or the other high-technology industries are examined in detail, it turns out that they cannot pass the test of quantification.

Robert E. Baldwin, for example, after examining several possibilities related to spillovers, such as labor force training and research and development, demonstrated a strong presumption that protection was unlikely to internalize the spillover.[1] If a high-technology firm is likely to lose workers once it has trained them before recovering the cost of training, it is not clear that a higher price of output, provided by import barriers, will induce the firm to invest more in such training than it otherwise would. Similarly, if one firm's research and development results spill over to other firms, there may be more firms for the spillover to reach when the price of the output is higher, but it is not clear that a single firm's incentive for undertaking research and development is likely to increase, and so on.

In a similar vein, David Richardson surveyed the empirical research on the implications of imperfect competition for trade policy. He concluded that the gains from trade were larger under conditions of imperfect competition than they would have been with perfectly competitive markets, and that the empirical evidence offered no support for the view that trade intervention will improve welfare.

There is one particular respect in which the case for protection of high-technology industries based on the existence of external economies has been quite misleading. An important part of the output of high-technology industries is intermediate products, whose availability at reasonable prices is important to the pace of productivity and innovation in other high-technology-using industries—computer firms use semiconductors. Rather than promote productivity-raising spillover, policies that restrict the availability and raise the price of high-technology parts and components, as the new protectionism often does, may actually suppress them. The policy of the U.S. government in encouraging the formation of a price-raising semiconductor cartel is an important case in point.

POLITICAL REALISM AS AN ARGUMENT FOR MULTILATERAL FREE TRADE. Allowing trade flows to be determined largely according to the dictates of the markets permits the conservation of hard-to-get information. The new trade theories suppose an abundance of information that is difficult, and often impossible, to come by. This fact alone would be a grave shortcoming, but when combined with political reality, it is a fatal flaw. In governments everywhere the preservation of existing

---

1. Robert Baldwin, "The Case against Infant Industry Protection," *Journal of Political Economy*, vol. 77 (May–June 1969), pp. 295–305.

jobs and incomes carries, understandably, much greater weight than keeping open the potential for the creation of new jobs, even when the new jobs are likely, on the average, to be better jobs. If a deliberate policy of protection and industry subsidies were to be adopted, special interests would flock to political decisionmakers to press their cases by exploiting the absence of objective empirical criteria and information.

As noted earlier, a somewhat similar case can be made that a turn toward bilateral negotiations and an attempt to organize a whole series of free trade associations would run the danger of unleashing the political forces of protectionism. One characteristic of most of the proposals for bilateral bargaining over trade issues (for example, outcome-oriented, voluntary import expansion agreements) is that they rely on the threat of imposing additional trade restrictions as the bargaining chip to induce the other party to agree to the import expansion target. But some important domestic interests want trade restrictions to be made as tough as possible regardless of what the concessions are, and they will lobby accordingly. Thus, on a case-by-case bilateral basis, the occasions for protectionist outcomes multiply.

What Should American Trade Policies Be?

An important part of the argument for a move toward governmentally managed trade in the United States is expressed in the idea that the world of international trade is neither free nor multilateral, and that governments everywhere are intervening unilaterally or bilaterally in trade flows. If one accepts the conclusion that multilateral free trade is best, what policies should the United States pursue to advance the scope of a free trade environment, deal with other countries when they violate free trade principles, and answer the voices of the critics who use the shortcomings of the current system as an argument for abandoning it?

The critics of free trade are correct in noting that many European and Japanese trade and subsidy measures injure the United States. But, Krueger suggests, the United States is as much of a sinner as anyone, at least in formal barriers to trade. Therefore, large "gains in trade" could be made on all sides by aggressive and radical moves to lower existing trade barriers as part of the ongoing round of the General Agreement on Tariffs and Trade (GATT) negotiations. In steel, autos, textiles, agriculture, semiconductors, and a host of other sectors, nontariff barriers interfere with a huge volume of actual and potential trade and could form the raw material for a massive exchange of concessions. One possibility would be a multilateral agreement under which the industrial countries would undertake to remove all border restrictions on trade over a prenegotiated period.

There is further scope for an American initiative in the Uruguay round. It would call for a greatly strengthened GATT secretariat with enhanced surveillance and fact-finding functions. Conceivably, the initiative might then go further and offer national treatment to foreign firms from countries that agree to codes of conduct for national policies affecting foreign firms in their own jurisdiction.

Summary of Robert Kuttner

Kuttner's discussion of the Krueger paper first set forth his own views on the question of trade policy and then offered a critique of Krueger. According to Kuttner, nineteenth-century laissez-faire economic policies promoted a boom and bust cycle leading to protectionist responses with contractionary consequences. The Bretton Woods regime of the first two and a half decades after the Second World War was successful, not because it restored a laissez-faire trade regime but for two other reasons. First, Bretton Woods was built on a framework not of laissez-faire but of mixed economies, with governments taking responsibility for ensuring economic growth and stability. Second, the success of the liberalized trade regime required the hegemonic power of the United States, which was willing to make asymmetric trade concessions as a means of securing its other geopolitical aims. That hegemony no longer exists. The classic case for free trade has broken down because other countries are pursuing strategic trade policies that provide advantages to their own technically dynamic industries, while getting a free ride from the U.S. persistence in trying to follow free trade rules. The United States should recognize this reality and use its bargaining power to bring a balance of benefits to the system, so as to retain for the United States competence and competitiveness in key dynamic industries while making the process of decline in older industries socially bearable.

Kuttner makes five principal criticisms of the Krueger paper. First, the traditional comparative advantage case for free trade has become much weaker because resources matter less and knowledge matters more in modern economies. Other nations use various interventionist devices to capture the gains from advances in knowledge by promoting and protecting their knowledge-intensive industries. Second, many of the arguments against old-fashioned protectionism are no longer relevant, precisely because much of modern protectionist measures are part of broader national policies to favor dynamic high-technology industries. Third, even when protectionist devices are used to protect older industries under competitive attack, such as in the steel and textile industries, free trade advocates ignore the higher investment and associated productivity gains that are forthcoming under the umbrella of trade protection. Fourth, the Krueger argument that acceding to the infant industry argument for protectionism opens a Pandora's box of special interest protectionism ignores the fact that around the world Pandora's box has long been opened, and the United States simply cannot ignore the results. Failing to come to grips with all of these realities, argues Kuttner, leaves the United States with a fourth-best world of Super 301 bilateralism. It is better that the United States recognize the nature of the modern trading world and develop a much superior regime of sensibly managed trade.

The Case for Bilateralism
by Rudiger W. Dornbusch

Dornbusch argues that U.S. trade policy should have two chief objectives: rolling back the increasing amount of protectionism that now takes place by way of nontariff barriers at home and abroad; and preventing the emergence of restrictive trade blocs. He argues that aggressive bilateralism is the way to do this. He perceives bilateralism as strategy for freeing international trade more rapidly than would be possible under continued adherence to the GATT framework of multilateral negotiation, which operates too slowly and is being circumvented by trade policy initiatives in Europe and Asia. Since other countries manage trade to restrict access, the United States should impose performance measures in judging the success of trade policy. In particular, he favors a policy of making continued access to the U.S. market contingent on equal treatment for the United States abroad.

Dornbusch begins his paper with some prefatory remarks on what trade policy can and cannot do. He believes that a primary objective of trade policy should be to raise real incomes by raising U.S. terms of trade, improving the efficiency of resource allocation, and providing larger markets (hence higher profits). But trade policy is not an appropriate approach for dealing with a nation's trade balance, which is determined by domestic saving and investment decisions. He notes, however, that if the United States reduces its fiscal deficit, net exports will have to improve. In that circumstance improved market access could serve as a useful complement to the necessary domestic macroeconomic adjustment since it would allow the United States to make that adjustment with less real devaluation than otherwise.

Opening Japan

Dornbusch says the United States should pursue a different policy approach to Japan than to other nations. He believes the United States should try in an uncompromising fashion to open the Japanese market. He argues that Japan has an unusually low level of import penetration that has not risen over time. In particular, imports of manufactures remained in the range of 2 percent to 3 percent of gross national product (GNP) throughout the 1965–88 period with no apparent trend. Although the degree of import penetration increased in other industrial countries after each successive round of GATT negotiations, it did not in Japan. Furthermore, Japan engages in unusually low intraindustry trade.

Dornbusch perceives business-government collusion as a principal cause of the low import penetration. These restrictive practices and patterns of business behavior should be attacked, according to Dornbusch, by using import performance targets. But another reason for Japan's low imports is not because of formal barriers or government nontariff barriers but because Japanese consumers and firms "prefer" Japanese goods. This behavior seems particularly evident in the purchase of capital goods. Japanese multinationals located outside Japan buy almost exclusively from Japan, whereas other multinationals operating in third countries display a much wider dispersion of purchases.[2] Dornbusch argues that the source of the low import penetration does not matter; and, if these buy-Japanese preferences indicate unusual Japanese tastes, then they should be rooted out by price and nonprice measures (that is, import subsidies and import performance criteria).

Dornbusch advocates a very aggressive and unilateral U.S. approach to Japan. He argues that the countries in the European Community are ambivalent about discriminating against Asia in general and Japan in particular; thus, they would make poor partners in an effort to open Japan. The United States should, therefore, act on its own, using Super 301 as the primary policy weapon. He would set targets for the growth

---

2. Mordechai E. Kreinin, "How Closed Is Japan's Market? Additional Evidence," *World Economy*, vol. 11 (December 1988), pp. 529–42.

rate of Japanese imports of manufactures from the United States during the next decade. He suggests a target of 15 percent annually. If apparent consumption in Japan grew at a 5 percent rate, the U.S. share would rise from 2.5 percent to 6.0 percent of apparent consumption of manufactures, or by 1 percent of GNP.

This demand would be enforced by an automatic sanction system—either selective discrimination against particular Japanese exports or, preferably, an across-the-board tariff on Japanese exports. He hopes that Europe would make the same demand.

Dornbusch would not mind if Japan responded to the issue of purchase from American firms by locating Japanese firms in the United States and exporting products back to Japan, since he argues that what is important is good jobs at good wages, rather than ownership. Similarly, Dornbusch finds no problem if the logical response to a rise in Japanese imports is an increase in Japanese exports. He recognizes that implementation of the tariff would have serious foreign policy concerns but feels these issues may as well be faced.

Building a U.S. Trade Bloc

The second part of the paper is devoted to suggestions for building a U.S. trade bloc. Dornbusch reviews the theoretical literature and argues there is no strong case in favor of a multilateral rather than a bilateral approach for obtaining freer trade.

In practice, he says, the GATT is eroding because of growing protectionism in the form of nontariff barriers. He also points out that the GATT has done little to open heavily protected less-developed countries. Moreover, it has not prevented trade discrimination, which occurs increasingly through measures such as the Europe 1992 actions and recent Japanese efforts to build a de facto trading area in Asia.

He then looks at theory and points out that, as Robert Mundell has shown, these customs union measures can give their members terms-of-trade benefits at the expense of the rest of the world. Dornbusch argues that the formation of trade blocs does not decidedly undermine negotiations on intellectual property or services on a multilateral scale. So he suggests, all in all, there seem to be few costs and could be great benefits.

The concern of course is that if the United States set off on this approach, there might be a risk that other nations would develop competing blocs. But Dornbusch dismisses this fear as a reaction to the untried; the concern simply reflects an outmoded U.S. sense of being the custodian of a policy tradition, while other countries have an interest in perpetuating the U.S. naiveté.

Having failed to find strong theoretical or practical arguments against building such a bloc, he looks at positive reasons for doing so. First, he argues that Europe and seemingly Japan are doing so already. If the United States builds some blocs of its own, it could reduce the risks of being excluded from an Asian bloc. Second, he points out that Europe 1992 will almost certainly have negative terms-of-trade effects for outsiders. He brings out the point that, if the United States started along similar lines, at least the issue of compensation for the terms-of-trade impacts on third parties would surface as an issue for international negotiation. He adds that if Europe 1992 reinvigorates the European economy, the same should be true elsewhere. Finally, the United States already has low tariffs and has little further to offer in international negotiation over tariffs. However, it can offer potential partner countries exemption from any nontariff barriers and future protection against U.S. fair trade laws.

Dornbusch then considers with whom these blocs should be negotiated. His first candidate would be to offer the European Community unrestricted free trade by 1992. Such a challenge, "bypassing the tedium of GATT," would find strong resonance within Europe among those who fear protectionism and "add an edge to the skinning of the Japanese onion."

Free trade areas with Latin American countries could also be fruitful—in particular, with Brazil and Mexico. Mexico's potential is indicated by the increase of Mexican imports from the United States of $6 billion in just a single year. A free trade association with Latin America would allow the United States a privileged status in these markets, at least for a while, until the proliferation took place.

In Asia, Korea and the Philippines might be the place to start. Their markets are large, growing rapidly, and highly protected. Such a move would enable the United States to check Japan's attempt to build a trade bloc of its own.

Summary of Robert Z. Lawrence

Lawrence disagreed strongly with both of Dornbusch's policy proposals. Although the closed Japanese market was a problem for the world economy, he argued, the Dornbusch approach could make matters worse rather than better and could prove counterproductive. Lawrence emphasized that imposing quantitative import targets would require Japan's Ministry of International Trade and Industry to organize buying cartels. They would therefore strengthen precisely the cartel-like behavior the rest of the world does not like. He questioned if a market run through quotas could be thought of as "open."

Lawrence observed that Dornbusch's policy to target trade between the United States and Japan would clearly discriminate against third countries and would divert trade rather than open up Japan. He pointed out that if tariffs were imposed on Japanese exports, without a change in the underlying saving-investment balance, a reduction rather than an increase in Japanese imports would occur. Lawrence also stressed that Japanese imports of manufactured goods had grown rapidly over the past four years. Their 21 percent growth rate exceeded the Dornbusch goal. He questioned the need for a dramatic and risky policy change in dealing with Japan precisely when the current policy of strengthening the yen and negotiating the removal of barriers seemed to be paying off.

There was also criticism of Dornbusch's suggestions for new free trade areas. Multilateral approaches have many advantages over those that proceed bilaterally. In particular, the political costs for the United States would be lower; and, as U.S. experience with Japan has shown recently, using multilateral approaches can be more effective. Some issues (for example, agricultural subsidies) cannot be solved bilaterally. They were a conspicuous omission in the U.S.-Canada agreement.

Lawrence was skeptical of the view that the United States would not impose its fair trade rules on countries with free trade agreements. Again he pointed to the special panel that was instituted in the case of the U.S.-Canada arrangement—an arrangement required because the United States was not willing to waive its antidumping and other "fair trade" laws. The Dornbusch approach, he argued, could lead to a proliferation of special rules with different partners that would be complex to administer.

The Case for Managed Trade
by Laura D'Andrea Tyson

In this paper Tyson argues that from both a positive and a defensive standpoint, untrammeled free trade is not a viable alternative as a national trade policy, especially when it comes to high-technology products. Domestic high-technology industries confer important benefits on the rest of the economy in stimulating technological advance and productivity growth. The political reality is that governments around the world are pursuing strategic policies to secure shares of the world market for their own high-technology industries, and if the United States stands by and merely watches, its high-technology potential may be irreversibly harmed. Trade in these products will inevitably be "managed." Such trade can be managed deliberately and well or haphazardly and poorly. The only way to achieve the former is with an explicit, thoughtful policy that shapes how the government manages trade in these products.

Rationale for Managed Trade

Tyson identifies four main reasons why government should play an important role in managing trade flows for high-technology products: First, growth in high-technology industries generates important spillover benefits for other high-technology firms and for the economy generally, which do not show up as profits for the firms generating these benefits. Thus, the unaided operation of the private market will not provide enough incentives for the growth and expansion of these industries. Moreover, because of the high fixed costs for research and development and the advantages that come through learning by doing, high-technology firms once established in the world market tend to have big advantages over potential newcomers. Thus, in the high-technology world, comparative advantage can be created. As a consequence of these characteristics, the fate of high-technology industries should not be left to market forces alone. Second, in view of this fact, governments all around the world, including the United States, have employed subsidies, protection, and other devices to promote such industries. The alternatives are not free trade versus managed trade but management through international agreements versus uncoordinated, beggar-thy-neighbor national policies. And because the advantages that trade policies and subsidies can confer on high-technology firms are not easily reversible, failure of the United States to pursue trade policies that support its high-technology industries, while other countries are doing so, can do long-lasting damage to American growth and competitiveness.

Third, high-technology products account for about a third of American nonfarm merchandise exports. Managed trade agreements that stimulate the exports and reduce the imports of such products could enable the United States to adjust its trade deficit with a smaller drop in the dollar's value and a smaller loss of real income. Finally, perceived efforts by the

U.S. government to support U.S. high-technology producers, in the face of trade barriers and policy intervention abroad, may moderate protectionist pressures at home. Failure to pursue such policies is causing some traditionally internationalist high-technology firms to become much more aggressive in seeking trade relief under U.S. antidumping and related laws, leading to a privatized trade policy that is far from optimal for the country as a whole.

Definitions of Managed Trade

There is no single definition of managed trade. It includes proposals calling for both bilateral and multilateral agreements. Such proposals can be macroeconomic or sectoral in focus, and they may be structured with rules for the conduct of trade, or they may attempt to target outcomes directly. Their most common feature is that trade is controlled, directed, or administered by government policy. The serious policy debate, however, has concentrated on proposals for microeconomic policies that are targeted to industrial sectors deemed to be of strategic importance to the U.S. economy.

Advocates of managed trade argue that the GATT pays insufficient attention to such widely used practices as rules of origin, local content, government procurement, and antidumping provisions, which are aimed at controlling trade outcomes. The focus of managed trade advocates on policies that target outcomes for specific industries represents the biggest area of difference with the advocates of the multilateral-GATT approach. Examples of such policies are the various voluntary export restraint agreements or the semiconductor agreement that specified a target for increased Japanese imports. This latter example of a voluntary import expansion agreement is argued not to be protectionist because it expands rather than restricts trade.

The Theoretical Case for Managed Trade in High-Technology Industries

Technology-intensive industries are marked by rapid reductions in costs over time and substantial barriers to late entrants that create imperfectly competitive market structures. In such cases, free trade is not necessarily the best policy from an individual country's perspective since a nation can attempt to exploit its ability to earn monopoly rents in industries with substantial competitive imperfections. In addition, the production of these industries is believed to generate substantial spillover benefits to other industries, and, it is argued, a healthy and sizable high-technology sector is essential for a nation's competitiveness and productivity growth.

Advocates of intervention in the high-technology industries emphasize a Schumpeterian view of competition and productivity gains that stresses competition in the dimension of new product and process innovations rather than through price competition. In such situations patterns of resource allocation that are most efficient in the static Ricardian sense, evaluated against current costs and prices, are not necessarily the most beneficial once the opportunities for future innovations are included in the calculation. This is particularly true if technological advance is a joint output of current production, as is true with learning by doing or other problem-solving activities. If industries differ in their opportunities for such technological innovations, the choice of current resource or industry mix can strongly influence the pattern of future growth. These potential gains will not be fully realized by private agents because the social returns to innovation exceed the private returns; capital market constraints limit the use of borrowing to finance research and development, requiring reliance on internally generated profits for investment in innovation; and the industries are characterized by increasing returns to scale.

The problem remains, however, of how to identify the industries in which these opportunities for dynamic gain might exist. The examples are largely based on ex post identification, and the theoretical models do not suggest a strong definition of the required characteristics of such industries. Moreover, ensuring that the correct policies to promote the industry would be followed in practice is not an easy matter from a political standpoint. Thus, even among those economists who agree that such dynamic considerations represent significant modifications to the standard comparative-statics case for open trading relationships, the range of views about the value of government intervention is broad.

Policy Proposals

Tyson begins her discussion of policy proposals by noting that the goal of governmental interventions in the high-technology industries is not simply to deal with the usual matter of trade policies—the trade balance or foreign barriers to imports—but to secure a share of world employment and production for such industries in order that the domestic economy may gain the spillover benefits they are perceived to generate. Managed trade policies are not just about international trade.

The paper puts forward three sets of proposals for managing trade in high-technology products. The first set of proposals addresses the imperfectly competitive nature of the high-technology industries and can be grouped under the broad label "competition policy." An ideal approach to antitrust policy would be the establishment of uniform antitrust rules in all the major countries, but this is a politically unrealistic goal. As a fallback, the United States ought to identify the elements in a country's economic institutions that impede foreign competition and negotiate for their removal—which is the basic idea underlying the Bush administration's negotiations with Japan under the title of the structural impediments initiative.

Also under this rubric, the United States should work to initiate industry-by-industry multilateral negotiations among the chief high-technology suppliers on new policy codes for the behavior of governments and of firms. An example is the Semiconductor Trade Agreement between the United States and Japan. Indeed, as a first step in the desired direction the United States should call for multilateral negotiations on the semiconductor industry, seeking to extend some of the essential principles underlying the agreement and bringing the European Community under the tent. Realistically, industry or sectoral policy codes will have to be negotiated among a limited number of countries, or, even in some cases, bilaterally. They could then be extended on a conditional most-favored-nation basis to any countries who wish to adhere to the policy rules and might eventually serve as a model for necessary changes in the GATT.

The second big area for the application of a policy of managed trade involves antidumping laws. Both Europe and the United States have increasingly been using antidumping laws to protect their high-technology interests against the inroads of low price imports, especially from Japan. Increasingly, dumping cases have been brought not on the traditional grounds of discriminatory pricing (export prices lower than domestic process) but as a response to below-cost pricing. In the European Community antidumping laws have been combined with very restrictive rules of origin, defining what is and what is not an imported product, to provide a high degree of protection against the inroads of Japanese semiconductors and other high-technology products.

Economists have traditionally been skeptical about the use of anti-dumping laws. The loss to consumers outweighs the gains to the protected producers, and most of those who have studied the issue discount the danger that foreign producers will be able to pursue a predatory strategy of driving out competitors and then charging a monopoly price. But, says Tyson, once the strategic nature of the high-technology industries is recognized, the arguments change. Because such industries generate highly desirable spillover benefits to a country, below-cost imports can inflict great damage; and because of high fixed costs and learning-by-doing phenomena, the damage may be irreversible. Ideally, it would be desirable to negotiate multilateral rules about government policy and firm behavior, along the lines just discussed. One component of such a plan would be rules that limit potentially predatory strategies by high-technology producers. Even on an optimistic assessment, however, development of agreement on such rules will take many years. In the interim, evidence of dumping by Japan could best be countered by providing subsidies to the threatened domestic industry. But since subsidies are not likely to be politically achievable, especially in view of the current federal budget situation, Tyson argues that an active anti-dumping policy can help protect American high-technology industries from irreversible damage. At the same time, the United States should press for multilateral negotiations to develop more precise and uniform antidumping procedures and standards by which to assess antidumping and countervailing duties. Current practices and procedures are highly variable among countries.

The final set of managed trade proposals espoused by Tyson involves the negotiation of voluntary import expansion targets for various high-technology industries with Japan or any other country where U.S. products are deemed to be denied "fair" access to markets. Ideally, as indicated earlier, multilateral arrangements for rules of government and firm behavior in the high-technology sector would include rules guaranteeing market access. But in the absence of such agreements, and even under the best of circumstances they will not be forthcoming for many years, it may be necessary to give priority to negotiating bilateral, outcome-oriented agreements that specify numerical goals for imports of American products into foreign markets where access is now encumbered by various structural barriers. Tyson recognizes that economists have traditionally been wary of such agreements because they threaten the cartelization of world markets and also violate the nondiscrimination principles of the GATT. But, she argues, if the target applies to a country and an industry in which there is ample evidence of market closure—as was the case, she says, with the Japanese semiconductor market—and if the import targets can be met by imports from any foreign country, then the agreement will promote rather than retard competition and will not be discriminatory.

Tyson sums up her views by stating a preference for the negotiation of multilateral rules to govern the conduct of what is already managed world trade in high-technology products. But given the difficulties of negotiating such arrangements, and the length of time it would take, she believes that the establishment of minimum shares of national markets for imports may be a necessary and desirable fallback option, and better than the highly protected markets that are likely otherwise to develop as the outcome of the rival strategic trade policies of the major countries.

Summary of Avinash K. Dixit

Dixit agreed with Tyson that orthodox and uncompromising free trade is no longer a viable policy alternative because of political realities. But he also argues that Tyson's proposals for a managed trade regime are equally unrealistic from a political standpoint.

Dixit sets out four basic organizing principles or criteria for the design of trade policy and uses them to evaluate the Tyson paper. First he says that market failures are best treated at their source. Many of the ills with the U.S. economy identified by Tyson call for domestic measures, macro and microeconomic, but not for trade measures. Thus, subsidies to U.S. producers to promote research and development or to compensate for injury are dismissed by Tyson as "pure fantasy," in current budgetary conditions. But dealing with the problems by trade protection, the imposition of countervailing and antidumping duties or the organization of price-raising cartels (as in the Semiconductor Trade Agreement) also provides subsidies to American producers through a tax, by way of higher prices, on American consumers.

Second, Dixit says, creating industries with a comparative advantage has costs as well as benefits; users of a product such as semiconductors whose domestic supply is reduced pay higher prices. Although Tyson asserts the existence of "dynamic Schumpeterian benefits" that will counter such costs, she offers, says Dixit, no empirical evidence. He also cites several situations in which dynamic considerations lower any spillover benefits that might have existed, thus reducing rather than increasing the case for government intervention. Third, Dixit states that the policy process must be conducive to strategic bargaining. In particular, bargaining threats must be credible and reversible (unless the

United States forgoes or reverses the threatened actions, foreign governments will have no incentive to make concessions). But the U.S. policy process makes it impossible to meet these criteria. The nation cannot move quickly or firmly and once it erects trade barriers as a threat, they take on a life of their own supported by the special interests who benefit from them.

Dixit's final principle is that the management of markets usually leads to its cartelization. This result, he argues, is amply supported by the history of U.S. regulatory agencies and by the recent management of trade in the automobile and steel industries, where U.S. imposition of voluntary export restraints has enabled foreign governments and firms to organize price-raising cartels. Tyson claims that the voluntary import expansion agreements she espouses are different and that how semiconductor trade is managed has increased the number of U.S. competitors in the market. But Dixit counters that when markets are shared by prearrangement or if generous minimum price arrangements are dictated, competition is stifled despite the higher numbers of firms.

Dixit then evaluates three of Tyson's proposals for managed trade in the following areas: high-technology products, antitrust and antidumping policy, and voluntary import expansion agreements. He first enumerates the serious difficulties of objectively identifying the industries that should be favored, a fact, he argues, that will make it easy for special pleaders to capture the process. As a second-best alternative to the unrealistic prospect of common antitrust rules in the United States and Japan, Tyson proposes bilateral negotiations with Japan that would specify "allowable rules for firm behavior" in world markets, along the lines of the semiconductor agreement. But Dixit notes that Europe and the emerging countries of the Asian rim are not about to let the United States and Japan dominate the high-technology world market. Once negotiations start, they are likely to lead not to improved competition but to a carving up of world markets, a process that will be harmful to the global economy.

Dixit also criticizes the Tyson proposals for the imposition of antidumping duties to protect American high-technology industries against potential Japanese predation. He argues that the surge in antidumping cases after 1985 (based on below-cost prices) arose from the sharp fall in the U.S. dollar—with volatile exchange rates it makes good sense for foreign firms to tolerate a period of prices below average or even marginal costs. And Dixit makes two criticisms about the voluntary import expansions agreements favored by Tyson. He reiterates the argument, made earlier, that market sharing arrangements lessen rather than increase competition. He also observes that the U.S. policy process is too cumbersome to allow the United States to play the necessary strategic negotiating game successfully.

Dixit urges two changes in current U.S. policy: budget deficit reduction that would lower U.S. trade imbalances; and changes in U.S. antitrust policy that would recognize increased international competition. He also recognizes two potential roles for strategic trade policy: inducing other countries to open their markets when the United States has a genuine export advantage (for example, rice, not autos, in Japan); and deterring other countries from closing their markets. But, he says, the United States would have to make its domestic policy process more flexible and less subject to special interests in order to operate successfully in this arena.

Commentary

Each commentator is summarized as follows.

Robert E. Baldwin

Baldwin was in strong agreement with the Krueger paper. During the last forty-five years, he says, whenever theoretical arguments for heavy governmental intervention in trade flows were implemented—in the socialist countries, the developing countries, or in some instances in advanced industrial countries—the results were nearly always a slowing in development and a loss of international competitive status.

Baldwin criticizes Dornbusch and Tyson for their arguments for managed trade and suggests that some of the problems in the current world trading order that they seek to remedy could be better handled through elaboration and refinement of the GATT framework. Others could be addressed through bilateral or conditional most-favored-nation arrangements of a type consistent with the GATT.

Baldwin notes that Dornbusch heavily and Tyson partially defend their proposals as a means of expanding U.S. exports and improving U.S. terms of trade in the face of a Japanese import market that is difficult to penetrate. But, he points out, of the three important empirical studies that have tried to answer the question about whether the Japanese market is unusually hard to penetrate for manufactured imports, two come to a negative conclusion. And even the study that does find the Japanese market to be an "outlier" estimates that the gains to foreign exporters would be quite small even if the Japanese market were to be converted to an average market in terms of import penetration. Tyson relies on the spillover benefits from high-technology industries to justify a policy of managed trade. Baldwin agrees that a theoretical case for government intervention exists if such spillovers are an important aspect of productivity growth in the modern economy. But Baldwin then points to Tyson's recognition in her paper that most of the empirical studies of government subsidies justified on these grounds conclude that the subsidies were counterproductive.

Baldwin offers several criticisms of various elements of the Dornbusch and Tyson proposals. It is highly unlikely, he believes, that it would be politically feasible to eliminate the application of U.S textile, apparel, steel, auto, and similar quotas to countries with whom the United States negotiates free trade arrangements, as Dornbusch seems to think possible. It is equally unrealistic, he argues, to assume that once fixed export amounts for U.S. products are put in place, they can later be dismantled in favor of a liberal trade policy. What the United States would get is a set of export quotas that would prove as hard to dismantle as the current import quotas. And it is equally naive, he says, to believe that the United States could successfully negotiate discriminatory policies to increase exports without other countries following suit with similar beggar-thy-neighbor policies, undoing any advantages the nation might have secured and leaving the whole world worse off. And finally, Baldwin argues that the combination of managed trade and bloc building policies would create an atmosphere in which international economic relationships were increasingly seen as zero-sum games in which each country tries to increase its power, or the power of its bloc, at the expense of the others. He briefly spells out several scenarios in which this result could pose serious dangers to world trade and conceivably to world peace.

Baldwin devotes the final part of his commentary to the proposition that some of the objectives of the Dornbusch and Tyson proposals can be achieved under the aegis of the GATT. The creation of free trade agreements are consistent with the GATT if they apply to substantially all of the trade of the partners, do not raise barriers against third countries, and are more trade creating than trade diverting. Although multilateral arrangements are generally best, free trade associations that are genuinely liberalizing are welcome. Similarly, although unconditional most-favored-nation arrangements are generally preferred, conditional most-favored-nation agreements, in which trade concessions or trading rules apply to a subset of countries, are sometimes permitted under the GATT, as was true of the government procurement code negotiated at the Tokyo round.

As an alternative way of handling the problem of subsidies, with which Dornbusch and Tyson are rightly concerned, Baldwin proposes a new procedure under the GATT. Each country would make specific requests of other countries to reduce or offset the subsidies it believed were harming it. Each country would also announce the countervailing duty actions it was prepared to take if bilateral or multilateral negotiations were not successful. Countries who believed that some or all of their subsidies did not violate the GATT rules could appeal to GATT-appointed panels of experts to issue advisory rulings on the pertinent questions. A comprehensive negotiation based on these claims and submissions would then take place. Baldwin describes this approach as "aggressive multilateralism." Finally, to deal with the contention that Japanese business practices, as opposed to government rules, tend to restrict imports unfairly, Baldwin notes that a code on restrictive business practices was considered but not accepted in multilateral discussions during the early postwar years, and he suggests that it may be time to consider the negotiation of a GATT code dealing with the matter.

I. M. Destler

According to Destler, too little attention has been paid, by either economists or political scientists, to the fact that American political leaders during the 1930s, and even more strikingly after the Second World War, fashioned a liberal-leaning trade strategy that dominated the political scene for more than forty years. Though commentators on trade politics typically paint a gloomy picture of how susceptible trade policy is to capture by special interests and protectionist lobbies, during those forty years, American governments of both parties developed a political strategy that achieved round after round of trade liberalizing measures.

According to Destler, a key element of that strategy was that it succeeded in turning the trade policy agenda from how much to limit imports to how best to reduce foreign barriers and promote exports. It was thus able to enlist large segments of the business community in promoting trade liberalizing measures. Free trade policy took the political offensive, rather than concentrating on damage-limiting tactics against special interests.

But the very success of this strategy and its export-promotion orientation, when confronted with the persistent trade deficits that the United States ran in the 1980s, combined to produce many of the pressures for aggressive mercantilistlike policies that characterize today's scene. Export-oriented industries, subject for many years to competitive pressures from an overvalued dollar and even afterward finding it difficult to sell in Japan or to compete against the Japanese and others in third markets, shifted from unequivocal to conditional support of free trade— the condition being reciprocal access to foreign (especially Japanese) markets. And since successive earlier rounds of trade liberalization had reduced or eliminated a large part of official barriers to imports, it was impossible to offer mutual liberalization as a bargaining device. It was natural to turn to the threat of limiting access to American markets as the only effective negotiating weapon—thus Super 301, the Semiconductor Trade Agreement, and proposals for results-oriented, quantitative trade targets. In a similar vein, those who believed in an industrial policy to promote strategic American industries began looking to export promotion and protection against what were seen as predatory strategic policies of other countries.

One of the consequences of these developments has been that many of the elite, internationally minded business supporters of free trade have come to support, as a negotiating tool, not old-fashioned protectionism but aggressive export promotion strategies involving unilateral threats to restrict access to the U.S. market.

Destler concludes by framing two alternative futures with respect to trade policy. One, the U.S. superaggressiveness in trade policy may be simply a short-term and understandable response to the U.S. trade deficits of the 1980s. As they disappear, the aggressiveness would relax and trade policy would revert to something near its earlier status. Or two, the current turmoil in trade policy may signal a transition to a new mercantilist emphasis by the United States, perhaps with an integration of trade policy and an industrial policy promoting high-technology industries.

Finally, Destler also notes that the critics of liberal trade policy must do more to establish their case than merely demonstrate the presence of economics in the trade practices of other countries. Rather it is necessary to show that persistence in liberal trade policies by the United States harms the nation and the alternatives would help. And even if the

United States concludes that technology advance is an important good in which firms tend to underinvest, that does not prove that trade intervention is the appropriate response.

Robert B. Reich

Reich starts by noting that the definition of free trade is difficult. Even in the absence of any barriers erected explicitly to keep out imports, a host of regulations, limits, and requirements that governments impose for health, safety, environmental, and other reasons may in fact advantage domestic firms relative to foreigners. Business practices initially adopted for various domestic reasons may have the same effect. Witness the formidable difficulties that the Japanese distribution system puts in the way of imported goods. Free trade is not some natural condition of a market but can only be defined by formal agreements among governments about what it means.

As a prelude to discussing the papers, Reich distinguishes both trade agreements and their goals along several different dimensions. Trade agreements may be rule or outcome oriented; they may be differentiated by sector or be uniform in their application; they may be aggressively enforced, using the threat of market access to ensure compliance (or even to secure agreement in the first place) or passive in nature, relying on previously agreed rules and procedures for enforcement. And finally agreements may be bilateral or multilateral. There are, thus, many alternative combinations of ways in which trade may be managed.

Reich argues that the choice of a desirable trade strategy from among this set of choices depends on the goals that one seeks to accomplish through trade, and he sets forth five possible goals (many of which are not necessarily exclusive). The first is simply more trade. Reich finds that to some extent Dornbusch, but especially Krueger, puts much weight on this goal without explaining why this aim is appropriate. The second possible goal is to enrich the nation in a zero-sum gain at the expense of other countries. According to Reich, this aim is a major goal of Dornbusch's aggressive bilateralism in relation to Japan. But there are problems with trying to attain this goal. It may not be a sustainable goal since it will breed political resentment and reduce other nations' willingness to cooperate on trade matters. Moreover, the gains from U.S. leadership in promoting cooperative arrangements are so large that the nation should not abandon that role even in the face of some "free riding" by Japan on U.S. willingness to abide by multilateral free trade rules.

Although it is not a goal proposed by any of the authors in this volume, Reich notes that much of the discussion about American trade policy seems to assume that the United States should seek to improve the profitability of American-owned corporations. But as American-owned corporations locate more and more facilities abroad, while, conversely, more and more U.S. citizens work in the American plants of foreign-owned corporations, a policy of increasing the profits of U.S. firms is not the same thing as raising American living standards. American living standards depend much more on the kind of jobs made available to American workers than on the returns earned by American capital.

Finally, Reich notes that a possible goal for national trade policy is the one Tyson proposes—that of securing for the United States an appropriate share of world production and employment in high value-added industries that generate knowledge and other spillovers that improve American productivity and living standards. But this goal, argues Reich, should not be formulated in a beggar-thy-neighbor, zero-sum strategy that would aggressively use bilateral outcome-oriented agreements and other trade measures to aggrandize American high-technology and high value-added industries. Rather it should be formulated positively to seek multilateral, rule-oriented negotiations to allocate high-value jobs among nations according to agreed-on criteria.

Reich then comments on what he believes to be the excessively pessimistic views of most economists about the capacity of government to carry out a managed trade strategy, without succumbing to special interest pressures. Other governments, notably Japan, have proved capable of successfully pursuing a strategic trade policy, making choices not dictated by special pleaders. The United States has been capable of pursuing rational and strategic policies in the international trade arena overriding special interest demands for favored treatment. Witness the leading U.S. role in the creation of the GATT, the International Monetary Fund, the World Bank, and other Bretton Woods arrangements. Many of the United States' most successful industries were created with the help of, or within, rules designed by government—aerospace, aircraft, telecommunications, biotechnology, and so on. And finally, some governmental agencies, by common repute, have enjoyed a high degree of competence for years, such as the Antitrust Division of the Department of Justice, the Securities and Exchange Commission, and the Congressional Budget Office, to name only a few. And finally, notes Reich, if U.S. political capacity for making strategic selections is weak, while other nations are being more "strategic" about their trade policies, to the detriment of the United States, it behooves the nation to change its ways.

Free Trade Is the Best Policy

Anne O. Krueger

THE CASE FOR a policy of free trade can be based on both positive and negative grounds. On the positive side are arguments stressing traditional comparative advantage and world welfare, as well as the unchallenged proposition that every country is better off in a world of free trade than in a world in which all countries practice highly protectionist policies or engage in "strategic trade management." Perhaps even more important, free trade provides a competitive environment that induces greater economic and technical efficiency in domestic firms.

On the negative side, the U.S. political process is bound to capture any attempt at strategic trade management and undermine its economic aims for political reasons.

The positive case for free trade has at least four components. I consider each one in turn: the straightforward comparative advantage case, amended to take account of the increasingly complex structure of modern industry, which greatly strengthens the case; the recognition that protection of some industries inevitably disadvantages others, often unintentionally; the fact that free trade strengthens competitive pressures in any economy, with favorable results for dynamic efficiency; and the proposition that clearly all countries will lose when all are sufficiently protectionist, and free trade is a consistent policy for domestic and global welfare.

The case against alternative trade policies is somewhat more difficult to put, because advocacy of protection originates from many different vantage points. First, I consider the current pattern of protection, which almost all agree is highly inefficient. Thereafter, I elaborate the case against sectoral protection, emphasizing the difference between advocating "some" measures and defining processes and criteria that would

I am indebted to David Orsmund for valuable comments and research assistance.

68

implement these measures. Finally, I discuss the political economy of protection. Once protection is accepted as a legitimate policy instrument, the political process is bound to seize it and use it far more intensively and with many more negative consequences than advocates of protection anticipate.

Several alternative stances have been advocated as paths toward a more open, multilateral trading system. First, some observers support the Uruguay round GATT negotiations, and policies toward that end. Second, some people advocate aggressive measures, such as Super 301, as mechanisms for opening up foreign markets. Third, some argue that multilateral efforts to achieve freer trade are unlikely to succeed, and that bilateral free trade agreements represent another way of achieving the goal of free trade. Each stance is considered in the final section, where I conclude that efforts to strengthen the GATT, and work directly within its framework, offer much greater hope of success than the suggested alternative approaches. Indeed, the alternatives are more likely to increase global protectionism than they are to improve the openness of the international economy.

The Positive Case for Free Trade

The straightforward comparative advantage argument for free trade needs little elaboration to an audience at Brookings. Unless a country has monopoly power in trade, it will always be able to attain a higher level of welfare if it permits trade at international prices, producing those commodities that are comparatively cheaper at home and exchanging them for those that would be relatively more expensive to produce.[1] When there is monopoly power in trade, using an optimum tariff to take advantage of it can improve a country's welfare. Even then, the tariff must not be too high or welfare can be even lower than it would be at free trade, and other countries must not be able to retaliate "too much." However, in the context of U.S. policy discussions, the optimal tariff

---

1. If there are domestic market distortions, first-best policy is to correct those distortions at their source. There has been no serious advocacy of protection in the United States as a policy to improve welfare in the presence of domestic market distortions, and that line of argument is not considered further. The case for adjustment assistance—which is based on very different analytical underpinnings—is discussed.

argument has not been used as a basis for advocacy of protection, and I will therefore not consider it further.[2]

The comparative advantage case for free trade is independent of why there might be cost differences. It simply asserts that, if foreigners can produce something relatively more cheaply than it can be made at home, it pays to produce something else and trade it for the item in question. Comparative advantage could arise from factor endowment differences (Heckscher, Ohlin, and Samuelson), from differences in technology (for whatever reasons), from product differentiation with increased market size, or for other reasons.[3]

To say that policy A is better than policy B, however, is not enough. If the difference between the two is very small, then noneconomic considerations may override the (small) gains to be had by choosing policy A. The size of the gains from free trade (or equivalently the losses from protection) is determined by the sources and magnitudes of the differences. In modern economic life, productivity gains, and therefore economic growth, largely depend on increasingly precise specifications of products, with specialized uses and markets. The greatest productivity gains are now being achieved with specialized electronic components, adapted for particular functions, specialized chemicals for differentiated processes, and specialized materials. Cost savings are possible by producing a microchip more adapted to a particular need, or a robot with specifications that fit a certain task. Individually, many of these savings are fairly small, but competition in the international economy, and

2. If one had to guess, one would guess that the United States had monopoly power, if at all, in the imports of some primary commodities and in the export of some high-technology manufactures. The optimum tariff argument would then imply that imports of those primary commodities should be subject to tariffs and exports of high-technology manufactures should be *taxed*. The advocates of protection in the United States are advocating protection to high-technology industries. The American tariff structure is escalated in such a way that primary commodities are imported duty free or at very low duty rates, which is the opposite of the policy that would be adopted if monopoly power considerations were the motivation for protection.

3. The development in economic theory that has called free trade into question is not the comparative advantage proposition: it is the assertion of the possibility that cost differences are created by government policy, and that, in particular, the first to enter may achieve a market size and cost advantage that permits the country to capture the rents arising in a monopolistically competitive situation. It is not sufficient that there be new lines in which comparative advantage may be developed; for protection to be an economically defensible policy, the development of this comparative advantage must be privately unprofitable (because otherwise individual firms would in any event undertake it and reap the rewards) but nonetheless publicly profitable.

especially in high-technology, frontier items, is intense, and cumulatively, access to lowest-cost specialized items can mean large cost savings.

There are two implications for trade policy. First, the size of the production run for each specialized item influences its cost and price. Second, any competitor without access to the lowest-cost source for specialized parts and components will not survive long in the international marketplace. Any proposal for protection should contain provisions that insulate domestic using industries from the high costs that would otherwise be incurred if producing industries are protectionist. However, the bureaucratic complexities of so doing usually make that an impossible task, so from the potential gains—if any—from protecting a particular industry should be subtracted the potential losses to using industries—an impossible task.

These considerations together imply that the costs of protection in the frontier industries are likely to be high: if some domestic firms are protected, users of their output will be subject to higher costs than their international competitors. In turn, as users' competitive positions deteriorate, they will demand less of the individual parts and components and therefore raise costs of individual production runs still further: the risk of a cumulative downward spiral in the industry may be high.

For an economy such as the American one, where comparative advantage surely lies in the "frontier" industries that are also principal sources of growth, the costs of protection of advanced industries may well be the inability of firms using advanced technology to compete with their foreign competitors. But the case against protecting lagging industries is equally strong. Because economic growth is associated with rising real wages, it is likely to be the labor-using industries that are under pressure both from the growth process and from the competition with the same industries in countries well behind the United States in per capita incomes and growth. To protect the labor-intensive industries[4] is to slow down the process of shifting resources into activities with higher real rewards. Sufficient protection of existing industries would imply a failure to free real resources for the new activities on which growth is likely to be based, and would curtail growth for lack of fungible resources, quite aside from the effects on incentives.

In a modern economy, it is almost impossible to find a system of

4. There is an important distinction between protection and provision of assistance to workers and others who are strongly disadvantaged by the growth process.

protection for some industries that does not confer negative effective protection on others.[5] Attempting to protect the American semiconductor industry through trade policy, for example, would disprotect all American industries using semiconductors, thereby eroding their competitive positions.

In today's complex modern economic structure, trade barriers are probably incompatible with sustaining growth and a high level of productivity. Certainly, there seems to be a political consensus in both Australia and New Zealand—the developed countries in the OECD with the highest levels of protection against manufactures—that earlier protective policies in those countries bore great responsibility for their lagging per capita incomes and low growth rates relative to other developed countries.[6] The important notion of effective protection rates—wherein nominal tariffs are used to calculate the levels of protection (both positive and negative) accorded to domestic value added—was developed in part to demonstrate the crucial role of interdependence of economic activities in a modern economy: it is simply not possible to impose tariffs on imports of goods that are used further downstream in other productive processes without negatively protecting the user industries. And, as is well known, if an attempt is made to "protect everything," the result would be exchange rate appreciation that would offset the impact of the effort: if some industries are protected, others will necessarily be deprotected.

One can readily go one step further and argue that policymakers and bureaucrats cannot have enough information on which to base decisions about which industries to protect and what the side effects will be. As Adam Smith knew long ago, the individual entrepreneur has information that is simply not accessible to bureaucrats. Any effort to elicit infor-

---

5. It could be argued that this problem can be resolved by subsidizing the activities whose protection is desired. Certainly, the economic costs of protection would be considerably reduced if an industry received a subsidy rather than protection. This is because the impact on user industries would be reduced, the consumer cost would be lessened, and also because, on political economy grounds, the cost of protection would be far more visible. The chief arguments against subsidies are the standard efficient resource allocation one, and also that, once subsidies are started, all will claim them. Entrepreneurs will devote their efforts to seeking subsidies, rather than to increasing their profitability through market activities. The greater visibility of the economic costs of subsidies, and the restraint upon their magnitude imposed by budgetary considerations, however, makes them far less objectionable than tariffs or quotas.

6. See Kym Anderson and Ross Garnaut, *Australian Protectionism: Extent, Causes and Effects* (Allen and Unwin, 1987).

mation about which industries to protect is likely to encounter immediate problems of incentive compatibility: whatever criteria are set forth will affect entrepreneurial behavior, usually in undesirable ways. If protection is to go to high-cost industries, the incentive for cost-reducing behavior is greatly reduced. Yet, if it is argued that protection should go to relatively low-cost industries, an immediate question is why they should need it. Again, modern business practice usually makes it impossible for corporate executives and top managers to forecast accurately their costs and prices. Decisionmaking inherently takes place in an atmosphere of uncertainty. It is unreasonable, therefore, to expect that bureaucrats can correctly forecast whose costs will fall in the future, where productivity increases will be greatest, or which activities will generate the largest technical advances.

One of the lessons of the past quarter century has been the importance of competition as a force for cost reductions and productivity gains. The perfect competition of the textbook is not what I mean by competition, but rather the availability of enough actual and potential alternatives so that a firm's managers and employees are aware that their future fortunes depend on the ability of the company to innovate, reduce costs, and keep producing products demanded in the marketplace. Although the lesson has perhaps come home with greater force in developing countries than developed, it has certainly been an important component of the drive for deregulation and privatization.

Especially with the type of growth process just described, in which specialized parts and niches are becoming more and more important as sources of cost reduction and new product development, a global market is imperative. Otherwise, production runs will not be large enough to overcome indivisibilities; simultaneously there is unlikely to be enough competition to induce adequate development of new products and specifications. Even the United States, despite its large domestic market, needs competition from the rest of the world, in addition to its need for international markets for the products in which it is competitive.

The argument for a policy of free trade is essentially an argument that each country will, in self-interest, find it an appropriate policy. To protect because others do so is to shoot oneself in the foot.

In addition, however, a strong argument exists that an international economy in which countries are protectionist, or negotiating among themselves about what fair trade is, makes the world inherently less attractive. Such a world is politically more dangerous than one in which an open, multilateral trading system operates under agreed-on rules, such as most-favored nation, overseen by an organization such as the GATT (or, preferably, a strengthened GATT). Even in the best of circumstances, trade disputes can be highly contentious. Given America's leadership role and its interests in the international political order, Americans should be the most interested in dealing with such disputes in an agreed-on international framework rather than unilaterally alleging, and acting on, "unfair trade practices." It is counterproductive and unseemly to have contentious trade relations at the center of diplomatic discussions between the United States and Japan, or the United States and the European Community. The damage to American relations with Korea over trade issues is enormous. It is also counterproductive for the United States to exhort Brazil to service its debt while simultaneously calling the country to task under Super 301, when Brazil's politicians are also being urged to stimulate exports in order to maintain debt-servicing obligations. Even if, because of monopoly power, for example, it were in one country's interest to adopt protection of a particular industry or industries, it is much less likely to be in its interest if retaliation is possible. Moreover, if all countries are protectionist, the gains from trade will clearly be smaller for all of them than if they are all free traders.

This consideration bears greater weight for the United States than it would, for example, for Australia. Although the United States is not as large an economic power as it was twenty or thirty years ago, the United States is still the single, largest trading nation, and as such, can influence the international economic policies of other countries more than most other countries can. If the United States exercises that leadership for free trade both by exhortation and by leadership, the gains from other countries' reduced protection could be considerable. Furthermore, the United States' avowed adherence to free trade while simultaneously using Super 301, the Multifiber Arrangement, sugar quotas, and a host of other protective instruments is perceived as hypocritical, and it undermines American influence. Especially with the European move toward harmonization by 1992, American actions on trade policy may have a significant impact on the ultimate openness of the European Community.

The Case against Protection

The varied and even internally inconsistent arguments in favor of protection present a serious difficulty to those making the case against protection. The case for protecting textiles, clothing, and labor-intensive industries, for example, is the direct opposite of the case for protection or assistance to high-technology frontier industries.

Consequently, I first examine some of the big problems with the existing system of protection. Next, some of the chief arguments for protection are set forth and examined, including the argument that protection is necessary because of the American current account deficit, the argument that protection is needed to offset other countries' protection of their industries, the arguments for managed trade, and the argument for selective protection of new industries. Finally, I argue that once some protection is accepted as policy, the political process, far from being able to accept a technocratic criterion for protection, will seize whatever protectionist argument is put forth and use it toward very different ends.

A look at the important sectors in which the United States has adopted protectionist policies over the past several decades does not reveal a single instance of major economic gains. Since it is doubtful that there are many defenders of the present protective structure, a brief rundown is sufficient. Consider protection of textiles and apparel, footwear, steel, autos, sugar, and modems.

Protection against imports of textiles and apparel has existed since 1955. By 1985 bilateral negotiations within the framework of the Multifiber Arrangement had set quotas on imports of 650 different commodities from thirty-one different countries. In 1984 the protection to domestic textile and apparel producers was estimated to be equivalent to a 30 percent tariff, costing Americans about $27 billion annually. The economic cost of this protection was estimated as around $280 per household and exceeded $11,000 per (low-wage) job in the industry.[7] Much of the verbal defense for this protection was based on the goal of avoiding hardships for American workers in these low-wage industries, yet the protection offered by the Multifiber Arrangement provided an umbrella under which the textile and apparel industry in the United States moved from north to south; the North Atlantic region's share in textile and

---

7. Although jobs may be "saved" in protected industries, this does not imply that aggregate employment increases as a result of protection. Protection pulls resources away from other industries and into the protected ones. It is ironic that the persons holding the jobs saved may be different from those who were employed in the industry when protection was conferred. The jobs saved in textiles and clothing were largely new jobs in the South, while employment continued to diminish in the regions whose politicians had pressed for protection.

apparel employment fell from about 30 percent and 60 percent in 1959 to 20 percent and 34 percent respectively by 1976.[8]

Besides the aggregate gains and losses, internal inconsistencies and contradictions characterize the efforts to protect textiles and apparel. Domestic apparel producers, for example, have been negatively affected by restrictions on imports of textiles; the Hawaiian apparel industry was strongly opposed to the latest set of restrictions because it cut the industry off from Far Eastern sources on which it based its comparative advantage. Similarly, the effort to restrict imports has led to ridiculous situations. Possibly the best-known example is ramie, a coarse, itchy fiber. When imports of textiles and apparel made with traditional fibers were restricted in the early 1980s, apparel producers began experimenting with ramie as an alternative in women's sweaters. From zero in 1983, ramie imports rose sharply; by 1986 ramie was included in the Multifiber Arrangement review, with quotas set for exporting countries.[9] Disputes have also arisen about labels of origin with Far Eastern exporters, with a strong suspicion in the United States that quota rights extended to some countries have indeed been used by others. At the global level, the arrangement provides higher textile and apparel prices to producers in Korea, Taiwan, Singapore, and Hong Kong. Consequently, they are producing more textiles and apparel long after their development would otherwise have resulted in a shift out of these industries. That situation not only harms the development of those countries, but it also restricts the economic development of other nations, who might otherwise be able to expand their exports more rapidly. The recent spectacle of the United States imposing Multifiber Arrangement restrictions on Bangladesh's exports to the United States was grossly inconsistent with the stated American concern for Bangladesh's economic development. Ironically, American foreign aid officials had been advocating the adoption of economically efficient, market-oriented policies, especially including a shift in incentives toward production for exports.

8. Data are from *Economic Report of the President*, February 1988, pp. 148–49; Gary Clyde Hufbauer, Diane T. Berliner, and Kimberly Ann Elliot, *Trade Protection in the United States: 31 Case Studies* (Washington: Institute for International Economics, 1986), pp. 14–15, 139; and Anne O. Krueger," Protectionist Pressures, Imports and Employment in the United States," *Scandinavian Journal of Economics*, vol. 82, no. 2 (1980), p. 143.

9. Richard Wightman, "Quota Curb Fear Spurs Ramie Flood," *Women's Wear Daily*, November 4, 1986, p. 10. The main quota, of 74 million square yards, was allocated to China.

Although textiles, especially, have a few user industries other than apparel (such as furniture and automobiles), they are by and large consumer goods, which at least limits the cost of protection. By contrast, steel is almost exclusively used by other producers, which makes protection of it costly to other American industries. Steel was subject to trigger-price protection in the late 1970s and early 1980s, under which imports were permitted only at prices above the cost of production in Japan plus transport costs.[10] It is estimated that, ironically, American trigger-pricing protection raised profits of Japanese steel producers by more than $200 million in the 1970s—about half of Japanese expenditures on research and development in steel.[11] Although the trigger-pricing mechanism had not helped the industry, the industry nonetheless pressed for protection in the early 1980s. Most analysts have attributed a significant share of steel's troubles to "poor management, awful labour relations, bad investment decisions and the habit of looking to price rises, not better productivity, as a source of wage increases."[12] Nonetheless, in 1984 and 1985,"voluntary" export restraints on forty different steel products were negotiated with twenty-nine steel-producing countries.[13] The agreements were designed to restrict steel imports to about 20 percent of the U.S. market during the period 1985 to 1989.

It took fifty-five officials to administer the voluntary export restraints, and a strong perception developed that "bureaucratic capture" had occurred: when domestic users were unable to obtain domestic supplies and applied for imports additional to the quota, there was a pronounced tendency to find in favor of steel producers.[14]

By 1988, using industries had been confronted with steel shortages and delays in obtaining shipments. Prices of steel were 20 percent above their level of a year earlier. A 1987 International Trade Commission study estimated that voluntary export restraints in steel might have saved about 17,000 jobs, but that over 52,000 jobs in steel-using industries

---

10. Robert W. Crandall, "The Effects of U.S. Trade Protection for Autos and Steel," *Brookings Papers on Economic Activity, 1:1987*, pp. 271–88. Trigger pricing was finally abandoned as U.S. producers filed suits against U.S. steel exporters.

11. *Economic Report of the President, February 1985*, p. 117.

12. "Plea Bargaining," *Economist*, May 20, 1989, p. 79.

13. Already in 1985, it was estimated that the voluntary export restraints (VERs) resulted in a divergence between domestic and foreign steel prices equivalent to a tariff of about 30 percent.

14. Gary Hufbauer,"Wean the Steel Barons from Protection," *Wall Street Journal*, December 27, 1988, p. A10.

were probably lost because of smaller demand resulting from higher prices. It is estimated that the cost per job of steel protection is $22,000. Meanwhile, industries such as farm machinery, automobiles, machine tools, and other steel-using activities are paying a penalty, which led to the formation of a steel users' group, centering around Caterpillar Tractor Corporation.[15]

Despite all-time high profits, the steel industry pressed for a five-year extension of protection through renegotiated export restraints. Not surprisingly, opposition from users mounted rapidly.[16] However, President George Bush committed himself to continuation of protection during the 1988 presidential campaign, and it was anticipated that the voluntary export restraints for steel would be continued.[17]

Steel, like automobiles, is an industry in which relative wages were driven well above their counterparts in other producing countries during the 1970s and 1980s.[18] In both industries, part of the competitive disadvantage was attributable to the high wages. Even so, it is estimated that the cost per job "saved" of protection was $105,000 in autos.[19] The increase in price to American users was estimated by 1984 to be more than $2,400 a vehicle for Japanese automobiles and between $750 and $1,000 for American-made automobiles.[20] Of course, Japanese quality upgrading resulted from quantitative limits, and, arguably, protection of automobiles, like that of steel, assisted foreign producers at the expense of American producers.[21]

Not all American protection is for manufacturing. Most observers

15. Paula Stern, "They Make Us Uncompetitive," *New York Times*, March 18, 1989, p. 27. See also Clifford Winston and associates, *Blind Intersection: Policy and the Automobile Industry* (Brookings, 1987); Hufbauer and others, *Trade Protection*, pp. 14–15; and Jonathan P. Hicks, "Big Cast of Characters in Steel Quotas Debate," *New York Times*, May 29, 1989, p. 32.

16. Hicks, "Big Cast of Characters in Steel Quotas Debate."

17. For the Bush letter promising protection to Senator John Heinz (of Pennsylvania), see *Wall Street Journal*, December 27, 1988, p. A10.

18. For the U.S. steel industry, employment costs run about 75 percent over the U.S. manufacturing average, compared with around 50 percent in Japan, 30 percent in Canada, 20 percent in France, and 10 percent in Germany. See Donald F. Barnett and Louis Schorsch, *Steel: Upheaval in a Basic Industry* (Ballinger, 1983), pp. 68–69.

19. Hufbauer and others, *Trade Protection*, pp. 14–15.

20. Crandall, "The Effects of U.S. Trade Protection," p. 276.

21. It is ironic that one of the arguments used for protection of autos and steel is that "producers need profits to reinvest" to make them competitive. Clearly, voluntary export restraints (VERs) increase foreign profits by more than American profits.

believe that American protection of sugar may be the single worst protective measure in the United States. Among other things, the mechanism through which sugar is protected is so complex that it requires a specialist to understand it.[22] In brief, there are about 12,000 sugar farms in the United States; average payments per farm for sugar under the sugar program, which restricts imports so that the domestic price is about twice the world level, are estimated to be more than $260,000. The chief beneficiaries appear to be areas in Florida that are now opening up for cane growing.[23] Sugar prices have been supported at a level at which high fructose corn syrup (HFCS) is an economic substitute; sugar consumption has fallen from around 90 percent of total caloric sweetener consumption to less than 50 percent during the past decade: corn producers are now said to be the chief supporters of the sugar program. Meanwhile, it is estimated that it costs $76,000 to "protect" each job in sugar, with most jobs filled by immigrants. The total cost to consumers is estimated to be $3 billion annually. As a result of diminished demand and substitution of HFCS for sugar, the United States no longer imports much sugar. Economic benefits from foreign aid for the Philippines and the Caribbean Basin have been offset by their losses in sugar exports.[24]

All four of the industries discussed thus far have been subject to protection for some time, and it is therefore relatively straightforward to put up a case against protection as it has evolved. One of the unfortunate characteristics of protectionist pressures, however, is that the claims made for protection of new industries are based on the premise that it will somehow evolve differently than those protected in the past. Consider the particulars of one case in which protection is currently being advocated: telecommunications with Japan. As late as 1984, Japan did not produce modems. The American product was far superior to the acoustic coupler available in Japan for $260 and was on the market for about $130. For unknown reasons, American companies did not attempt to market in Japan, and the Japanese began production in 1985, selling modems at $290—still well above the American price. The American modem manufacturers made no move to export. By 1986 the Japanese

22. See Anne O. Krueger, "The Political Economy of Controls: American Sugar," in Deepak Lal and Maurice Scott, *Public Policy and Economic Development, Essays in Honor of I. M. D. Little* (Oxford University Press, 1990).

23. The environmental cost of this expansion is apparently very high.

24. Robert McGough,"Sweet Charity," *Financial World*, April 4, 1989, pp. 26–27.

had produced a faster-speed modem, priced at $245. Still, American modem manufacturers did not attempt to sell in the Japanese market. Later that year, the Japanese announced that they would produce a modem compatible with the leading U.S. brand, Hayes Microcomputer Products. By 1987 the Japanese had virtually caught up with the United States and lowered their prices to $185. By 1988 they began exporting to the United States. Now, as the market has widened and the Japanese are exporting, American firms are charging that the Japanese market is closed to them, and they are advocating protection. Why didn't the American manufacturers attempt to export to Japan when the Japanese did not even produce the item?[25]

Until recently, the case for protection was usually based on appeals for the welfare of those workers disadvantaged by imports in low-wage industries. There was little challenge to the basic proposition that free trade was desirable; proponents of protection instead pointed to the distributional implications, and especially to the hardship of laid-off workers, as a basis for their appeal.

In recent years, however, three additional arguments for protection have been advanced.[26] Some proponents say that the American current account deficit is unsustainable and must be corrected through trade policy. Some base the plea for protection on the argument that other countries engage in "unfair" trade practices of one sort or another and that protection must therefore be conferred to American producers to shield them from "unfair" competition. Finally some argue for "managed" trade, or "sectoral" trade policies.

The first argument, that protection must be used to help reduce the American current account deficit, is perhaps the most popular and also the most erroneous. Economists unanimously reject it. The current account deficit is a macroeconomic phenomenon. It is incurred because of an excess of expenditures over output in the United States. Currently, private saving in the United States is not large enough to finance both domestic investment and the governmental fiscal deficit. Americans are therefore importing capital from abroad, in the form of the current account deficit, to finance additional investment.

---

25. Data are from Michael Burger, "U.S.-Japan Trade Parable," *San Francisco Chronicle,* June 20, 1989, p. C4.

26. I discuss the proposal for aggressive bilateralism in the following pages. As it is put forth, it is advocated as a means to advance toward free trade, so that proponents do not contest the desirability of a free trade policy; they are essentially advocating bilateral free trade arrangements as a way to get there.

If additional protection were conferred to American industries under present circumstances, the effect would be to reduce imports and thus induce an appreciation of the dollar. That, in turn, would reduce the incentives for exporting and offset some part of the protection that had been conferred to imports. The net result would be an appreciated exchange rate, fewer exports, and fewer imports. The current account deficit would remain substantially unaltered unless a change occurred in the fiscal-monetary policies of the United States or in private saving.

Thus, those who hope for some improvement in the American current account deficit when advocating protection are misinformed. The current account deficit is the result of macroeconomic, and not microeconomic, factors, and cannot be significantly affected through protection.

The second "new protectionist" argument, that other countries engage in unfair trade practices, and that protection is a logical response, is more difficult to address. Obviously, industries wanting protection are quick to find instances of unfairness, whether they exist or not. And, even when they exist, protectionist interests are likely to overstate their magnitude and impact. Thus establishing what is "unfair," and ensuring that unfairness does not become a slogan behind which protectionist interests hide, is a serious problem.

Even if unfairness could be established, however, the problem of interdependence of industrial costs again arises. *If* country X subsidizes the production of widgets and sells them worldwide, a decision to protect American widget producers unilaterally against competition from X will leave American producers who use widgets as an input at a cost disadvantage in comparison with their foreign competitors who are buying widgets from X.

For this and other reasons, it is vastly preferable to work through the GATT to establish and enforce codes of conduct for the various governmental activities that are alleged to be unfair and to seek redress through the GATT procedures. Trade policy cannot be based on allegations of country-specific unfair trading practices; not only is country-specific protection difficult to administer and contrary to the essentials of an open, multilateral trading system, but it leaves each country in the position of being its own judge, jury, and executioner with regard to other countries' trade policies.

Almost all advocacy of protection is based on the premise that an industry, or an identifiable subset of industries, is confronted with special circumstances that warrant protection. These circumstances may be "unfair competition" from poorly paid labor abroad (textiles, apparel, footwear), lack of a "level playing field" because of government subsidies and assistance abroad (steel, semiconductors), need to assist domestic industries in attaining worldwide oligopolistic power (presumably high-technology biotechnology), and so on.

The sophisticated case for protection is usually based on some variant of the infant industry argument: that there may be market imperfections that inhibit a new industry or dynamic externalities from undertaking particular activities. As an example of market imperfections, newly emerging industries might not be able to secure the very long-term financing needed to see them through the initial period of low or negative profits to which they would be subject if imports were unrestricted. If externalities are given as the reason for protection, they must accrue to firms other than those undertaking the investment (or else the investor would stand to gain and the investment would be privately profitable); and they must be dynamic, taking place only over time. Until recently, the infant industry argument was usually appealed to as a basis for protection in developing countries, although many infants became senescent before growing up.[27]

However, even in theory, many questions were raised.[28] The dynamic externality had to be of sufficient size so that later gains, after removal of protection, would repay the initial "investment," defined as the losses that would be incurred because of the static costs of producing when the protected items would be obtained more cheaply from abroad. Further, it was always recognized that the appropriate form of protection would always be a producer subsidy, rather than a tariff or other border protection, simply because the excess costs to consumers could be avoided.

More fundamental, perhaps, were questions about whether and why the protection of an infant industry, even if undertaken by producer subsidy, would achieve the desired results. Here, identification of the source of the market imperfection or dynamic externality, and its magnitude, becomes crucial. With respect to sources, Robert E. Baldwin considered several possibilities: imperfect capital markets and dynamic

27. See Anne O. Krueger and Baran Tuncer, "An Empirical Test of the Infant Industry Argument," *American Economic Review*, vol. 72 (December 1982), pp. 1142–52.

28. The classic paper is Robert E. Baldwin, "The Case against Infant Industry Tariff Protection," *Journal of Political Economy*, vol. 77 (May–June 1969), pp. 295–305.

externalities arising from labor-force training, from the need for research and development, or from uncertainty. He demonstrated a strong presumption that protection was unlikely to overcome the source of the imperfection or externality: if a firm is likely to lose workers once it has trained them without recovering the cost of training (a peculiar presumption in light of the human capital analysis of on-the-job training), it is not clear that a higher price of output will induce a firm to invest when it otherwise would not: entry of a second firm might be more rapid at a higher product price than at a lower one. Similarly, if research and development results will spill over to others, there may be more firms for the spillover to reach when the price of the output is higher, but it is not clear that a single firm's incentive for undertaking research and development is likely to increase, and so on.

In current American discussions of protection, these same issues arise. Possibly, an industry or industries might be profitable once started, even though not privately profitable to begin with. A key question is how such industries are to be identified ahead of time. What bureaucratic procedures or mechanisms will help identify potential candidates for intervention? It is not enough to say "it is obvious" that industry has desirable externalities. Unless a procedure can be proposed for systematic evaluation of the existence and magnitude of such externalities, and a formula presented for determination about whether protection should be accepted or not, the argument for intervention in high-technology industries becomes as ad hoc as every other protectionist argument. Different groups will assert the existence of important externalities in banking and finance, semiconductors, telecommunications, biotechnology, pharmaceutical products, new materials, paper for fax machines, and so on.

Without an agreed-on set of rules and procedures—which could then be debated—to argue any variant of infant industry is to open Pandora's box for protectionist interests. Indeed, even if the infant industry case is valid, excess protection could result in a greater welfare loss than laissez-faire. Quantification is essential, not only for establishing a case at all, but for determining how much protection might be warranted.[29]

29. This assumes that protection is the appropriate instrument in the presence of an externality. For reasons outlined by Baldwin, that assumption is already questionable. However, it is well known that, when a first-best instrument of intervention is not available, a second-best instrument may prove welfare improving contrasted with laissez-faire. Advocates of protection for strategic industries might claim alternative instruments were unavailable.

To date, such quantification of the arguments for strategic trade has been largely lacking, and what little there has been does not suggest that any conceivable gains could possibly be worth the costs of protection.[30]

More fundamentally, as the Richardson survey demonstrates, the empirical techniques used to estimate the magnitude of gains and losses under imperfect competition are far from agreed on. Until they are, it is difficult to deduce what proponents of strategic trade policy have in mind: one must trust the political process, or alternatively, a group of intelligent bureaucrats, with determination of where dynamic externalities lie and their magnitude. As just argued, placing trust in a judgment process is to invite capture by special interests and an outcome far worse than an open trade policy.

At issue is not whether there should be American policies to improve the quality and quantity of resources available for production, and the efficiency with which they are used. The question is whether government intervention should be industry specific, or should instead be limited to the financing of education, research, and other activities that support all economic activity, and to the provision of generalized incentives on the basis of which firms may judge where to use the assistance.

Not only are techniques for ascertaining which industries are deserving of support singularly unreliable, but the record of picking the winners has usually been unsatisfactory. Simultaneously, ample evidence exists that investment in education, infrastructure, and research offers an ample payoff. If one were to advocate appropriate policy for the United States, it would be one of strengthening the quality and quantity of resources available generally, leaving the allocation of resources for specific industries to the market.[31]

Even if there were an agreed-on eligibility procedure for special assistance, problems would remain. Once such a formula were put forth, it would provide incentives for producers to behave, or to forecast the

---

30. See J. David Richardson, "Empirical Research on Trade Liberalization with Imperfect Competition: A Survey," *OECD Economic Studies*, no. 12 (Spring 1989), pp. 8–44. The empirical work surveyed generally showed that the gains from trade were larger under imperfect competition than they would have been with perfectly competitive markets and offered no support for the view that trade intervention will improve welfare more in the presence of imperfect competition.

31. This is not to state that the market allocates resources perfectly. It is to argue that the choice is between an imperfect market and an imperfect government, and that, once the political process intervenes in the determination of industries eligible for special favors, it is likely to be far more imperfect than the market.

future of their activity, in such a way as to increase their chances for eligibility. Especially when a criterion for receipt of benefits now is expected behavior in the future, forecasts are likely to be influenced in ways that increase the probability of receiving favorable treatment. If, for example, a subsidy were to be given for research and development in the widget industry, questions would immediately arise about why widgets and not doodads. Resources would probably be pulled into research in the designated industries, but no guarantee exists that those resources would have high payoff. Many expenditures would be reclassified as research and development in widgets, and the marginal subsidy cost of encouraging genuine research would be far greater than the average cost.

Until the advocates of strategic trade intervention put forward the criteria and procedures by which decisions will be made, it is difficult, if not impossible, to forecast consequences. It is almost surely inevitable, however, that political pressures will arise to expand the scope of policy beyond that intended and devised under the criteria and procedures. It is in the nature of the political process that there will be pressure for extending favorable treatment to ever larger groups than those initially intended for eligibility. Although this is a danger in general, it is even more a danger when discussion of specific sectoral issues arises: identity bias implies that the political process will work to favor the particular interests about which it knows something (steel workers, auto workers, and so on) than about those many anonymous economic actors who, if their activities were as large and as visible, might be equally favored.[32]

Trade policy is made in the political limelight. Only a strong intellectual defense of free trade has provided resistance to protectionist pressures of all kinds. Political scientists have long since recognized the iron triangle of politics, between politicians, bureaucrats, and their constituents.[33] Trade policy, especially one in which a sectoral component is a

32. See my "Asymmetries in Policy between Exportable and Import-Competing Goods," in Ronald W. Jones and Anne O. Krueger, eds., *The Political Economy of Protection: Essays in Honor of Robert E. Baldwin* (Basil Blackwell, 1990), pp. 161–78.

33. See Morris P. Fiorina, *Congress: Keystone of the Washington Establishment* (Yale University Press, 1977). The iron triangle is explained as follows. Bureaucrats like to have large activities to administer. Constituents like to see these activities in their districts and will vote for representatives who deliver more of these activities. Politicians seek election, so support the bureaucrats' efforts to expand their activities. In the case of trade policy, activities are protection (VERs?) of steel, autos, textiles, and so on. Constituents vote for those politicians who obtain protection for those

key feature, runs the serious risk that it will be captured by the iron triangle, as members of Congress vote for protection for the items important to their constituents, and trade votes with representatives of other districts whose voters are concerned about other sectors.[34]

The virtual impossibility of securing the complex information needed to decide precisely where and how much the government should intervene with a strategic trade policy interacts with the politics of protectionism to guarantee an outcome at whose prospect the academic protagonists of managed trade would shudder. In the absence of information required to satisfy objective economic criteria for intervention, producer pressure groups would have a field day cooking up specious arguments to justify favored treatment.

Alternative Approaches to Freer Trade

In the current climate, many thoughtful individuals will agree with the line of reasoning spelled out thus far. They will, however, ask, but what should be done when the rest of the world distorts trade flows with protectionist measures, subsidies, and other devices that harm *our* industries? The question is legitimate: free trade would no doubt benefit other countries, as well as the United States.

There is some doubt, however, about whether the American economy as a whole would be better off if other countries removed all of their interventionist policies: to the extent such policies in other countries are encouraging the perpetuation of high-cost industries and reducing productivity, American firms are more competitive than they would otherwise be. As an offset, the higher foreign incomes that would be associated with a removal of protection would increase the size of the market for American goods and simultaneously provide a lower-cost source of some imported items whose cost of production would fall as a by-product of

---

activities in their districts. Any policy aimed at sectoral identification must confront this fundamental fact.

34. Any protectionist policy is also subject to another dilemma. Industries that have comparative advantage are presumably already low cost, whereas those at a comparative disadvantage are high cost. It is extremely difficult for politicians to explain why low-cost activities merit special treatment, and thus a built-in bias exists for protection of high-cost activities. Once that bias is recognized, the incentives for cost reductions and for efficiency increases that would otherwise confront producers become less strong, as success in increasing profitability through cost reductions is at least partly offset by reduced access to political profitability through protection.

free trade abroad. It is a judgment whether the larger foreign market overseas that would result from universal free trade would offset the higher productivity levels that would result from a removal of all protectionist interventions, border and otherwise.[35]

Some advocates of managed trade would argue that the United States now faces something quite different from old-fashioned protectionism abroad. The interventionist policies of some foreign governments enable their high- technology industries to exploit world markets to the advantage of their own countries and at the expense of U.S. high-technology industries, promotes productivity growth abroad, and depresses it in the United States. But as shown in the previous section, it is not at all clear that the externalities from high-technology industries are sufficient to warrant subsidy or prohibition. Nor is it clear that the U.S. government would have sufficient information or the political will to identify and select the firms or industries that ought to be subsidized and protected.

To say that the United States should be protectionist, because the rest of the world is, is analogous to arguing that, because other peoples' drug addictions hurt me, and because other people will not stop taking drugs, I should become addicted to them. Although nonaddicts are harmed, the harm of addiction is greater still. And the same is true of trade policy.

Those who believe in free trade, but bemoan its absence in other countries, generally advocate one of three policy lines. One, negotiate bilaterally and use American bargaining power to attempt to induce the reduction of foreign trade barriers. Two, attempt to find trading partners willing to negotiate free trade agreements bilaterally and form free trade areas as an alternative to an open, multilateral trading system. Three, pursue the Uruguay round trade negotiations as vigorously as possible, supporting an open, multilateral trading system to the hilt and adopting an open, multilateral trading system no matter what the outcome of the Uruguay round is. In this section, I argue that bilateralism, in any form, is not a substitute for an open trading system. Moreover, many of the

35. This same judgment would have to be made vis-à-vis the single market of Europe after 1992 even if the European Community did turn protectionist. If 1992 and its associated deregulation result in more rapid European economic growth, the increased demand for foreign goods associated with that growth would serve as at least a partial offset to any increased protection in Europe. However, whether Europe is protectionist or not depends on several factors, including the success of the Uruguay round of trade negotiations.

complaints made by Americans against the foreign trade practices of other countries cannot be addressed satisfactorily in a bilateral framework.

Undeniably, foreign measures adversely affect many American activities. European and Japanese agricultural policies are perhaps the largest instance, but those clamoring for protection in the United States also cite industrial subsidies, state-owned (loss-making) manufacturing activities, and restrictive trade practices (including border protection) as actions that harm American producers. Although those claims are not necessarily wrong, they are probably somewhat exaggerated: anecdotal evidence by the seekers of protection often is. In addition, most of the complaints are not really amenable to bilateral resolution. Moreover, American protection and intervention are somewhat greater and more pervasive than those advocating "retaliatory" protection normally recognize.[36] American protection is actually far more legalistic than is protection in most of Europe and Japan: antidumping, countervailing duties, and now Super 301 retaliation have significant, if unmeasurable, protectionist content. If one also takes account of barriers to foreign construction firms provided by voluntary export restraints, agricultural intervention in dairy products, meat, sugar, and citrus fruit, it is not obvious that American policy is so much less protectionist than that of other countries. A big difficulty in assessing calls for protection because of "unfair" practices abroad is that some of those demanding protection are "old-fashioned protectionists," whereas others are genuinely concerned with foreign competition. Even so, a tendency to underestimate American protection and overestimate foreign protectionist practices prevails.[37]

Regardless of the relative culpability of the United States and foreign countries, however, the question about what American policy should be is a legitimate one. Those who adhere to the notion of free trade if there is a level playing field advocate the aggressive bilateralism contained in Super 301 and in "results-oriented" bargaining. Under these policy proposals, the United States would use its bargaining power to induce the offending parties to either alter their behavior or face trade sanctions

---

36. Some observers claim that American protectionism in the 1980s increased more than that of U.S. trading partners. See, for example, "America's Trade Policy: Perestroika in Reverse," *Economist*, February 25, 1989, pp. 59–60.

37. See, for example, Gary R. Saxonhouse,"The Micro- and Macroeconomics of Foreign Sales to Japan," chap. 9 in William R. Cline, ed., *Trade Policy in the 1980s* (Washington: Institute for International Economics, 1983), pp. 259–304.

from the United States. Brazil, India, and Japan have already been named under Super 301, and the semiconductor agreement with Japan is said to be results-oriented because 20 percent of the Japanese market is targeted to be the purview of American firms.

It is, of course, possible that countries named under Super 301 will alter their trade policies. Indeed, the trade regimes of India and Brazil are highly restrictionist. Undoubtedly, those two countries would be much better off if they opened up their trade regimes. Whether Super 301 will induce them to do so is an open question. The question, equally problematic, is what will happen to their trade balance with the United States when they open up their trade. Arguably, at least for India, Indian exports of textiles and clothing to the United States might meet more resistance (from the Multifiber Arrangement quotas) than American exports meet in India. Whether a more liberalized Indian or Brazilian trade regime would result in more imports from Europe, the United States, Japan, or other nations is equally problematic.

Will being named as Super 301 targets improve the climate for trade liberalization in Brazil and India, or will a political backlash occur? To date, neither Brazilian nor Indian authorities have reacted in ways that would result in a more open trading system as a consequence of their targeting.

Japan is more complex. The Japanese trade surplus with the United States has substantially followed the fluctuations in the real yen-dollar exchange rate.[38] There is little evidence that Japan has taken restrictionist measures in the 1980s. Thus it is difficult to understand how Japan's trade restrictions could have influenced the course of events, especially the increasing trade surplus with the United States. In response to this state of affairs, most informed observers now recognize that the Japanese government has imposed few formal trade restrictions.[39] They state, however, that informal practices by industrial organizations shelter Japanese producers.[40]

38. For documentation of this view, see C. Fred Bergsten and William R. Cline, *The United States-Japan Economic Problem* (Washington: Institute for International Economics, 1985).

39. Gary Saxenhouse's analysis concludes, "Looking at the United States and Japan, it is difficult to argue that American producers of industrial goods are protected by fewer overt barriers than are their Japanese counterparts." Gary R. Saxenhouse, "Japan's Intractable Trade Surpluses in a New Era," *World Economy,* vol. 9 (June 1986), p. 240.

40. See Saxonhouse," Micro- and Macroeconomics," pp. 270–71, for an elaboration

Although, in most cases, it is clearly in Japan's self-interest to eliminate such practices, it is not evident how the Japanese government can take measures to achieve such outcomes. Insofar as there are Japanese preferences for dealing with Japanese firms, or Japanese tastes for Japanese products, it is difficult to understand how the Japanese government can take direct policy actions to alter these preferences.

Even if it does so, the Japanese will not necessarily prefer American rather than European or alternative imports. If a results-oriented approach, such as that advocated by Rudiger W. Dornbusch, is adopted, several problems arise. First, the Japanese might achieve the required increase by trade diversion from other trading partners. For the Japanese to give preference to American imports over those from other sources would entail serious problems with other American (and Japanese) trading partners. European, Australian, and other exporters would not willingly acquiesce to trade diversion of that magnitude. If instead they attempted to ensure a 15 percent annual increase in imports from the United States while simultaneously maintaining most-favored-nation treatment for other trading partners, one wonders how rapidly their imports would have to grow from other countries.[41]

Sectoral, results-oriented arrangements are equally problematic, as is evidenced by the Japanese-American Semiconductor Trade Agreement. Ironically, advocates of open markets believe that the Japanese should simultaneously fail to intervene in their economy and guarantee that private Japanese companies purchase from U.S. sources. The question becomes even more acute when it is recognized that many American firms purchase from Japanese sources. Certainly, American firms are not pressured to buy from Japanese sources, and yet they continue to do so. Surely that is evidence of the limited degree to which purchases of Japanese goods by the Japanese demonstrates "irrational" preferences.[42]

---

of these informal practices. They include the large volume of postal savings and the consequent governmental impact on the financial system, the existence of large bank-centered industrial groups, the existence of very large industrial group-trading companies, the highly inefficient distributive system, treatment of Japanese labor as a fixed cost, and so on.

41. If Japan's global imports grew at 15 percent annually for ten years, while real GNP grew 5 percent annually, Japan's import share would be 26 percent of GNP by the year 2000, contrasted with 10.5 percent in 1988 (and 15.7 percent in 1985, before the appreciation of the yen). This would constitute more than twice the American share of imports in GNP.

42. The discussion of Japanese preferences is reminiscent of the discussions of

Furthermore, bilateralism offers no scope for a solution in several important sectors. These include agriculture, the Multifiber Arrangement, and other quantitative restrictions on trade. The experience with the Canadian free trade area is illustrative.

In sum, results-oriented aggressive bilateralism has scope for big disruptions of the international trading system and little potential for enhancing the efficient flow of goods and services in the international economy. Although bilateralism may result in an occasional reduction or removal of a trade restriction, it will certainly not make a serious difference for American trading prospects and greatly impairs the prospects for an open, multilateral trading system.

The second alternative, forming special trading relationships with particular trading partners, has been suggested as another means of achieving freer trade. Once several large trading nations have agreed on a free trade area among themselves, the rationale goes, other countries will find the attraction of the large, unfettered market irresistible. Therefore, if the United States moves toward free trading arrangements with particular countries, that will not constitute an abrogation of the principles of an open, multilateral trading system. Rather, it will be the beginning of an important free trade area.

Canada can and should be regarded as a rather special case. Clearly, geographic and other links between Canada and the United States would permit the formation of a free trade area without abrogation of the spirit of the open, multilateral trading system. Consideration of what could and could not be covered in the Canada-U.S. free trade area is instructive of the limits of bilateral arrangements. First, many of the principal nontariff barriers to trade (such as in agriculture) are not addressed in the free trade agreement because of the infeasibility of a bilateral approach. Second, the United States essentially bargained for reduced Canadian protection in return for assurances that any future protective measures would not apply to Canada. In this sense, the United States offered a "standstill" for Canada in return for reduction in preexisting Canadian barriers.[43] It was simply not possible to bargain bilaterally to reduce existing protection that applies, after all, to many countries.

---

dollar shortage in the late 1940s and 1950s when it was widely believed that there was a persistent tendency for the United States to remain perpetually in current account surplus.

43. See Jeffrey J. Schott, *More Free Trade Areas?* (Washington: Institute for International Economics, 1989), especially p. 12.

If one considers how bilateral free trade areas might cover additional countries, the problems would be compounded. As one example of the difficulties, consider how the Canadians, who bargained for better access to the American market in some agricultural commodities, might react if the United States now bargains with Australia for access to that same market on the same terms. Canadians might properly feel that they had lost something they had bargained for. As the number of countries involved in bilateral free trade areas rose, the potential for problems would be enormous. The advantage of trade concessions made in multilateral bargaining is that the negotiating parties have a chance to know what they are giving and getting.

The bilateral commission charged with resolving trade disputes between the United States and Canada could also lead to complications. Though one such commission can readily resolve disputes, what would happen with several such commissions? What would occur if the decisions of different commissions were inconsistent?

Finally, the regions with whom it is proposed that the United States form a free trade agreement are not usually those with whom the United States has the most trade frictions: Japan and Europe. Bilateral free trade agreements cannot be a solution to American trading problems, while Europe and Japan are left out. Some proponents of free trade agreements argue that the preferences they give other countries will induce Japan to join in free trade arrangements. But this argument is doubly fallacious: first, most other countries who are usually mentioned as candidates for a free trade agreement—Mexico, other Latin American countries—are not very competitive in the goods that Japan exports to the United States. And, second, most U.S. trade difficulties with Japan arise for reasons other than governmentally imposed trade barriers, which are the only thing that can be the subject of free trade agreements. Consideration of the difficulties likely to be encountered in extending the coverage of bilateral free trade agreements is perhaps the strongest argument for an open, multilateral trading system.

The GATT system has served the international economy well, although not perfectly, during the past four decades. As the number of significant economic centers in the world economy increases, the need for an international institution under which all trading participants can seek redress for their grievances, and develop acceptable codes of conduct, is all the greater. Though minor victories may be won in aggressive bilateralism, they cannot compare with the gains that can be achieved through the strengthening of the open, multilateral system.

Moreover, many trading problems require a multilateral solution. Among them, prominently, is that of subsidies in world agricultural trade. Given that Europe, Japan, Korea, and Taiwan are all serious protectors of their agriculture, while the United States, Canada, Australia, and other countries are significant exporters, the problem is inherently multilateral. Not only can interventions not be satisfactorily negotiated away on a bilateral basis, but the necessary adjustments will be much less painful if undertaken multilaterally.

The same considerations apply to several other areas, including government subsidies to particular industries, services trade, intellectual property rights, financial services, and so on. Only in a multilateral context can agreements be reached that may have the potential for redressing the perceived inequities of countries' policies at the present time.

There is a significant danger that the world could divide into trading blocs. If it does so, there is certainly likely to be a European bloc and a North American bloc. An important question is whether there would be a separate Asian trading bloc. If there were, that would carry significant implications for the politics and economics of the twenty-first century. If instead there were to be a Pacific area, the question is why one cannot work out a multilateral trading agreement.

A Trade Policy for the United States

It must be concluded, therefore, that the United States should pursue a policy of free trade and support for the GATT and an open, multilateral trading system. The case for removing existing interventions has already been made. The costs of protection for steel, autos, sugar, beef, textiles, clothing, construction, citrus fruit, and other sectors are high, and protection to those activities achieves no visible social purpose. Many of these protectionist measures have resulted in additional resources moving into these sectors (as in the case of textiles in the South), and there will undoubtedly be costs of reducing protection.

That there may be costs of removing protection is an argument for gradual (perhaps three years) removal of restrictions; it is not an argument for failing to remove them.[44]

---

44. The extent to which the protected industries would contract is questionable. However, the costs of adjustment would be greatly reduced if other countries simultaneously removed their protection. This is one of the reasons why the diplomatic route to freer trade has great appeal.

However, the reality of short-run adjustment costs for affected workers and employers raises the question of social policy toward trade-affected industries. In general, a strong argument can be made that social policy should be geared to treating all individuals in the same circumstance—loss of job, illness, and so on—in the same way, regardless of the cause of the circumstance. Trade is no exception: it is in principle impossible to determine who loses his job because of, for example, imports, and who loses his job because of poor management, regional relocation of a company, or other factors. Further, the plight of an unemployed person does not depend on the cause of the job loss.[45] Moreover, no evidence shows that imports are a more important source of employment disruption than are other factors.[46] Since modern economic growth increasingly depends on the flexibility and responsiveness of an economy, measures to assist displaced workers generally may be desirable social policy.[47] However, were a policy of dismantling trade barriers over the near term decided on, one can well imagine that temporary, additional adjustment assistance might be warranted during the interim period. To the extent possible, such assistance should be targeted to easing the transition (for example, assisting with moving and relocation expenses, subsidies to search costs, high unemployment compensation for a transition period, assistance with retraining expenses, and so on).[48] In the longer term, however, it is difficult to understand why those affected by foreign competition should be treated any differently than those affected by technological change, changing tastes, or other variables. Policy should therefore be part of overall social policy.

Finally, international diplomacy is important. The United States has not only the direct economic interests just discussed, but also political interests in the international economy. A healthy international economy is beneficial for developing countries on political and economic grounds. A healthy international economy can also help reduce tensions between the United States and American trading partners. As a large trading

---

45. Plant managers frequently cite foreign competition as a reason for plant closings; this writer has never seen poor management used as an explanation. It may be human nature to blame foreigners, rather than local conditions, when announcing plant closings.

46. See Krueger, "Protectionist Pressures," for some evidence.

47. The well-known difficulty, of course, is that if assistance is sufficient to compensate, the incentive for relocation is significantly diminished, if not lost.

48. One might even contemplate permanent assistance for those over a specified age, possibly 55 or 60.

nation, the United States has some scope for leadership in the international economy.

In the early postwar years, that leadership was exercised in favor of free trade in the context of an open, multilateral trading system. The result was a spectacular success for the entire world economy. In recent years, the American position has been more that of an aggrieved victim of protection than that of a world leader. "Japan bashing" has been a sorry spectacle. The United States' strategic interests in Japan, which extend well beyond trade policy, also suggest that existing trade policy is inappropriate for a leading country. On the present path, a serious diplomatic confrontation with Japan over trade issues is not unthinkable and would represent a foreign policy disaster.

Yet, unless some initiative is taken, the international economy, which contributed so greatly to world economic growth in the decades after World War II, could conceivably become fragmented into trading blocs. Such an event would represent a sizable economic loss for the United States, and an even bigger political loss.

As Europe moves toward the integration that will accompany 1992 and beyond, American behavior will be a chief determinant of the extent to which the European Community is a single market open to the rest of the world, or whether instead it is more closed to the outer world. If the United States continues to lean toward protectionist, retaliatory, or strategic responses, a more closed Community would surely be one response. That in itself would negatively affect American economic and political interests, but it would also accelerate a drift toward bilateralism. Such a drift would inevitably witness serious quarrels and confrontations between the United States and Japan over trade policy, with countries in Latin America, the rest of Asia, the Middle East, and Africa finding it even more to their advantage to join one trading bloc or another than they now do. That would negatively affect their economies and American political interests in several regions.

The alternative is a significant strengthening of the open, multilateral trading system, which was one of the great contributions of American leadership to the postwar world. In this context, the Uruguay round of trade negotiations is currently proceeding under the GATT. Although the United States has supported the Uruguay round, it has been tempered by Super 301 and other American actions that cast doubt on the American commitment to the GATT. There are complex issues in establishing codes of conduct for new areas of importance, and attention to these issues has been distracted by focus on Super 301 and possible bilateral trading arrangements. Although the United States has indicated a willingness to negotiate, the stance has been one of "being ready to consider" proposals that are made.[49] Even within the Uruguay round discussions, there has been only limited if any progress on abandoning the Multifiber Arrangement (within a reasonable time horizon), an interest of great concern to the developing countries. Nor has there been any indication that traditional barriers to foreign construction firms working in the United States might be removed or relaxed.

Aside from the strong political imperatives for a less confrontational American trade policy, there could be significant reductions in the extent to which dismantling of trade barriers requires domestic adjustments if all countries simultaneously reduce their barriers. The required agricultural adjustment for Europe, Japan, and the United States, for example, would be far less severe if all removed their agricultural protection simultaneously. The pressures on any one country's textile and clothing market would also be greatly reduced if all simultaneously abandoned the Multifiber Arrangement.

There is scope for American leadership and a serious diplomatic initiative on both political and economic grounds. It would call for a strengthened GATT secretariat and strengthened surveillance functions; it would call for the removal of all border restrictions on trade, with negotiability about the time frame for removal.[50] An initiative might then go beyond that to offer national treatment to foreign firms in countries that agree to codes of conduct for national policies affecting firms.

However, as long as American policy continues on the dual track of aggressive bilateralism and the Uruguay round, American support for the GATT sounds lukewarm and is unlikely to command great support from other nations. Regaining the momentum of the trade liberalization (and rapid-growth) years of the 1960s and early 1970s would contribute much to American economic growth, and even more to the economic health of many countries in which American foreign policy has a strong interest.

49. This was not true with agriculture, an area in which the American proposal was to abandon all subsidies over a ten-year period. Such a proposal would have had a better chance of success had it been part of a package proposal, including the Multifiber Arrangement, other VERs, construction work, and other areas of interest.

50. For example, developing countries might undertake to remove all quantitative restrictions within five years, then reduce tariffs over the following five years, while industrial countries could undertake to remove all quantitative restrictions, including VERs, and tariffs within a five-year period.

Discussion by Robert Kuttner

To my surprise and delight standard economics is becoming more open to historical, institutional, and inductive methodology. In this vein, I would like to open my remarks by asking you to consider the following propositions. First, "International trade remains a political act whether it takes place under a system of free trade or protection, of state trading or private enterprise, of most-favored-nation clause, or of discriminating treatments."[51]

Albert Hirschman wrote that statement in 1945, and it is still quite relevant. He went on to say that when you have a world of sovereign nation states which exercise sovereignty within their borders but not outside their borders, trade is, by definition, a political act. Second, but now in my own words, nations have different national economic interests that differ from the economic interests of their trading partners, even if those trading partners happen to be geopolitical allies in what used to be called the Cold War. The invisible hand will not settle those issues, especially when the real world is a subtle and complicated mixture of laissez-faire trade and managed trade.

Let me start with a brief outline of the generic case against laissez-faire trade. The case against a laissez-faire trade policy rests on historical, geopolitical, and empirical grounds, and increasingly on grounds provided by economic theory. Historically, the classical system of free trade in goods and capital, linked to a gold standard and mediated solely by private market actors, may have produced gains to allocative efficiency in a static sense. But even at the theoretical level it left out the issues raised by technological progress. And it was unstable. It was subject to bouts of boom and bust, and it was deflationary. In the real world of nation states, that instability and deflation led to responses that were protectionist and indeed contractionary.

I think the assumption that the effective choice is between free trade and multilateralism, on one hand, and unilateralism or bilateralism and protection, on the other, is inconsistent with the historical record. Bretton Woods was indeed an effort to restore flows of commerce and

---

51. Albert O. Hirschman, *National Power and the Structure of Foreign Trade,* expanded edition (University of California Press, 1980), p. 78.

payments and multilaterialism, but not to bring back classical liberalism or a simple gold standard or an unfettered laissez-faire.

Bretton Woods aimed at a multilateralism that was respectful of the economics and politics of high growth, of domestic stabilization, and of Keynesianism—before the neo-Keynesians got hold of it.

For twenty years the regime worked very well because it was supremely a regime of a mixed economy, a regime of freer trade but not a regime of nineteenth-century free trade.

The second article in the case against laissez-faire trade is geopolitical in nature. There has been much recent work in political science, which has demonstrated that unless countries have greater willingness to cede sovereignty to transnational authority than has been evident in the modern world, a liberal trading system requires a hegemonic country willing to take responsibility for the goals of the entire system, sometimes at the expense of its own national goals. That country must also make asymmetrical concessions to secure the loyalty of other partners to the free trade system.

This was certainly true in the post-1944 world. The willingness of the United States to make asymmetrical concessions to develop a liberal trading system was intensified because the United States was also the leader of the Western alliance in the Cold War. There is a long history of the United States putting Cold War goals first and seeing trade concessions as bargaining items in that pursuit, while other countries put trade goals first.

The Europeans have never had the idealistic, Wilsonian view of free trade as the summum bonum that the United States has had. Europe has always been somewhat more oriented to realpolitik in its economic policy, as have the Japanese and many of the Asian newly industrializing countries as well.

Empirically, the classical case for free trade as the optimum arrangement breaks down because of overwhelming evidence that several emerging nations have done rather well by practicing strategic trade policies rather than Ricardian trade objectives and by playing the role of free rider on a system in which the United States is the world's residual and most open market.

In a world in which the most important ingredient for national wealth is the availability and economic application of knowledge, it is awfully hard to make a case that relative factor endowments among countries determine trade flows. In today's world, competition is not perfect, it is possible to capture advantages, and learning curves matter more than factor endowments. Thus it is possible to gain an initial foothold in the most technically dynamic industries and then to deny competitors the necessary ability to capture the rents from innovation, which they need to finance research and development.

There is a whole literature on the new "strategic" view of trade. I find it intriguing that the typical new-view paper invariably ends with a disclaimer that even though the paper has blown a big hole in the theory of comparative advantage, the authors certainly do not mean to give aid and comfort to mercantilists and are certainly not about to suggest that governments are competent to plan or to improve market outcomes for a whole congeries of reasons given in a footnote. I do not know whether this approach reflects a need to keep the union card, but one increasingly finds such disclaimers, contradicting the body of the papers.

I think the practical test is to adapt trade policy to the real world, with respect both to what the United States seeks in negotiations about the world trading system and to the specific trade measures the United States takes in its national interest. I think the chief trading nations should bring to the world trading system a balance of benefits and work to bring about a system biased toward growth, a system in which poor countries are not shackled by debt.

If other countries want to practice the sort of selective mercantilism that the United States has indeed practiced, then instead of using up scarce diplomatic and economic bargaining chips to tutor those countries about the error of their ways, the United States should be using its resources to bring a balance of benefits to the system.

The United States should also use trade policy, as well as other national resources, to retain for the United States competence and competitiveness in key, emerging, dynamic industries, to make the process of decline in older industries coherent and socially bearable; and to move toward a system, if not of free trade, then certainly of freer trade.[52]

Finally, some see the dissenting view on trade as merely a set of special pleadings, whether from the AFL-CIO or the American Iron and Steel Institute or any other group. But this dissenting view deserves respect. It is a different conception of how the international political economy operates, drawing on political science, diplomatic history,

---

52. I have spelled out these ideas in a recent paper. See Robert Kuttner, "Managed Trade and Economic Sovereignty" (Washington: Economic Policy Institute, 1989).

institutional and developmental economics, and, of course, John Maynard Keynes.

One of the distressing things about the Krueger paper is not just that it argues against special interest pleadings in trade, but that it argues against politics itself.

The same concerns about special interests in trade can be applied to macroeconomics, to labor market policy, and to virtually anything that a democratic polity gets to decide.

Aristotle said that only the gods and the beasts can live in a world without politics. If human society is not a political society, it must be a totalitarian one.

Even in economic terms, the straightforward case for comparative advantage, as both an empirical description of what is and a normative description of what ought to be, has never been weaker than it is today, primarily because resources now matter less and knowledge matters more. Furthermore, postwar history is replete with nations using various mercantilist measures to capture advantage.

The idea that a country needs cheap inputs to be competitive is a kind of static view. After the war several countries could have bought their inputs cheap from the United States. In effect, they faced make-or-buy decisions. They decided that, for the long run, it would be better to make the product in their own countries, to develop some competence and some knowledge in it, and to get on the bus, even though at that particular time, it would have been cheaper to buy from Zenith or General Motors.

The Krueger paper has a conception of protection that is purely defensive. But the real problem is not so much pure protection—in the sense of keeping out the other guy's exports—as it is mercantilism. It is not that Japan or South Korea or the European Community puts up walls against U.S. products. They have a whole strategic conception of what is good for their national economy. They wield an array of subsidies, selective market closings, coerced technology transfers, and the like in a strategic effort to capture advantage for their economies.

I quite agree with Anne O. Krueger that if one simply makes a checklist of policies that are protectionist in the literal sense, the United States is as bad a sinner as other countries; but other countries do it more systematically and thereby capture advantage for their economy.

The static calculation of the costs of, say, the Multifiber Arrangement or voluntary export restraints in steel—and I know this is a standard methodological exercise—fails to capture one important aspect of the problem.

Take textiles, which is probably the worst case to try to defend. When Krueger states that the cost of textile protection is $11,000 per job, what she doesn't say is that textile protection, in the United States and in western Europe, allows firms to invest in more efficient capital. The U.S. textile industry has had a rate of productivity growth twice that of the average industry and second only to electronics, in part because textile producers have had some assurance that they will have a market next year. No one knows what the rate of productivity growth in textiles or the rate of capital investment in textiles would have been in the absence of the Multifiber Agreement in Europe or in the United States.

To pursue the case of textiles still further, reliance on cheap labor as a source of efficiency is a static concept because cheap labor does not get more efficient over time. To rely on smarter capital as a source of efficiency is dynamic. And so, the whole conventional way of looking at the Multifiber Agreement misses the point.

Krueger claims, "The American product was far superior to the acoustic coupler available in Japan. . . . For unknown reasons, American companies did not attempt to market [modems] in Japan and the Japanese began production in 1985. . . . By 1987 the Japanese had virtually caught up with the United States." By 1988, according to Krueger, the market had widened, the Japanese were exporting, and American firms were accusing Japan of closed markets and advocating protection.

The whole story, however, is in what Krueger leaves out. The reasons are not unknown. It is no accident that telecommunications was one of the targets for the Market Opening Sector Specific talks. Telecommunications was an industry in which the United States did not have a comparative advantage, and the Japanese markets were notoriously closed. It was not a matter of the United States being too lazy to go to Japan and say, "Hey, get your modems and get them while they are hot." The United States could not compete in telecommunications because of barriers.

I want to quote one passage at length because I think it gets to the whole story. Krueger writes, "Without an agreed-on set of rules and procedures . . . to argue any variant of infant industry is to open Pandora's box for protectionist interests. Indeed even if the infant-industry case is valid, excess protection could result in a greater welfare loss than laissez-faire."

But Pandora's box is already open. There is probably more managed trade in the world than free trade. A lot of foreign industries get a free ride on the unwillingness of the United States to have a strategic trade policy. To argue, as the Krueger paper does, that it is unseemly to have spats over trade policy is to assume that the spats are not out there. And in fact they are there.

In sum, being devout about free trade does not relieve one of the need to sort out issues. Those who maintain the traditional economist's devotion to free trade would have the nation pursue not a second but a fourth best. They would have the United States revert to the nineteenth-century Cobdenite idea that unilateral free trade is the optimum, while even the GATT is really built around a more mercantilist concept that concessions are supposed to be reciprocal in the real world and that countries simply do not open their markets to the export of other countries unless there is some broad degree of balance and reciprocity in the system as a whole.

That approach worked very well for the first twenty years of the GATT. The chief problems, as Rudiger W. Dornbusch suggests, is that for the past twenty years most of the world's actual mercantilist practices have been fairly impervious to the norms of the GATT. Because of U.S. fealty to the free trade ideology and geopolitical interest in having other countries support it, the United States has in practice stopped negotiating for serious reciprocity.

The result has been to leave the United States with a fourth-best bilateralism (like the Super 301), which came into existence, I think, because the United States was fearful of a balance-of-benefits concept under multilateralist auspices. The European Community suggested such an approach in the early 1980s, and the United States rejected it because it was seen as Japan bashing. The idea of "balance of benefits" was that major nations would maintain rough balance in their accounts with the trading system as a whole. The idea was never fleshed out, because the United States strenuously rejected the entire concept.

Now the United States is left with a fourth-best bilateralism, when it could have had a mixed system under multilateral auspices.

General Discussion

The Uruguay round GATT talks were discussed. Jeffrey Schott stressed the goal at the GATT was not to achieve absolutely free trade, but to move toward freer trade. Julius Katz felt the round could be completed by the end of 1990. He noted that the U.S. position was that "everything was on the table." It was up to other countries to respond and make offers. Contrary to the impression given by Krueger, he stressed that this position included U.S. trade in steel and textiles. Krueger was more skeptical about U.S. positions. She felt in some cases, such as agriculture, the United States was using extreme free trade rhetoric instead of adopting realistic negotiating positions. She feared that, by making extreme demands, the United States was gambling that others would not go along with it.

Krueger argued that regardless of how the Uruguay round was concluded or what other countries were doing, it made no sense for the United States to become protectionist. But Robert Kuttner commented that her embrace of unilateral free trade seemed to contradict her support for the GATT, which is based on reciprocal reductions of trade barriers. Laura D'Andrea Tyson also argued against unilateral free trade. She said the United States paid a high cost in allowing other nations to be free riders. Inevitably, in response to foreign actions, the United States has been forced to respond, too late, with intervention of its own. As an example, Tyson suggested that the recent development of more cooperative relationships among U.S. firms, particularly in DRAMS, was a protective response to the environment faced by U.S. firms rather than the initiation of a new system of collusion.

The discussion also considered U.S. trade protection. Fred Bergsten argued that to avoid protectionism, trade policy must be consistent with exchange rate policy. Under the Reagan administration, the administration embraced a policy of free trade, but it also adopted an exchange-rate policy that produced a large overvaluation of the currency, giving rise to huge protectionist pressures. Bergsten argued that to restore or maintain a free-trade approach, it was necessary to restore macroeconomic equilibrium and adopt a credible commitment to maintain it in the future. Krueger agreed with Bergsten that macroeconomic forces were important in generating protectionist pressures in the United States. She pointed out that protection was an inappropriate response to a macroeconomic disequilibrium because it would simply divert the pressures into some other area such as domestic inflation.

Tyson argued that as U.S. interests have shifted away from free trade, the free trade ideology has not provided a counterweight to political pressures. Krueger observed that the United States was particularly vulnerable to capture because of its political system. Mussa noted how political pressures resulted in the B-1 bomber being manufactured in all fifty states. Gary Horlick agreed that U.S. trade protection has failed to reflect a strategic vision. Protection has been granted to strategic sectors, such as semiconductors and machine tools, and to nonstrategic sectors such as steel, softwood lumber, and apparel. Horlick observed that a Republican administration was particularly unlikely to embrace a coherent theory of strategic industrial policy.

Claude Barfield also said that the rationale for U.S. government support has been weak. He argued that Sematech was supported, not on the basis of a reasoned analysis, but on the basis of the assertion that semiconductors are the key to all electronics. Soon thereafter, he noted, it was argued that high-definition television was the key to the electronics sector. Krueger mentioned that the discussion over high-definition television created such uncertainty that it delayed research on the subject. Krueger took issue with Kuttner's defense of textile industry protection. The intent of the policy, she emphasized, was to save jobs rather than promote investment or encourage efficient production. But the policy failed because originally the jobs were in New England, and the investment took place in the South.

Krueger supported some general forms of intervention, particularly for public goods such as health and safety standards. Currently, she felt the most important U.S. problem was the educational system. She opposed policies that discriminate in favor of domestic firms and promote particular industries and felt that sector-specific policies could be readily captured by special interests. Krueger was also skeptical that the experience of Japan and Korea supported the case for sector-specific industrial policies. She stressed most industrial assistance by the Korean government was for exports in general rather than for specific industries. She recalled that in the 1950s, Japan's Ministry of International Trade and Industry tried to close down the automobile industry in Japan.

The discussion also focused on what kind of intervention is legitimate in an open market. Robert Baldwin pointed out that the new trade theory with imperfect competition and economies of scale suggests that liberal trade policy is best. New empirical studies show relatively few cases in which the theoretical arguments favoring protection apply. Compared with studies that assumed perfect competition, the newer studies indicate much greater benefits from liberalization and much greater costs from protection. Barry Bosworth emphasized the benefits of intense competition in international trade—international competition forces a country to be efficient. Only in the tradable-goods industries has the rest of the industrial world caught up to the United States, whereas in the nontradable-goods industries, countries are not making any progress to close the gap. If the U.S. automobile industry had not been subject to competition from Japan's manufacturers, U.S. autos would not be nearly as good as they are today. Robert Blecker criticized Bosworth's example of the automobile industry. He pointed out that protection and intervention had also helped U.S. automakers to catch up to their foreign competitors. He mentioned that Chrysler was saved by U.S. industrial policy. He also argued that Japan's success occurred partly because of home market protection.

Robert Pastor suggested a serious difference between Krueger and other participants was the degree to which they believed the United States was more protectionist than other countries. He felt it necessary to define protectionism with sufficient precision that would allow for comparisons and judgments on the kind and degree of protectionism. Michael Mussa suggested that threats and acrimony were natural parts of the process of trying to achieve open markets. However, he felt that actions under the Super 301 sections of the 1988 Trade Act had focused on areas in which the payoff was too small to justify the political heat engendered. Avinash Dixit emphasized the importance of credibility for strategic policies such as Super 301 to be effective. He voiced concern that such measures, which start out as temporary actions, could become institutionalized and grow into long-term protectionist mechanisms.

Robert Reich asked how to deal with the entire panoply of government policies that may have discriminatory effects but are motivated by other concerns such as health, safety, and environmental regulations. Krueger stressed that she favored health and safety standards but not those whose intent was to discriminate against foreign products or firms. Kenneth Flamm asked what rules should apply to spending on research and development. He emphasized that such spending was inevitable because, besides the rent-shifting motives, governments had legitimate reasons for research and development spending that were motivated by the difference between private and social rates of return. Claude Barfield suggested that distinctions be made between the things that one might do on the research side and those on the development side. He expressed skepticism, however, that the political process could predict effectively where social and private returns diverge.

Policy Options for Freer Trade: The Case for Bilateralism

Rudiger W. Dornbusch

U.S. TRADE POLICY should aggressively seek freer trade, complementing the GATT process with bilateral initiatives. The policy should aim at rolling back domestic nontariff barriers, securing the opening of markets abroad, and forestalling the emergence of trade blocs harmful to U.S. exports. How should these goals be achieved? Unfortunately, the public debate portrays trade policy as if there were only two options: the status quo of "GATT and the open, multilateral system" (which is neither quite open nor uniformly multilateral) and "managed trade" (the GATT-is-dead crowd). There is no middle ground. Anyone arguing for bilateral liberalization falls into the crossfire between protectionists who see the risks for vulnerable industries, and never see the potential of extra exports, and multilateralists who fear for the process. Not surprisingly the debate in black-and-white terms has failed to convince anyone and has kept off the table productive options that ensure freer trade. Congressman Richard A. Gephardt is right when he argues, "Nowhere is there less analysis and more intellectual paralysis than on the critical issues of foreign trade. The dominant voices are both dogmatic and outdated; they insistently echo a past that probably never was, a past that in any event no longer exists and will not come again."[1]

In the United States, commitment to the GATT process has become an objective in itself. Americans automatically object to bilateral initiatives, even ones that are plainly within the GATT rules and actively practiced in Europe. Few among the protagonists of the status quo ask whether the protracted GATT process—negotiations take a decade or more—will deal adequately with the biggest problems facing U.S. trade policy. The beneficial effects of the status quo are taken for granted and

---

1. Richard A. Gephardt, "Fooling Ourselves about Free Trade," *Wall Street Journal*, April 12, 1988, p. A34. Of course, I do not agree with his policy prescription of protectionism and bilateral trade balancing.

the only counterfactual is a world without trade. Those who favor the status quo rationalize the violations of the open trading system by Japan with the argument that Japan is "already" opening up. Bilateralism practiced abroad, as in the Europe 1992 initiative, is welcomed, even if the same policy used by the United States is seen as a threat to the system and the process. Any bilateral proposition is presumed subversive and argued to death on grounds it violates U.S. principles, is impractical, is politically infeasible, or has insignificant effects.

If there are two dirty words in international trade diplomacy, they are "aggressive" and "bilateral." The notion of aggressive policy offends in a world where negotiation, balance, and rules—diplomacy rather than bully thy neighbor—are supposed to reign. Although unilateral action, associated with Smoot-Hawley and the implosion of world trade in the 1930s, is considered the worst kind of action, bilateral action is not far behind. The liberal trading system, in this view, is fragile and might not survive the challenge of a bilateral trade strategy. If the system suffers, who can be sure that it will not revert to the 1930s with pervasive impediments, collapsing trade, and a world depression? Indeed, bilateralism conjures up the discriminatory trade practices of the 1930s such as Imperial Preferences or the Schacht agreements.[2]

But the disdain for bilateralism is not warranted. Bilateralism received a bad name when it was an instrument for restricting trade, but open bilateralism or plurilateralism (a term I use interchangeably with bilateralism) can be an effective instrument for securing more open trade. Indeed, if trade is open in the sense of allowing conditional most-favored-nation access, a bilateral initiative can become a vehicle for freer trade on a multilateral basis. Third countries excluded from an initial agreement should be welcome to enjoy its benefits on condition they adhere to its terms.

The gains from the multilateral approach in the past have been significant and are not in question; and in some areas, such as intellectual property or services, the multilateral approach still holds promise. But the pace at which the process delivers extra gains is slowing down and the liberal trading system is eroding. Trade policy initiatives in Europe and in Asia are working quite possibly to the detriment of U.S.-located production. The increasing tendency to restrict trade by nontariff barriers

---

2. For an excellent sketch of trade history in the light of multilateralism versus bilateralism, see William Diebold, Jr., ed. *Bilateralism, Multilateralism, and Canada in U.S. Trade Policy* (Ballinger, 1987) and the references given there.

and voluntary export restraints needs to be reversed. And the problem of Japan needs to be addressed. Japan actively participated in the GATT tariff-cutting rounds but avoided opening its market through keeping in place a second layer of trade restriction. It is time for countries like Japan to open or face trade restrictions on their exports.

In this environment, the search for more effective U.S. trade policy assumes special importance. To reap the real income gains that freer trade can offer, the United States must not be confined by the relatively unproductive GATT process. The policy I advocate is to use aggressive bilateralism to push the world economy toward freer trade, complementing the GATT process when it still heads in that direction or filling a vacuum in the quest for freer trade when the GATT has tacitly accepted the status quo or even a slide into protectionism. In such cases, a more forceful trade posture, exemplified by the Super 301 remedy and negotiations of free trade areas, is desirable.

A bilateral approach should be oriented toward results. If other countries manage trade to restrict market access, then U.S. policy must impose performance measures in judging the success of trade policy. The United States should make continued, and preferably even less restricted, access to the U.S. market contingent on equal treatment in targeted countries abroad. Japan would be an obvious candidate, so would Korea, Mexico, and other newly industrializing countries.

What Trade Policy Can and Cannot Do

How can trade policy help advance U.S. welfare? Short-run responses to restrict imports are deficient. But over the proper time frame for trade policy, which is a decade or more, an outward-oriented growth strategy that focuses on developing export markets can raise the standard of living. Before I discuss such a strategy for the United States, I review what trade policy *cannot* do.

Trade Policy and the Trade Balance

The U.S. trade deficits have unfortunately become central to the discussion of a more active trade policy. Trade policy should not be used to bring about trade balancing, as the U.S. trade balance reflects not only market access for U.S. goods abroad, and for foreign goods at home, but primarily national saving and investment. By confusing the issues of market access with those of trade balance, politicians such as

Table 1. *Bilateral Trade Surplus with the United States*
Billions of U.S. dollars

Region	1980	1988
World	19.5	19.8
Japan	10.1	52.1
Germany	0.9	12.2
Italy	−1.1	4.8
Canada	0.7	10.6
East Asian newly industrializing countries	3.0	28.4
Mexico	−2.6	2.6

Sources: International Trade Administration, *United States Foreign Trade Highlights* (Department of Commerce, July 1989), table V.3A.

Gephardt are open to attack as protectionists and have weakened the legitimate U.S. pursuit of markets abroad.

The focus on bilateral imbalances, which emerged from Representative Gephardt's protectionist legislative proposal, is particularly fortunate. The concept of bilateral balancing originated in the 1930s in Hitler Germany, was subsequently used in planned economies, and was the rule for a while in the Eastern bloc. It was also used in the immediate postwar period in Europe before the Marshall Plan and the European Payments Union brought back multilateral approaches. Bilateral balancing is a primitive organization of international exchange that is almost tantamount to barter trade. There is simply no excuse for such a focus, and it is embarrassing that the U.S. administration perpetuates the use of this Schachtian notion in negotiations with Japan. It has no place in a market economy. Even the Soviets have given up on it.

Even if eliminating bilateral imbalances was a sensible goal, it is hard to interpret the data in a way that suggests trade impediments abroad are a source of the imbalances. Table 1 shows the bilateral balances in 1980 and 1988. The bilateral imbalances with most foreign countries have grown in this period. Is this to suggest that they have all erected new trade obstacles to U.S. exports? And if the problem is Japan's land use, business practices, and distribution systems, have these only become obstacles in the past few years? And what has happened in Germany and Canada to increase their bilateral surplus?

The $100 billion deterioration of the U.S. trade balance in the 1980s reflects domestic macroeconomic misalignment, not trade impediments. U.S. trading partners rightly question how the United States can possibly expect to achieve trade balance without macroeconomic correction.

They rightly fear that any trade improvement without accompanying fiscal restraint would translate into inflation, higher interest rates, dollar appreciation, and yet more commotion.

Concretely, if Japan tomorrow decided to import an extra $50 billion from the United States, it would represent a 1 percent increase in demand for U.S. goods and services. The increase in real demand, including moderate multiplier effects, would push the U.S. unemployment rate down by a full percentage point, well into the region of red hot over-heating. Moreover, since in many industries there is currently not enough excess capacity to respond to the demand increase, increases in prices would result. The sharp increase in inflation, and the Federal Reserve response in the form of tight credit, would raise interest rates, drive down investment spending, and bring about further dollar appreciation. These results would nullify the expected improvement in the trade balance.

The trade balance will improve only if the net effect of market opening abroad, taking into consideration the adjustment of the entire world economy, is to raise U.S. saving relative to investment or to improve the budget deficit. The national income identity shows that external imbalances reflect macroeconomic imbalances: net exports = saving − investment. Trade improvement requires an increase in national saving or a decline in investment. Neither event is in any obvious and tight way linked to U.S. market access in Japan.

It is remotely conceivable that market access abroad could improve the trade balance. Firms might invest only some of their increased profits. They might pay more taxes that the government did not spend. But such an outcome is not certain, particularly when the economy is substantially at full employment, as is true in the United States today, so that more exports create a shortage of resources and lead to more imports. It is doubtful that the United States can really afford a trade improvement today without first undertaking a significant correction in the budget that frees the required resources.

The Real Income Squeeze

Unlike bilateral balancing, real income is a serious issue. As table 2 shows, since the 1970s real hourly earnings have been stagnant. The moderate growth in per capita real income that took place in the 1970s and 1980s represented increasing employment (from increased labor

Table 2. *The U.S. Middle-Class Squeeze*
Average percent increase per year

Income	1950–59	1960–69	1970–79	1980–88
Real per capita disposal income[a]	1.6	3.0	2.1	1.8
Real hourly earnings[b]	3.0	2.6	1.0	0.1

Source: Author's calculations based on *Economic Report of the President, February 1990*, tables, C-27, C-46.
a. Private, nonfarm business sector.
b. Hours in private, nonfarm business.

force participation of women and the entry of baby boom cohorts into the labor force) rather than growth in real wages.

The deterioration in real income performance is further highlighted by focusing on median real income. In the 1980s families stayed in place if they were lucky, but it is evident that for many families the real income position deteriorated.[3] So far the real earnings squeeze has not translated itself into politics, presumably because employment growth permitted real per capita incomes to rise. But this mechanism is unlikely to operate in the years ahead, and hence the question of where real income growth can come from, or how to avoid shrinking real incomes, is indeed critical. If real income does not grow, redistribution and counterproductive economic populism are a serious risk.

The concern for real income growth is not only a reflection of the lack of achievement in the past. It is also influenced by the inevitability of fiscal adjustment that lies ahead and its effect on living standards. When fiscal adjustment finally does occur, there is a need to offset the contractionary impact of smaller deficits—crowding-in—to maintain full employment. This objective can be achieved through a combination of lower real interest rates or a gain in competitiveness that leads to an increase in demand for U.S. labor. There are four ways to bring it about:

—A real depreciation of the dollar and hence a decline in U.S. real wages.

—Protection.

—Foreign direct investment in the U.S. traded-goods sector, which helps reduce imports and increases exports. To the extent that foreign direct investment is conditioned by either incipient protection (tariff

3. For an extensive discussion of the middle-class squeeze, see Frank Levy, "Incomes, Families, and Living Standards," in Robert E. Litan, Robert Z. Lawrence, and Charles L. Schultze, eds., *American Living Standards: Threats and Challenges* (Brookings, 1988), pp. 109–53.

factories) or depreciation, it may only be a beneficial side effect rather than an independent adjustment.

—Improved market access abroad, which raises demand for U.S. goods without the need for real depreciation.

If crowding-in has to take place, one way or another, improved market access abroad assumes special importance because it accommodates the fiscal adjustment at minimum cost. Enlarged access abroad might dispense with the need for a 15 percent or 20 percent real depreciation that would otherwise be required to sustain full employment.

What Trade Policy Can Do

Trade policy has become synonymous with protection. That is an unjustified connotation because, to the contrary, it can be a source of growth in real income.[4] Trade policy has been given little credit for raising real income in the United States. Edward F. Denison, for example, attributes to trade policy only an impact of 1.5 percent of the level of GNP. But another strand of the profession attributes great benefits to an openness toward trade. The World Bank, for instance, represents this alternative view. Others have gone much further. Bernhard Heitger draws on cross-country evidence for less-developed countries to argue that protectionism slowed down growth (through various identified channels) on average by as much as 1.9 percent a year.[5]

Clearly, any effects of trade policy for the U.S. economy are much lower than this estimate, but they are worth looking at because every bit of growth counts. Trade policy could raise real income through four separate sources.

—Trade policy could improve the home country's terms of trade and hence real income.

—Trade policy could improve the efficiency of resource allocation. A

4. Trade policy as employment policy is fundamentally misdirected; employment problems that arise from structural change in the world economy should be handled by adjustment assistance, not protection. Lawrence and Litan develop this argument. See Robert Z. Lawrence and Robert E. Litan, *Saving Free Trade* (Brookings, 1986); and Lawrence, "Protection: Is There a Better Way?" *American Economic Review*, vol. 79 (May 1989, *Papers and Proceedings, 1988*), pp. 118–22.

5. Edward F. Denison, *Trends in American Economic Growth* (Brookings, 1983); World Bank, *World Development Report* (Washington, 1987); and Bernhard Heitger, "Import Protection and Export Performance: Their Impact on Economic Growth," *Weltwirtschaftliches Archiv*, vol. 123, p. 257.

more efficient geographic specialization raises the real income associated with a given resource endowment.

—Trade policy, by opening markets, could allow export firms to sell more. Larger markets mean more profits.

—Trade policy influences the extent of capital accumulation and the efficiency of capital accumulation (understood broadly to include not only plant and equipment but also research and development, skills, learning by doing) and in this way can raise the growth rate of labor productivity and hence the potential for real income growth.

The implications of a different U.S. trade strategy are easily exaggerated and political discussions almost systematically do so. Estimates of the benefits of Europe 1992—an important trade project if successful—run to a cumulative gain of 4 percent to 6 percent of European GNP. In the United States, the effects of trade policy on real income, even if it includes agriculture, are unlikely to achieve such magnitudes. But even so, few sources of real income growth are as free as those from a more open trading system.

The next question is what kind of trade policy to pursue. Two directions are explored. One is an uncompromising opening of the Japanese market, the other a policy of building a U.S. trade bloc.

The Welfare Costs and Benefits of Trade Restriction

The benefits of free trade compared with protection are widely accepted. But it is also commonly believed that economic theory has demonstrated that welfare would be improved by *freer* trade achieved through a multilateral approach. In fact, no strong theoretical case can be made in this direction.

The central feature of trade policy for a large country is its ability to affect, through trade impediments, the equilibrium terms of trade.[6] In a world with perfect competition (no externalities and no other distortions such as infant industry issues), there is no other reason for trade restriction. The focus on the terms of trade highlights a basic conflict between a national and an internationalist perspective. Nationally, better terms of trade redistribute world income toward the home country and

6. I am not concerned with two other possible motives for commercial policy: strategic trade policy in the context of imperfect competition to which managed trade may or not be the answer, and national security.

Figure 1. *Real Income and Protection*

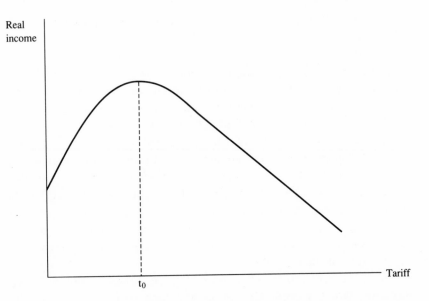

that is desirable. But trade restriction also carries a cost in that it introduces a distortion between the prices faced by firms and households and world price. Thus the benefits from trade restrictions must be traded off against this cost, and there is an optimal level of restriction—the optimal tariff.

Figure 1 shows real income as a function of the tariff rate. For a large country, there is an optimal tariff, t, which maximizes real income. The optimal tariff implicitly assumes no retaliation. But other countries will respond to another country's optimal tariff strategy, and the outcome would be a tariff-ridden world. A typical situation is shown in figure 2 where the strategic interaction between two countries, each of which sets its optimal tariff, taking the behavior of the other as given—results in a Nash equilibrium. The points t_0 and t^*_0 are the optimal tariffs for each country as in figure 2, when the other country practices free trade. The reaction functions in a Nash game are t_0R and t_0R^* for countries 1 and 2 respectively. The Nash equilibrium is at point E where both countries practice tariffs.[7]

7. The equilibrium may not be unique. For discussion see John McMillan, *Game Theory in International Economics* (Chur, Switzerland; New York: Harwood Academic Publishers, 1986).

Figure 2. *Trade Equilibria with Protective Games*

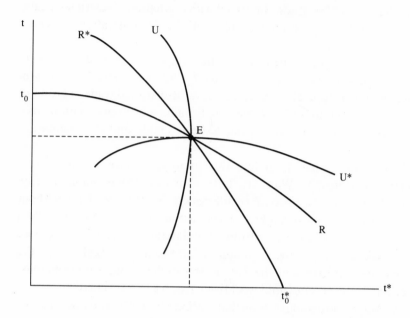

For our purposes it is interesting to ask what statements can be made about welfare in a situation such as E. As John McMillan shows, two results can be demonstrated:

—At E a mutual (small) tariff reduction (not necessarily proportional) will increase each country's welfare. This potential for gain from cooperation is a characteristic of the Nash equilibrium because that equilibrium is the outcome of noncooperative strategies.

—Complete liberalization is not necessarily in each country's interest. One country may be better off at the restricted trade equilibrium than at free trade.[8]

The theoretical foundation for reciprocal tariff cutting at E is thus established. Unilateral tariff cutting is definitely inappropriate, in this game. Since E is that point at which each country individually optimizes, unilateral tariff reduction would simply induce a lower level of welfare. What is not established by this theory is where to stop in the reciprocal tariff cuts. Specifically, going all the way to free trade need not be beneficial for everyone. At some point the argument for further tariff

8. McMillan, *Game Theory*.

cuts runs out of steam unless each individual country believes it might benefit from full free trade compared with a situation of restricted trade. In practice it would be impossible to offer a demonstration or even a presumption either way.

The theoretical argument for multilateralism, as viewed by a single large country, is even weaker than that for full free trade. The question arises whether, for a given situation of tariff-distorted trade, a group of countries can improve its welfare by forming a customs union or free trade area. The literature on the issue is ample and the results are important.

Plurilateralism has the potential to improve welfare. As Murray C. Kemp and Henry Y. Wan, Jr., have shown, customs unions can be formed that are Pareto-welfare improving for the members without reducing welfare for outsiders.[9] Thus customs unions are potentially a move toward freer trade even from a multilateral perspective. Of course, as McMillan argues, the situation is intrinsically unstable since the incentive exists to expand the membership of the union, reaping increasing gains in the process until worldwide free trade is reached.[10]

Of course, the demonstration that there are Pareto-improving customs unions does not imply that members will, in the process of forming a union, forgo their ability to restrict trade. As Robert Mundell has shown, the process of granting tariff preferences affects the terms of trade of union members relative to the rest of the world, and it thus distributes gains toward the members over and above what is gained from a more efficient allocation of resources. This is the basis for the argument cautioning against bilateralism, which Paul Krugman has developed.[11] The same terms-of-trade issue that might stop an individual country from going all the way to free trade could stop a union from expanding until it encompasses the world.

In Krugman's analysis an ingenious model of intraindustry trade is developed to show that few blocs are worse than many, three being the worst. The result is striking in view of much talk about a tripolar world.

9. The basic trick is that in addition to the internal lump sum transfers the external tariffs are adjusted so as to maintain trade with the rest of the world unchanged. Murray C. Kemp and Henry Y. Wan, Jr., "The Gains from Free Trade," *International Economic Review*, vol. 13 (October 1972), pp. 509–22.

10. McMillan, *Game Theory*.

11. Robert A. Mundell, *International Economics* (Macmillan, 1968); and Paul Krugman, "Is Bilateralism Bad?" Working Paper 2972 (Cambridge, Mass.: National Bureau of Economic Research, May 1989).

But it is important to look more closely at this result. The analysis relies critically on two ingredients. First, there is symmetry in the world so that blocs are rigorously equal sized. Second, in the transition to fewer blocs each bloc responds to the changing trading world by an increase in its optimal tariff in a Nash game. But consider the case in which bloc building is not accompanied by an increase in the optimal tariff. Is there still a welfare loss? Krugman's result continues to hold in that a reduction in the number of blocs, maintaining full symmetry so that blocs are always equal sized whatever their number, does reduce welfare. But when tariff rates are low, the welfare loss is very moderate, amounting to 1 percent or less of the free trade level of welfare.

The critical point I want to emphasize is that theory does not suggest that a plurilateral freeing of trade is a bad idea. Clearly, when it is done with the (unlikely) stricture that trade with the rest of the world should be unaffected—leaving trade creation as the pure result, nobody could possibly but applaud. In the same way, holding initial tariffs constant, the same result seems to follow at least in symmetric models of intra-industry trade.

The Multilateral Trading System

Supporters of a multilateral approach—the GATT, the Uruguay round, unconditional most-favored nation—argue two points. One, the approach has served the United States well in the past. Two, alternative approaches, including a dual track strategy, would weaken and even undermine the multilateral approach. In that case, they would throw their undivided support to the multilateral approach. In this section I question the extent to which the system is open and multilateral.

Rising Protectionism

Crediting the multilateral trading system with reconstruction of world trade after the breakdown of the 1930s, and with the growth of world trade at higher rates than world real income, would certainly be overdoing it. The reconstruction of world trade started on a bilateral basis. In Europe a dual track strategy has been followed all along, and Japan and many, if not most, less-developed countries (LDCs) have never really liberalized.

But there is no need to deny that the GATT certainly helped. The relative question is whether the GATT today still has substantial forward

Table 3. *Trade Restrictions in Industrialized Countries*

Restrictions	United States	Japan	European Community
Number of voluntary export restraints	62	13	138
Share of trade subject to hard-core, non-tariff barriers[a]	15 (17)	29 (22)	13 (22)

Sources: Margaret Kelly and others, *Issues and Developments in International Trade Policy*, Occasional Paper 63 (Washington: International Monetary Fund, December 1988), pp. 11, 13, 93; and *Economic Report of the President, January 1989*, p. 164.

a. By source of importing. Imports refer respectively to those from industrial and developing countries.

momentum or whether it is being eroded at the margin. It is not hard to bring evidence that the liberal trading system is slipping; trade is growing, but so is protectionism by nontariff barriers. Table 3 shows the proliferation of trade restrictions in the main industrialized countries. The GATT process as it is unfolding in the Uruguay round certainly will do little to stem this rising trend of trade restriction.

The GATT also does little to open up heavily protected developing countries. For reasons that are hard to understand today, pervasive inefficiency in the countries least able to afford it is thought to be a desirable feature of the GATT.[12] Korea, or Brazil, or India remains heavily protected. The GATT has made no provision for their liberalizing.

It is difficult to characterize the extent of protection in LDCs, but table 4 conveys some idea. For middle-income LDCs, average statuary tariff rates range between 34 percent and 54 percent, and between 36 percent and 83 percent of tariff positions are affected by nontariff barriers.

The liberal trading system has not only failed to check marginal protectionism and to open up LDCs, it has also failed in one of its chief assignments: avoidance of discrimination in international trade.

In the past thirty years, despite the GATT, Europe has used bilateral approaches over and over again, from the European payments union to the Common Market and the European Free Trade Association (EFTA), and to the Europe 1992 initiative. Few questions have been raised about

12. Of course, when industrial countries vote in the International Monetary Fund and the World Bank they take an entirely different view of protection of less-developed countries.

Table 4. *Trade Restrictions in Less-Developed Countries*
Percent

Restrictions	Per capita income		
	$500–$1,000	*$1,001–$1,500*	*$1,501–$5,000*
Average tariff rate	41	54	34
Tariff positions subject to nontariff barriers	77	83	36

Source: Kelly and others, *Issues and Developments in International Trade Policy*, tables A-22, A-23.

the wisdom of that strategy, whether it meant deepening the extent of integration or widening the scope to include Greece and Portugal, North Africa, and Turkey. Developments in Eastern Europe offer the prospect that this region, certainly East Germany, will soon enjoy a preferred trade status with the Common Market just as all of the EFTA already does.

Regional Initiatives

The principal regional effort in which Europe is involved removes the argument that a U.S. free trade bloc policy would undermine an otherwise intact multilateral system. The Europe 1992 project so clearly foreshadows trade discrimination that the EFTA partners are scrambling to get inside the deal for fear of being left out in the cold. A U.S. policy of building a trade bloc may be the undoing of further progress along the multilateral road. It certainly is not the first or decisive trespassing.

Advocates of the multilateral approach, beyond general invocations, have really not demonstrated what particular prospective gains, under active and promising negotiation, are being undermined. Formation of trade blocs does not, decidedly, undermine negotiations on intellectual property or services on a multilateral scale. Moreover, it can be argued that a bilateral approach can help create more enthusiasm about multilateralism simply because it demonstrates the gains from participating rather than being left out.

These considerations suggest that the United States ought to approach formation of a trade bloc or bilateral trade liberalization on a cost-benefit basis rather than on abstract principle. The argument that only regional integration is allowable is an entirely unreasonable restriction on moves toward freer trade even if it offers a superficial obstacle to U.S. initiatives in Asia or South America. Europe does not seem overly impressed with

Table 5. *Post-Tokyo Round Tariff Rates*
Percent

Region	Raw materials	Semifinished manufactures	Finished manufactures
United States	0.2	3.0	5.7
Japan	0.5	4.6	6.0
Canada	0.5	8.3	8.3
European Community	0.2	4.2	6.9

Source: *Economic Report of the President, January 1989*, p. 156.

the regional restriction. Thus, if on cost-benefit grounds a bilateral or plurilateral free trade approach is promising, there are no principles that can be effectively argued against it.

The Closed Japanese Market

Perhaps the most striking failure of the GATT system is the continuing closedness of the Japanese market. Although the country did participate in the various rounds of tariff cutting, Japan's economy remains basically closed in manufactures trade and, of course, in agriculture. Tariff protection or explicit quotas are not at issue as table 5 shows. Japan seems to be somewhat of an onion with multiple layers of protection of one kind or another.[13] As a result, a market that constitutes one-fifth of the industrial world effectively remains closed.

The statement that Japan remains a closed economy is supported by the trendless, low level of import penetration in manufacturing (figure 3). Whereas all industrialized countries show serious increases in import penetration, for Japan the level is lower than everywhere else and shows no sign of rising over the past decade.

Traditionally, three explanations have been offered. One is that Japan as a resource-poor country is an exporter of manufactures and an importer of materials. That argument leads one to expect that the manufacturing content of exports should be far higher than that of imports, but not the near absence of manufactures imports. But clearly resource endowments are not the only source of trade. Intraindustry

13. On the closedness of the Japanese market, see Robert Z. Lawrence, "Imports in Japan: Closed Markets or Minds," *Brookings Papers on Economic Activity, 2:1987*, pp. 517–54; and Bela Balassa and Marcus Noland, *Japan in the World Economy* (Washington: Institute for International Economics, 1988).

Figure 3. *Manufactures Imports, 1967–88*
Percent of GNP

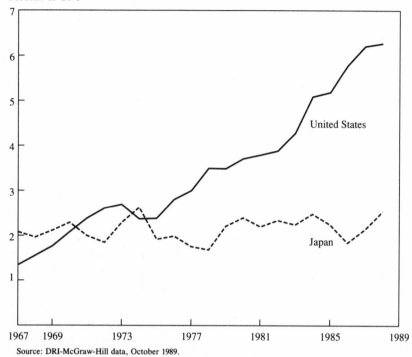

Source: DRI-McGraw-Hill data, October 1989.

trade is also based on gains from variety. For all industrialized countries other than Japan, much of the increase in import penetration reflects precisely this channel, whereas in Japan it is virtually absent. Resource endowments then cannot be the explanation.

Table 6 compares an index of intraindustry trade for the United States and Japan. The index is defined in equation 1 and ranges between zero and unity. It is apparent that if in a commodity group the value of exports equals that of imports ($X - M = 0$), the index assumes a value of unity; conversely, if trade is all in one direction only, the index is equal to zero.

$$(1) \qquad \text{Index of two-way trade} = 1 - \frac{|X - M|}{X + M}$$

It is apparent that, in every commodity group, Japan is more nearly a one-way country than the United States, and when the United States seems to be a one-way country, it is because it is hardly exporting anything. In Japan, by contrast, clothing is the only area of manufactures in which the country is a net importer. The striking absence of two-way trade in Japan is part of the evidence of an anti-import bias.

Table 6. *Measuring Two-Way Trade, 1987*

Index	United States	Japan
Manufacturing	0.72	0.40
Engineering product	0.78	0.21
Machinery for special industries	0.88	0.24
Office and telecommunication equipment	0.93	0.24
Road motor vehicles	0.49	0.08
Other machinery and transportation equipment	0.95	0.38
Household appliances	0.26	0.12
Textiles	0.65	0.70
Clothing	0.10	0.25

Source: GATT, *International Trade, 1987–88*, vol. 2 (Geneva, 1988), tables AB8–9.

A second argument for the low level of manufactures imports is that government nontariff barriers stand in the way of imports. That has clearly been true for public procurement and more generally for anything that required facilitating regulation. But the third reason is probably more important. It goes under the heading of "culture" and as such seems almost acceptable—Japanese consumers and firms "prefer" Japanese goods.

A striking piece of evidence of this effect has been brought by Mordechai E. Kreinin, who reports on a survey of capital goods purchases by multinational firms located in Australia.[14] Whereas European and U.S. multinationals purchase their capital goods anywhere in the world, based on price and quality, Japanese firms buy their capital goods virtually without exception in Japan. There might be a presumption for Japanese firms purchasing a relatively larger or even very large share of their capital goods in Japan, but the exclusive purchase in Japan draws attention.

The mechanisms of the buy-Japanese attitude are diffuse. They range from familiarity and ease of business relations, inertia, and a taste for discrimination to the social pressures applied to deviant behavior by a business community that consciously administers a redlining policy against imports.

Gary Becker has developed an economic theory of discrimination,

14. Mordechai E. Kreinin, "How Closed Is Japan's Market: Additional Evidence?" *World Economy*, vol. 11 (December 1988), pp. 529–42.

and the model applies perfectly to what is happening in Japan. As Becker notes of his theory:

> This theory can be applied to "discrimination" and "nepotism" in all their diverse forms . . . since they have in common the use of nonmonetary considerations in deciding whether to hire, work with, or buy from an individual group.
>
> Individuals are assumed to act as if they have "tastes for discrimination," and these tastes are the most immediate cause of actual discrimination. . . . When a consumer discriminates against products, he acts as if he incurs nonpecuniary, psychic costs of consumption by consuming them.[15]

It does make a difference whether low import penetration is a reflection of this taste for discrimination or whether it is mostly the outcome of a government and business policy of trade restriction. In the former case one can choose from two views: one perspective is that one cannot argue with tastes. If Japanese consumers are willing to forgo variety or pay more for made-in-Japan labels, so be it even if it comes at a terms-of-trade cost to the rest of the world. Or one can take the position that in an open world society, discrimination is a bad habit (taste), a reflection of ignorance, that should be rooted out by price and nonprice measures. In this perspective, import subsidies in Japan and import performance criteria would be the right response. But if the preferences of Japanese consumers are not the primary explanation, leaving the range from ignorance and inexperience to business-government conspiracy as the principal source of low import penetration, there can be no reason to accept the state of affairs and import performance targets should be set.

In reality some of each of the underlying motives are likely to be at work. In particular, Japanese consumers are not hostile toward or skeptical of foreign products. Any time Japanese consumers have a chance of getting close to superior products (German scissors in the 1950s, BMWs, Mercedes, Gucci, or Hermes products today) they make abundant purchases. Insistence on a process of continuing, substantial opening of the Japanese market is therefore appropriate.

15. Gary Becker, *The Economics of Discrimination* (University of Chicago Press, 1971), pp. 3, 153.

Opening Japan

It would be preferable for the United States to act in concert with the European Community in opening Japan, and that option should be explored. However, the United States should not hesitate to act on its own, using Super 301. This is far more preferable than the administration's structural impediments initiative, which is poorly targeted and has failed to deliver any progress on the central issue: increasing exports to Japan.

A target should be set for growth rates of Japanese imports of U.S. manufactures. Monitored on three-year moving averages, Japanese manufactures imports from the United States should grow at an average (inflation-adjusted) rate of 15 percent a year during the next decade.[16] During the reference period, assuming a 5 percent growth of apparent consumption, the share met by U.S. supplies would rise from about 2.5 percent today to 6.0 percent of Japanese apparent consumption of manufactures. The import share of U.S. manufactures would rise from 0.7 percent to 1.7 percent of Japan's GNP.

An automatic and effective sanction mechanism should be put in place to ensure a timely response and a complete Japanese understanding that adjustment is required. Inevitably the sanction must include restrictions on Japanese market access in the United States. There are two possible routes. One, maximize the disruptive effects for Japan and minimize the costs to U.S. consumers. This objective could be served by developing a list of commodities for which substitute producers could easily and rapidly replace Japanese shipments. Or use across-the-board tariff surcharges on Japanese imports, triggered automatically and proportionate to the shortfall of Japanese import growth. Such a mechanism has the attraction of minimizing the political intervention and fallout and is therefore preferable.[17]

The policy raises several issues. The first question is whether Japan would simply shift demand from European to U.S. goods. If so, what would the European response be to Japan and to the United States? One

16. In 1987 Japan imported $55 billion of manufactures of which $16.5 came from the United States. Japanese GNP in 1987 was about $2,366 billion. Over the period 1985–88 the average growth of U.S. manufactures exports to Japan was 21.1 percent. GATT, *International Trade, 1987-88*, vol. 2 (Geneva, 1988), table AB9.

17. It would be understood that early completion of the target would end the process. Likewise, if Japan's import penetration reached the average of OECD countries, the process should end even if the United States is not the chief beneficiary.

would hope that Europe would make the same demand and, in exchange, forgo the growing tendency to discriminate against Japanese goods. If so, Japan would be effectively faced with a multilateral challenge to open that, if met, will lead to freer trade.

What if Japanese firms located in the United States accounted for most of the exports? This event would not be a problem. What is of interest is "good jobs at good wages" for U.S.-located production. Whether the employer is a U.S. or Japanese firm is almost entirely irrelevant. Of course, it must be understood that the targets for trade growth must be substantially based on U.S. content.

Third, what if Japan considers the U.S. posture unacceptable and threatens to trigger the sanction? Economic questions might affect wider foreign policy and national security concerns. It would be an illusion to think that these issues are not just under the surface and in need of an answer. Japan has grown up and is trying to define a role commensurate with its economic strength. It may be useful to trigger the search for that identity now and let Japan choose whether it is willing to be part of an open trading system of OECD countries or look for another role. Japan does have alternatives—increased integration in Asia and possibly even with the Soviet Union.[18] It would be a mistake to postpone the policy challenge because, as these alternatives are being developed today, sanctions applied in the future could be too late.

Finally, an effective market opening of Japan would free resources in Japan, and one must ask what adjustment would be set in motion. Possibly, real income gains in Japan could raise total demand. Or resources made redundant by import competition might be absorbed in the export sector and thus increase Japan's export competitiveness. There is no problem in this result; the U.S. policy objective should be to open markets, not to defend the U.S. economy against cheap imports. Cheap imports make for a high U.S. standard of living; adjustment difficulties, either in the United States or in Japan, should not be allowed to obscure that fact.

A U.S. Trade Bloc Strategy

Concerns about pursuing the bilateral or plurilateral route are to some extent fears about the dynamics of the world trade game. If the United

18. I have explored these in "The World's New Order: A Moscow-Tokyo Bloc?" *Washington Post*, July 16, 1989 p. B1, and "Give Japan a Target and Say 'Import,'" *New York Times*, September 24, 1989, sec. 3, p. 2.

States were to pursue a bilateral route and set up preferential trade blocs, would there not be a risk of the formation of other, competing blocs? And if that were to happen, could one be certain that there would not be a 1930s-style decline in world trade?

The opposition to plurilateral approaches is thus more than anything a reaction to the untried. But it also seems that the principle of bilateralism is far more offensive and readily challenged than any particular implementation, and more so when it is suggested for the United States than anywhere else. The principle of multilateralism and the liberal trading system is so sacred because the United States sees itself as the custodian of a policy tradition that it helped create in the 1930s. And other countries that routinely infringe have, of course, a vested interest in the U.S. naiveté. A U.S. trade bloc based on conditional most-favored nation should be pursued for several reasons whose common denominator is the favorable effects of freer trade, with or without adverse side effects on outsiders.[19]

First, Japan and Latin America are already building blocs of their own. The Europe 1992 initiative highlights that tariff cutting is not enough to promote free trade; the agenda of completing the internal market draws attention to the pervasive nontariff obstacles to the free movement of goods. The completion of that project has adverse effects on production located outside the union. Much public discussion has focused on the risk of a fortress Europe policy. That is certainly not a foregone conclusion. But even without such a policy, adverse repercussions, arising directly from the increased competitiveness of internal supply locations, affect outsiders. The European Community in its report forecast a growth of intra-European output and trade combined with a 7

19. There is an ample supply of further reasons against a trade bloc scheme. Diebold, *Bilateralism, Multilateralism and Canada in U.S. Trade Policy*; Jeffrey J. Schott, *United States-Canada Free Trade: An Evaluation of the Agreement* (Washington: Institute for International Economics, 1988), and *Free Trade Areas and U.S. Trade Policy* (Washington: Institute for International Economics, 1989); Y. C. Park and J. H. Yoo, "More Free Trade Areas: A Korean Perspective," in Jeffrey J. Schott, ed., *Free Trade Areas and U.S. Trade Policy* (Washington: Institute for International Economics, 1989); Robert M. Stern, "Adaptation to Changing Trade Patterns in the Global Economy," in Randall B. Purcell, ed., *The Newly Industrializing Countries in the World Economy: Challenges for U.S. Policy* (Boulder, Colo.: L. Rienner Publishers, 1989); and Paul Wonnacott, *The United States and Canada: The Quest for Free Trade* (Washington: Institute for International Economics, 1987).

percent to 10 percent decline in imports for sources outside the Community. This reduces the demand for Community imports, shifting that demand to inside sources. In all likelihood the result is a deterioration of outsiders' terms of trade relative to the union.[20]

The second reason to explore a policy of free trade areas concerns the repercussion of the European initiative. The result of the completion of an internal market is likely to be a deterioration of the terms of trade for the outside world, including the United States. Moreover, the tensions caused by the increased internal competition and the application of the "social dimension" may well add to the temptation to practice some content protection, although not targeted on the United States. To avoid the implied risk of a terms-of-trade deterioration, the United States should likewise generate a union if this can be done without more than offsetting welfare costs.

A further reason for a trade bloc strategy concerns the favorable dynamics of a wider area. In Europe the internal market project has stimulated investment, both from inside and outside the European Community, shifting the mood from Eurosclerosis to Europhoria. U.S. multinationals are gearing up to invest in Europe not only because of the growth prospects and the increased locational efficiency, but also because of a latent risk of content protection.

A trade bloc strategy can also be used to roll back protection. Having already reduced tariffs to very low levels, and having an open, competitive, and deregulated market, the United States has little to offer as a temptation for prospective partners. But there are two clear items left: one is the exemption for partners from any existing nontariff barriers, and the other is the exemption from any future protection or excessive application of the U.S. "fair trade" laws.

Finally, besides the formation of a single market in Europe, trade blocs are also forming in Asia and in Latin America. Japan is actively pursuing a policy of expanding trade, through direct investment and sourcing, with Korea, Thailand, the Philippines, and other countries. If the bloc were allowed to form, it could easily be to the detriment of U.S. trade interests, just as European integration may have been. Considering

20. Mundell has shown that reciprocal reduction of trade impediments inside a union must worsen the outside world's terms of trade. See Mundell, *International Economics*. See also Michael Emerson and others, *The Economics of 1992* (Oxford University Press, 1992), table A6.

Table 7. *U.S. Trade, 1988*
Billions of dollars

	U.S. exports	
Region	*Total*	*Manufactures*
World	321.8	255.3
Developed countries	206.2	168.0
Japan	37.7	22.0
Europe	100.1	82.2
Less-developed countries	106.9	82.8
Western Hemisphere	43.9	35.7
Mexico	20.6	17.0
Brazil	4.3	3.8
Asia	46.1	35.3
Korea	11.3	4.7
Indonesia	1.1	0.7
Philippines	1.9	1.5

Sources: International Trade Administration, *United States Foreign Trade Highlights* (July 1989), tables v.1 and v.9.

a trade bloc with Asian newly industrializing countries could turn out to be a promising strategy that defuses these risks while offering market access abroad and the prospect of much freer trade at home.

Free Trade with Whom?

In selecting target partners for a trade bloc two considerations are relevant. One, which markets are desirable because they are not accessible today and also because they are large and offer the prospect of significant growth? Two, what can the United States offer to entice a partner country to grant preferential access?

An extensive literature now exists on all possible candidates, on certain advantages, and on the political and economic obstacles.[21] (Table 7 shows present trade patterns.)

When Mexico lowered import barriers last year, the United States benefited with an extra $6 billion of exports. If a trade coalition could be arranged that put together fifteen Mexicos, the U.S. ability to meet that demand would be more than strained. The goal is to achieve this once-and-for-all increase in U.S. exports and then to ride the high growth rates of the partner economies. In this perspective the optimistic expectations placed on free trade areas are not extreme.

21. See note 19.

North Atlantic Free Trade

A first bold step would be to offer the European Community unrestricted free trade, to be implemented by 1992. That would defuse many of the risks of Europe 1992 and represent a dramatic impetus for the freeing of trade worldwide. There is no reason to shy away from the challenge of the European single market. It is early enough to avoid a closing of Europe 1992 (if only by the internal market measures). In a few years it could be too late.

The step is a big one, but it is proportionate to the transformation of the world economy implied by an inward-looking European bloc. Such a challenge, bypassing the GATT, would find strong resonance in those circles in Europe that fear European protectionism. It would give a fresh impetus to a discussion of worldwide free trade and add an edge to skinning the Japanese onion.

The climate is rarely favorable for freeing of markets. Today the world is inclined to experiment in bold ways with free market ideas; North Atlantic unrestricted free trade would be an extraordinary idea whose time and opportunity has come and may quickly pass.

Free Trade with Latin America

It is common to argue that a tripolar world is forming—Europe 1992 (including the European Free Trade Association), an Asian coprosperity area encompassing the Tigers and Southeast Asia, and the United States with the leftovers, notably Latin America.[22] In this rendition the United States would not appear as the winner. Growth in Asia is expected to average 8 percent a year for the next decade. For the Americas, one is hard pressed to expect growth in excess of 2.5 percent, at least from the perspective of today where debt overhang, capital flight, and hyperinflation are the dominant characteristics of Latin America.

But it would be a mistake to write off Latin America. First, and perhaps foremost, Latin America represents a national security issue and as such deserves attention. If freer access to the U.S. market, and less restriction on trade, at least from the United States, can help reduce the economic problems of Latin America, then a useful purpose is immediately served.

Beyond this consideration one must surely take a longer perspective.

22. The Tigers are Hong Kong, Singapore, Taiwan, and South Korea.

Latin America's population is growing rapidly and is already more than twice that of the United States. If Latin America recovers economically, and the United States can certainly invest in that prospect, ultimately a significant market for U.S. exports exists. A clear demonstration is given by the (unilateral) Mexican trade liberalization in 1988. In a single year Mexico's imports from the United States increased by $6 billion. That represents a larger increase than the entire prospective gain from the U.S.-Canadian free trade agreement.

The Mexican trade liberalization is of interest because it highlights two features. The first, already noted, is that LDCs' markets are extraordinarily closed and hence, when trade is liberalized, offer a potential for big increases in U.S. exports. Second, the Mexican liberalization was multilateral and hence, even though it overwhelmingly benefited the United States, it also allowed other countries to participate. A free trade agreement with Latin America would yield for the United States a more privileged status, at least for a while until it became multilateral.

It might be argued that the Mexican gains are already in place and that Mexico is one of the larger countries so that little is left to gain. But Brazil, which is far larger, offers a striking opportunity from the perspective of the next twenty years. Brazil does have a strong interest in unimpeded access to the U.S. market, and it offers an important market for U.S. exports.

A useful approach to Latin America would be to target Brazil and Mexico for a free trade area, including Canada if possible. Once the principle is accepted and the outline of an agreement is in place, other Latin American countries could join.

Pacific Rim Free Trade

In Asia, the United States should also offer a free trade arrangement. The United States has leverage because the U.S. market continues to be important for these countries. The initial partners to start the process might be Korea and the Philippines. Their markets are large and growing but highly protected. They are thus obvious candidates for a free trade area, which would boost the rents of U.S. export industries.

Japan is emphasizing a new division of labor that encompasses Asian locations as cost-effective parts of a Japanese manufacturing strategy. A free trade agreement with the Pacific Rim is therefore all the more important because it offers a check to Japan's attempt to build a coprosperity area of its own.

By all accounts Asia will be the most dynamic part of the world economy in the next twenty years. It would be a serious strategic blunder not to keep an open door toward Asia and participate fully in that dynamism. The current policy of mostly open trade (with peripheral voluntary export restraints and nontariff barriers) here and pervasive restrictions abroad is unjustifiably unbalanced and therefore politically prone to protectionism. A free trade approach can help defuse the risks by yielding for the United States sharply improved trade access while liberalizing the already restricted imports.

General Agreement on Tariffs and Trade

The point of the GATT process is to find partners who are willing to engage in reciprocal lowering of trade obstacles. Moreover, this aim is to be accomplished on an open, conditional most-favored-nation basis. Accordingly, the process should be open to any third country or group of countries who might want to join because they are hurt by trade diversion or are attracted to the possibility of trade creation, or are simply looking for a good excuse to become more efficient in their resource allocation. The proposal for the open, conditional most-favored nation does not mean the creation of arbitrary, new protection measures.

Under such terms there may be more sympathy for the search for a better trade strategy in the form of a conditional most-favored nation. Gary Hufbauer and Jeffrey Schott strongly argued for conditional most-favored nation as a device to cope with the "free riders" and "foot draggers" who, they argued, encumber the GATT process. Similarly, C. Michael Aho and Sylvia Ostry favor plurilateralism, "None of the alternatives to a renewed and reinforced GATT in the Uruguay Round are attractive. Of these a series of bilateral initiatives is the most risky, destabilizing and systematically damaging. The least bad may be a revival of the old idea of a super GATT, i.e., plurilateral agreements housed in the GATT that could, over time, embrace the full multilateral agenda and GATT members."[23]

---

23. Gary C. Hufbauer and Jeffrey J. Schott, *Trading for Growth: The Next Round of Trade Negotiations*," Policy Analyses in International Economics 11 (Washington: Institute of International Economics, 1985); and C. Michael Aho and Sylvia Ostry, "Regional Trading Blocs—Pragmatic or Problematic Policy," in William E. Brock and Robert E. Hormats, eds., *The Global Economy: America's Role in the Decade Ahead* (Norton for the American Assembly, 1990), p. 177.

The concerns about the disintegration of the multilateral trading system in the face of bilateral or plurilateral trade opening initiatives are vastly exaggerated. Europe has pursued the strategy for too long to leave any doubt that just about everything that opens trade is GATTable. Even so, just as in the case of opening up Japan, conditional most-favored nation to help open trade should preferably be pursued in the framework of the GATT. But if that strategy is not productive, then the policy should be pursued nevertheless, in the hope that the GATT will adjust and become more aggressively oriented toward freer trade.

Concluding Remarks

In large, advanced, industrialized countries, trade policy is relatively inconsequential. The room for exploiting catching-up strategies is limited because the United States is advanced, and scale economies are typically exhausted at the scale of operation that the rich U.S. market can offer. Gains could be reaped from more efficient resource utilization, but such gains are small and trade policy is unlikely to offer even the most significant ones. The U.S. economic problems, as it becomes apparent in the aftermath of the prosperous 1980s, will need to be solved by scaling down expectations of living standards, increased efforts at improving education, skills, higher saving, and higher productive investment. Trade policy cannot solve these problems, however successful the United States is at opening Japan or other markets.

But even if the gains from trade policy are small, a good trade policy should be active and directed toward opening the economy on the import side while creating more and better export opportunities. A trade bloc approach would seem a fruitful strategy to give a new life to a strategy of freer trade.

The state-of-siege mentality that shapes U.S. trade policy is a reflection of U.S. vulnerability as an economy and as a world leader. It stems from deep-seated structural problems. To remedy these troubles is the most urgent priority. In the meantime the United States should develop a results-oriented trade policy. If the nation fails to put in place a sensible policy now, the next U.S. recession carries the risk of protectionism. The Uruguay round was invented as a counter to rising protectionist sentiment in the United States. It is failing to deliver sweeping results, and therefore the risk remains that at the sight of the next recession, protectionism will run high. Even beyond this near-term prospect, the extraordinary success in Asia in graduating ever more rapidly in manufacturing cannot be digested if the current state of mind prevails. A trade bloc, by providing a dramatic export boost, provides a fresh impetus to the view that trade is a good idea, not a problem. That lesson is beneficial for the world trading system.

Appendix

Daniel Gros and Paul Krugman analyze commercial policy in a model of intraindustry trade.[24] Gros showed that the gains from a trade restriction policy depend on a country's relative size. He noted in particular that a Nash tariff game pays only for a country that is at least 2.77 times as large as the rest of the world.

In Krugman's analysis the model is adapted to a world of N provinces organized in B trading blocs of equal size. Each province produces one unit of a single good. There is product differentiation in the world and this constitutes the basis for trade. Welfare of the representative agent is described by the Dixit-Stiglitz utility function:

(A-1) $$U = [\Sigma(c_i)^\theta]^{1/\theta}; \; 0 < \theta < 1$$

Suppose one starts with a symmetric equilibrium where each region charges the same external tariff t. Krugman shows that welfare in a fully symmetric world market equilibrium (up to a constant) can be written as:

(A-2) $$U = U(t,^\theta,B)$$

In free trade ($B = 1$, $t = 0$) the value of utility is unity.[25]

Suppose now an initial tariff rate of $t = 0.1$. For values of θ ranging from 0.1 to 0.9, implying elasticities of substitution between any two products between 1.0 and 10, it can be numerically verified that welfare depends on the number of trading blocs. Indeed, as in Krugman's analysis, welfare is at a minimum level for a relatively small number of trading blocs. But at a tariff level of 10 percent the welfare loss from blocs, compared with free trade, is only 1 percent of the free trade level

24. Daniel Gros, "Protectionism in a Framework with Intraindustry Trade," *IMF Staff Papers*, vol. 34 (March 1987), pp. 86–114, and "A Note on the Optimal Tariff, Retaliation and the Welfare Loss from Tariff Wars in a Framework with Intra-Industry Trade," *Journal of International Economics*, vol. 23 (March 1987), pp. 357–67; and Krugman, "Is Bilateralism Bad?"

25. Krugman, "Is Bilateralism Bad?"

of welfare. When the elasticity of substitution is small, the welfare loss is one-tenth of 1 percent of the free trade welfare level.

Discussion by Robert Z. Lawrence

Rudiger W. Dornbusch paints a bleak picture: the world trading system is falling apart and trade diplomacy is resigned to a holding position. On one hand, Japan, an important market, continues to be closed, and on the other, the European Community and Asia are forming trading blocs. Nontariff barriers and voluntary restraint agreements are widespread. To change the situation, Dornbusch advocates a two part program: first, get tough with Japan, and second, form a U.S. trade bloc and negotiate, piecemeal, with just about everybody else.

I believe, as Dornbusch does, in the goal of an open trading system without discriminatory barriers. I also agree with him that one cannot ignore the issue of Japan's trade practices nor will I differ with his argument that bilateral and multilateral approaches can help achieve these goals. However, I do disagree with Dornbusch's emphasis on how to achieve these goals. Dornbusch assigns virtually no role to multilateral approaches to dealing with these problems, whereas I believe they should have the highest priority, and bilateralism should be reserved for special exceptions.

Dornbusch finds Japan guilty of a closed market and to open that market, he believes, the United States must unilaterally insist Japan raise its manufactured imports from the United States at an annual rate of 15 percent for ten years. U.S. trade policy toward Japan must shift from demanding equal opportunity for U.S. products to affirmative action. The United States must demand preferential treatment, not for foreign goods but for U.S. manufactured goods in Japan.

But if Japan's Ministry of International Trade and Industry (MITI) ran buying cartels that forced the purchase of U.S. products along the lines Dornbusch seeks, Japan might buy more imports but it need not be more open in the most fundamental sense—a market that can be readily contested by new firms, both foreign and domestic. In fact, this situation would resemble even more the "Japan, Inc." that the United States so sharply criticizes. Dornbusch also finds nothing wrong with Japanese firms located in the United States and carrying out the increased imports, he only wants to be sure they create jobs in the United States that pay high wages. But if Japanese-owned firms continue to control Japanese trade, the cartelized nature of the Japanese economy could continue despite the increased import volumes. Finally, Dornbusch says that without a shift in macroeconomic behavior, more Japanese imports will mean more Japanese exports. Indeed, a policy that worsens Japan's terms of trade is designed to achieve such a result. But if Japanese firms dominate Japan's imports, Japan's political problems in persuading the world to accept its exports are unlikely to improve.

If Japan does not respond to these measures, Dornbusch suggests that the United States impose tariffs on Japan's exports. Yet, as he points out, without a shift in Japan's macroeconomic policies, a tax on Japan's exports would have precisely the opposite impact he desires as it would most likely lead to lower Japanese imports and a weaker yen. Therefore, such a policy could lead to a downward spiral of trade.

Surely, the Japanese market the United States seeks is one that is open to all potential entrants rather than just to the United States. If MITI diverted trade from other countries in favor of the United States, it might placate Dornbusch and improve the U.S. terms of trade, but would it really be a move of the trading system toward the multilaterally based system he strives for? It would shift Japan in precisely the wrong direction.

Thus far, the U.S. government's approach to trade with Japan, even when it has negotiated bilaterally, has been for multilateral opening. U.S. emphasis on the rules and a strong yen has paid off and should be reinforced. Particularly rapid growth in U.S. exports to Japan has occurred in sectors in which negotiations *to change the rules* have been concluded. Ironically, the report of the Advisory Committee for Trade Policy and Negotiations, which advocated sectoral import targets, showed that after ten years of pressure, virtually all barriers to the importation of tobacco into Japan have fallen.[26] The four sectors that were singled out for negotiation under the maligned Market-Opening, Sector-Specific (MOSS) talks in the mid-1980s have shown impressive growth in Japanese imports. According to the report, from 1985 to 1987, U.S. exports to Japan in the four product categories combined increased by 46.5 percent, well above the 24.8 percent increase in total U.S. exports to Japan during the same period. Tough, persistent, sectoral

---

26. Advisory Committee for Trade Policy and Negotiations, *Analysis of the U.S.-Japan Trade Problem,* Report to Carla Hills, Washington, February 1989.

negotiations are needed, as well as enough patience to let the results begin to build.

In summary, Dornbusch's approach would not lead to a more open Japan in the economically meaningful sense of the word—their markets might be more open to the United States but not necessarily to the rest of the world. Therefore, instead of shifting to a managed trade approach to open Japan, the United States should increase its emphasis on sector-specific and more generic rules changes—ideally in a multilateral setting.

Dornbusch's second principal initiative is to create a U.S. trading bloc. He suggests there are no compelling theoretical reasons to prefer multilateral negotiations over bilateral negotiations. This initiative, however, shows little awareness of the political sensitivity of trade negotiations. Dornbusch fails to appreciate the benefits of multilateralism as a bargaining device. He ignores the fact that if the United States' free trade goals are achieved multilaterally, then the political costs to the United States are much lower. Also, through multilateral negotiations, countries have greater ability and incentive to make concessions than they would if they were just negotiating with the United States alone. For example, when Japan is condemned by the United States for barriers to foreigners, such as in the structural impediments initiative, it can rebut these accusations as based on weaknesses in the United States— U.S. fiscal policy or poor competitiveness—but the case for a more open Japan can be made most compellingly and convincingly when it is made by multilateral institutions.

In Korea and the countries in Latin America that Dornbusch favors for free trade areas, the notion of submitting to American economic influence is not very popular. And it is precisely for this reason that Mexico can open up multilaterally by joining the GATT to reduce its dependence on the United States, when it would have great difficulties in opening up only to the United States.[27]

Bilateralism may also not produce the best economic results. The benefits of multilateralism are similar to the benefits of money over barter. Bilateralism, like barter, requires a double coincidence of wants. However, multilateralism allows a country to obtain a concession from

27. For excellent discussions of the problems of bilateralism see Jeffrey J. Schott, "More Free Trade Areas?" in Jeffrey J. Schott, ed., *Free Trade Areas and U.S. Trade Policy* (Washington: Institute for International Economics, 1989); and C. Michael Aho and Sylvia Ostry, "Regional Trading Blocs: Pragmatic or Problematic Policy?" in William Brock and Robert Hormats, eds., *The Global Economy* (Norton for American Assembly, 1990), pp. 147–73.

one country by providing a benefit to another. It can increase the number of potentially liberalizing deals. It also allows coalition forming that can ease deal making. A country may be prepared to lower its barriers in one product if it can obtain access in another to countries B and C, when it would be unwilling to do so if it obtains access to either B or C alone.

Moreover, in an interdependent global economy, many problems simply cannot be solved bilaterally. For example, though both Canada and the United States had a serious interest in reducing their agricultural subsidies when negotiating the U.S.-Canada free trade agreement, they could not achieve a meaningful result in their bilateral negotiations, because neither could see itself without these subsidies in third country competition.

A multilateral deal brings all interested parties to the table simultaneously. This is much simpler and more comprehensive than the piecemeal discussions that occur when a series of bilateral negotiations are implemented. The value of a benefit to a particular country depends on who is party to the deal. Countries will object if they conclude a special deal for free access to the U.S. market, if in a later agreement the United States reduces the value of this concession by concluding a similar agreement with their chief competitor. A sequence of bilateral deals may not be readily transformed into a multilateral system. Proceeding piecemeal may result in a complex, crazy-quilt system in which U.S. trade with different partners is subject to different regulatory regimes.

All of these problems with bilateral approaches suggest that the United States should give its highest priority to multilateral approaches and, therefore, the GATT should be used whenever possible to settle bilateral disputes and to negotiate new trade rules.

Finally, a few more of Dornbusch's points deserve comment. Dornbusch is particularly naive in his assumption that free trade agreements will allow the elimination of voluntary restraint agreements and exemption of certain countries from U.S. fair trade laws. This did not happen in Canada, and it is unlikely to happen elsewhere.

It is also extremely unlikely the United States would be prepared to grant a few less-developed countries, such as Korea and Brazil, exemptions from the nontariff barriers that currently exist in textiles and steel. The extent of the adjustment expected in the United States would be considerable. There could be massive trade diversion for other textile-importing nations. In my view, if this battle is to be fought and it should be, it could be more easily achieved in a more general package of important export market benefits on a multilateral level.

Dornbusch also exaggerates what can be done about subsidies. As happened with Canada, the United States is not going to offer a country complete exemption from U.S. free trade laws until it ceases to practice subsidies. But once a country is prepared to abandon its subsidies for the products that compete with the United States, it would in practice have to stop subsidies all together.

Given these considerations, I do not find the arguments that free trade areas would be able to remove the voluntary restraint agreements and nontariff barriers very persuasive in either political or practical terms. Dornbusch's writing off the current GATT system by arguing that it fails to deal with the important problems is premature. He is concerned about voluntary restraint agreements and nontariff barriers. The GATT currently has negotiations under way about a new safeguards code and textiles and agriculture, two principal areas of nontariff barriers, on its agenda. Issues relating to subsidies and other industrial policy matters that are so knotty are also being discussed.

Dornbusch sees free trade areas as helping bring about improvement in the U.S. terms of trade or a decline in the U.S. current account without a devaluation. But actually, there is no reason to expect such results. The bilateral balance between the United States and its partner in a free trade arrangement might improve or worsen. There might be offsetting improvements with third parties, but the outcome would surely depend on the precise nature of the agreement.

Finally, Dornbusch seems to feel that like the countries in his Nash equilibrium, the United States can simply take the GATT for granted. In the short term, I believe that what happens at the GATT and how the United States behaves could prove crucial to the decisions made by Europe. I also think if the United States embarked on a Dornbusch approach, declaring U.S. indifference to the GATT, the consequences could be serious for the long term. Remember the analysis of Charles P. Kindleberger about the 1930s: the trading system unraveled because of the abandonment by the United States, which was then a relatively less important player. Unless the United States keeps pedaling, the bicycle will fall backward, and the trade system would degenerate into a maze of bilateral and discriminatory arrangements.

General Discussion

Michael Mussa stressed that, in 1990, the GATT round should be the principal focus of attention because it deals with issues such as agriculture, intellectual property rights, and investment that are important in U.S. dealings with other countries, particularly Japan. He called for increased presidential support for the GATT and commented that Dornbusch's paper was an interesting example of what could happen if the GATT failed. Dornbusch responded that if the GATT solved the problems he had pointed out, he would be only too happy, but he remained skeptical.

Although critical in general of Dornbusch's proposals, Fred Bergsten did agree with Dornbusch's criticism that the GATT had allowed too many free riders through the use of unconditional most-favored-nation treatment. Bergsten supported the increased use of arrangements that included only those countries willing to adhere to certain rules and allowed access to other countries only when they met the agreement's conditions. Such conditional most-favored-nation treatment, Bergsten argued, preserves multilateralism and avoids discrimination but deals with the problem of free riders.

Gary Horlick noted that the Japanese "problem" has to do with investment as well as trade issues. In particular, allowing foreigners to acquire Japanese companies was needed. Kenneth Flamm suggested that to ensure similar practices, international standards for antitrust and other business practices are required. Robert Baldwin noted that Japan's unusually strong preferences for Japanese goods cannot be dealt with under GATT rules. He recalled, however, that the charter for the International Trade Organization in 1948 contained a code for restrictive business practices. Baldwin argued that incorporating such a code into the GATT was preferable to the drastic plan advocated by Dornbusch.

Kenneth Flamm noted that according to Dornbusch, Japan was the only country with whom lowering formal barriers would not work. Flamm asked whether cultural differences with other countries, such as Brazil, were also too great to permit common rules. Bergsten commented that Dornbusch favored free trade with every region besides Japan, which in effect came close to multilateralism. Anne O. Krueger reminded the conference that in the 1950s, many argued the United States was so different there would be a permanent dollar shortage. Krueger suggested the issue of Japanese differences would prove similarly short lived.

Dornbusch's characterization of foreign protectionist trends was questioned. Krueger voiced doubts that Europe was as protectionist as Dornbusch implied, but argued that if the United States became more protectionist, Europe would follow. Alain Morisset stressed Europe was not becoming a fortress—simply a huge, complete, internal market. He observed that in financial services, movement would be freer for foreign firms in Europe than in the United States. Fred Bergsten and Jeffrey Schott argued that Asia was not becoming a trading bloc. Schott noted that in the 1980s, interregional trade in Asia fell slightly as a percentage of total trade. Avinash Dixit cited Krugman's model of trading blocs, which concludes that the worst number of trading blocs is three. Dixit warned that the trading system could be divided into three as a result of the policies Dornbusch advocated. Mussa warned that the Dornbusch plan could freeze Europe out of the Japanese market.

Flamm noted that although they differed on the level of aggregation, both Dornbusch and Tyson sought quantitative targets. But I. M. Destler stressed that unlike Tyson, who emphasized strategic industries, Dornbusch's argument was the more traditional one—that by closing an important market, Japan hurt U.S. producers.

There was some discussion about the size of the benefits from Dornbusch's proposals. Bergsten felt that Dornbusch exaggerated the macroeconomic benefits of his program in the form of an improved trade balance or U.S. export growth. Free trade areas reflect agreements by the United States and a trading partner to open up, and there is no presumption such agreements will improve the aggregate U.S. trade balance directly. Bergsten suggested that the overall dollar size of the U.S. export growth to Japan demanded by Dornbusch was not very large. Destler agreed that the United States would benefit from more exports to Japan, but he cautioned that the United States might also be hurt if Dornbusch's plan forced sanctions against Japan's exports to the United States. Indeed, Claude Barfield recalled that when the United States had tried to retaliate against Japan in telecommunications, many U.S. companies objected, since they depended on Japanese products. Destler suggested it might be instructive to have quantitative estimates of the likely gain of an increase in manufactured exports under the Dornbusch plan as well as a calculation on the negative side if it failed. Krueger felt that major terms-of-trade benefits were not generally associated with the type of intraindustry trade Dornbusch was calling for. The benefits of intraindustry trade, she noted, come mainly through scale economies from longer production runs. Krueger argued that the Dornbusch proposal for Japan would be as difficult to administer as a multiple exchange rate system.

Horlick argued that Japan is not an issue only for the United States; Europe and other trading partners are also involved. Robert Kuttner agreed, advocating that a trade proposal with Japan should be approached multilaterally. Kuttner criticized the United States for avoiding the GATT in its efforts to change Japanese practices. He noted these practices were a threat to the system as a whole. It would also be a mistake, he stated, to have a bilateral free trade deal between Europe and the United States, because it would represent a ganging up against Japan. Robert Baldwin observed the United States had effectively used the GATT route to use other countries to pressure Europe to liberalize agriculture. He stressed multilateralism could be aggressive and activist.

Several participants expressed views on bilateral or plurilateral initiatives. Dornbusch gave credit to Super 301 in stimulating Japanese imports, but he felt a simple, clean, aggregate target would do even better. Support for the bilateral approach came from Robert Pastor who felt that Dornbusch should have emphasized that it makes sense to use the leverage of the U.S. market more effectively in bilateral negotiations to open up other markets. In particular, he argued, the only way Japan could be induced to override particular domestic interests that might be threatened by U.S. imports was to threaten other more important export interests with the loss of the U.S. market.

Robert Baldwin noted that the GATT allowed unilateral and bilateral actions such as countervailing and antidumping duties, and article 23 on Nullification and Impairment. Michael Mussa said bilateralism was useful in the free trade association with Canada, and Michael Aho felt Mexico would be the sole remaining candidate for a free trade area. But Jeffrey Schott was more cautious about prospects for achieving additional liberalization with Mexico and pointed out that most U.S. trading partners preferred the GATT to bilateralism.

Krueger and Horlick stressed that conducting sequential bilateral negotiations opens a Pandora's box after each series of negotiations. The value of preferential access changes as each new partner is included. Horlick argued that bilateralism would increase inefficiency. He described the difficulties that exist when tariff columns and rules of origin proliferate. Horlick also stressed that while the U.S.-Canada free trade association removed tariffs, it had been unable to deal with many other issues such as agriculture, intellectual property, services, and subsidies, which require multilateral agreement to be effective. Michael Aho pointed out that simply embarking on negotiations sets up expectations that make the previous status quo difficult to recover. He underscored the political problems in choosing some partners over others and the dangers of turning trade policy into foreign policy.

Managed Trade: Making the Best of the Second Best

Laura D'Andrea Tyson

MOST ECONOMICS textbooks, even graduate-level textbooks on international economics, do not contain a definition of managed trade. Yet most economists, without knowing precisely what managed trade is, instinctively dislike it. Indeed, among the few things that unite economists from different theoretical and political traditions are their support for free trade and their opposition to managed trade.

The optimality of free trade is a canon of economic thought, buttressed by elegant theoretical proofs. If free trade is usually optimal, then by implication government policies that somehow intervene in the trade process are suspect. It doesn't matter what form such policies take—the conclusion is usually the same. Hence the instinctive aversion to the notion of managed trade, whether defined or not.

In reality, the world of international trade is not a world of free trade. Governments control or manage trade in various ways. Even the regulations of the GATT, an organization championed by most free traders, are a concoction of negotiations among governments, not private traders. Trade decisions are guided by market signals that are heavily influenced by national and multilateral rules about what is fair and what is not. An ardent free trader might say these rules distort market outcomes; an advocate of managed trade might say these rules are required to "manage" or regulate markets. However characterized, such rules will continue to be a determining feature of international trade, as long as the world continues to be divided into sovereign nations.

For informed policymaking, the real choices are not choices between

The author thanks the Brookings Institution and the Berkeley Roundtable on the International Economy for financial and technical support for this project. Pei-Hsiung Chin provided expert research assistance. Stephen S. Cohen, Avinash K. Dixit, C. Fred Bergsten, Robert Kuttner, and Robert B. Reich made useful comments on an earlier draft.

pure free trade and protection—which most economists incorrectly equate with managed trade—but choices about the appropriate combination of liberalization and government intervention that will improve national economic welfare and sustain a more open, international trading system over time. To make the latter choices, more than elegant demonstrations of the properties of free trade under limiting, often irrelevant, theoretical conditions are required.

The truth is, there are no simple theoretical guidelines for making trade policy in today's world. To pretend that such guidelines exist as an alternative to acquiring knowledge of the issues in a particular trade policy decision is to court disaster.[1]

For example, free traders often argue that if foreign governments violate national or international trading rules to subsidize their domestic producers, other nations should do nothing. Foreign subsidies should be treated as a gift resulting from the ill-advised actions of foreign policymakers. This argument is based on the assumption that foreign subsidies always hurt the subsidizing country and always help other countries whose consumers benefit by access to cheaper foreign goods. Whether this assumption is correct, however, is a question of fact, and compelling reasons lead one to think that the facts do not support its application in various industries.

Free traders also frequently argue that foreign behavior that violates international trade rules should be overlooked—that tolerating such behavior is an admirable form of self-restraint that bolsters these rules. But such tolerance, though it may signal the nation's unilateral commitment to a liberal trading regime, may encourage other nations to act in ways that gradually but inexorably undermine it. Under some circumstances, strategic retaliation or deterrence rather than unilateral restraint may be the best trade policy. Once again, no general theoretical principles indicate the appropriate policy choice. An analysis of the relevant facts is required.

Apparently unconvinced by the elegance of trade theory and the impassioned pleas of the economics profession, most governments,

---

1. For an example of the uninformed nature of policy discussions on issues relating to U.S.-Japan trade in semiconductors in the Reagan administration, see the account of such discussions in Clyde V. Prestowitz, Jr., *Trading Places: How We Allowed Japan to Take the Lead* (Basic Books, 1988). The discussions reveal that many participants in the policymaking process relied on platitudes, such as industrial policy is always bad and Japanese subsidies are always good for American consumers, in lieu of any real knowledge of either the U.S. or the Japanese semiconductor industry.

including the U.S. government, are actively intervening in trade in various ways. There is widespread agreement that at most about one-half of world trade is currently covered by GATT regulations. The rest, encompassing much of the trade in products considered of great national significance by many nations, including the United States, is affected by national policies often at odds with one another and with the basic GATT principles of multilateralism and nondiscrimination.

If managed trade is defined broadly as trade that is controlled, directed, or administered by government policies, then much of this trade is managed in one fashion or another. Consequentially, in evaluating the wisdom of a particular managed trade arrangement, the correct standard of comparison is often not free trade but another form of managed trade that may have even more deleterious effects over the long run.

I present the case for some form of managed trade in high-technology industries for four distinct but interrelated policy reasons: to promote the competitive strength of such industries in the U.S. economy; to improve the management of high-technology trade in the presence of widespread government intervention around the world; to support an expansionary adjustment of the U.S. trade deficit; and to deflect growing protectionist pressures at home and abroad.

First, growth in high-technology industries generates important external economic benefits for the economy. Because of these benefits, the fate of these industries cannot be left solely to market forces, particularly when these forces are heavily influenced by activist government policies abroad.

Second, because high-technology industries possess these characteristics, they have increasingly become the object of trade disputes and interventionist policies by the United States and other governments. The policy instruments used to promote high-technology domestic producers extend far beyond the border measures that have traditionally been the focus of trade policy. Because of widespread and diverse policy intervention, free trade in high-technology products is a largely meaningless option. For such products, the real choice is not between free trade and protection, but rather between managing international trade by new international agreements and managing it by unilateral, uncoordinated, and often beggar-thy-neighbor national policies.

Third, high-technology products account for a significant and growing share of U.S. trade—approximately 38 percent of nonagricultural merchandise exports and 25 percent of nonpetroleum merchandise imports in 1988.[2] Managed trade arrangements that stimulate U.S. exports and reduce U.S. imports of such products can help adjust U.S. trade imbalances, in the most effective way, that is, to the extent that such arrangements succeed in breaking down foreign barriers to U.S. exports, the United States can adjust its trade balance with a smaller drop in the dollar's value and less of a loss in real income.

Finally, managed trade and other policy initiatives to support U.S. high-technology producers in the face of persistent market barriers and widespread policy intervention abroad may moderate protectionist pressures at home. U.S. companies, including several high-technology, multinational producers traditionally supportive of free trade, have become much more aggressive in seeking trade relief under U.S. law. They are reacting to serious competitive difficulties caused in part by the actions of foreign governments to support their domestic producers. Increasingly, the real alternative to an activist managed trade initiative in the United States is not free trade but what might be called "privatized or special-interest trade policy," resulting from the legal initiatives of the private sector. But privatized trade policy, while serving the short-run interests of those American producers who successfully win trade relief, may not serve the goals of American competitiveness in high-technology industries and realizing a sustained adjustment of the nation's trade deficit.

In this paper, consistent with my emphasis on high-technology industries, I present the case for a sectoral approach to managed trade. Priority should be given to developing managed trade arrangements specifying allowable "rules of the game" for business and government behavior on a sector-by-sector basis. Ideally, such arrangements should negotiate away illegitimate forms of national intervention that discriminate against foreign producers and hamper trade. Failing that, such arrangements should aim at greater consistency in the rules for national intervention, resulting in more efficiently and fairly managed trade, if not freer trade.

To the extent that such process-type arrangements cannot be negotiated or enforced in a timely fashion, managed trade arrangements stipulating quantitative outcomes for sectoral trade flows may be re-

2. These calculations are based on the figures in table 1 and on figures for nonagricultural merchandise exports and nonpetroleum merchandise imports for the United States reported in the *Survey of Current Business,* vol. 69 (June 1989), p. S-17.

quired. An outcome approach may be essential if, in the absence of such rules, barriers to critical foreign markets pose a serious threat to the competitive strength of domestic producers.

Finally, I argue that managed trade arrangements stipulating quantitative outcomes for aggregate trade flows—such as an arrangement specifying targets for the overall U.S.-Japan trade imbalance—should be avoided. Such arrangements do not address the underlying macroeconomic causes of overall trade imbalances and are doomed to failure. Perhaps even more important, their implementation could be particularly damaging to high-technology producers.

Obviously, the case for sectoral managed trade arrangements in high-technology industries depends on the importance of external economic benefits for an individual nation arising from a rapidly growing and vigorous set of high-technology producers. Therefore, after defining alternative forms and goals for managed trade, I focus on the special features of high-technology industries, the external economic benefits they generate, and the potential harm that may be done if the United States relies on market forces while other countries pursue interventionist policies to preempt world markets for their producers. I conclude with some recommendations for developing effective managed trade arrangements for high-technology industries.

What Is Managed Trade?

It is not an easy task to define managed trade. In the lexicon of economics, there are no generally agreed-on definitions. Several different types of managed trade arrangements can be distinguished in principle and in practice.

Managed trade agreements can be either bilateral or multilateral. The Semiconductor Trade Agreement is bilateral, while the Multifiber Arrangement is multilateral. In general, multilateral agreements are preferable—bilateral agreements by their nature discriminate against excluded parties and usually result in increased trade friction. Multilateral agreements allow a larger number of interested parties to negotiate, usually resulting in less discriminating outcomes.[3]

---

3. Sometimes, bilateral agreements that invite others to join become multilateral over time. On controversial issues, not currently covered by multilateral rules, such as trade-related investment measures (TRIMs) or trade in services, progress can often come only through bilateral negotiations.

Managed trade arrangements can have either a macroeconomic or a sectoral focus. A macroeconomic managed trade arrangement, for example, the recent Kissinger-Vance proposal for U.S.-Japan trade, designates a target for the overall bilateral trade imbalance.[4] The import and export adjustments undertaken by each nation to realize the target are not part of the agreement, but are left to be worked out by each of them. Such an approach, which also characterized the Gephardt amendment, rests on the assumption that only the overall trade imbalance with individual trading partners is of concern, not its sectoral incidence or overall composition.

There is little to recommend a managed trade approach at the macroeconomic level. The overall trade position of a nation is mainly a consequence of macroeconomic forces, and any attempt to change it by the imposition of an aggregate quantitative target would be undermined by offsetting adjustments in macroeconomic variables, such as the exchange rate. Nor is there any obvious reason why the aggregate trade imbalance between two trading partners, such as the United States and Japan, should be the target of a managed trade agreement. Multilateral not bilateral trade imbalances matter from a macroeconomic point of view.

If the bilateral imbalance is a meaningful issue, it must be because bilateral disagreements occur about trade practices or market access barriers in specific industries. Bilateral or multilateral negotiations and managed trade agreements that address these disagreements directly are an appropriate policy response.

Finally, a managed trade agreement at the macroeconomic level, such as the one proposed by Kissinger and Vance, gives the surplus country the power to determine the sectoral incidence of export cuts and import increases required to reach the macro target. When the surplus country is one like Japan, which has demonstrated that it has the capability to organize selling cartels and to think strategically about the composition of its trade, the choices made could be extremely harmful to the deficit country.[5] To realize the macro target, exports important to the strength

4. Henry Kissinger and Cyrus Vance, "Bipartisan Objectives for American Foreign Policy," *Foreign Affairs,* vol. 66 (Summer 1988), pp. 899–921.

5. For a detailed discussion of Japan's targeting strategy and its influence on Japan's trade structure, see Giovanni Dosi, Laura D'Andrea Tyson, and John Zysman, "Trade Technologies and Development: A Framework for Discussing Japan"; and Laura D'Andrea Tyson and John Zysman, "Developmental Strategy and Production Innovation in Japan," in Chalmers Johnson, Laura D'Andrea Tyson, and John Zysman, eds.,

of the U.S. economy could be cut, while imports of marginal products that pose no competitive threat to Japanese producers could be increased. The bilateral trade imbalance might improve, but at the cost of a deterioration in the U.S. terms of trade and with no improvement in the market access of competitive American producers to the Japanese market.[6]

In contrast to macro managed trade arrangements, micro or sectoral managed trade arrangements focus on regulating trade in particular industries or products. Two types of sectoral managed trade arrangements can be identified: arrangements that establish rules for trade—and foreign direct investment—in particular industries; and arrangements that establish target outcomes for such trade.

The distinction between managing rules and managing outcomes is an important one, which discussions of managed trade, at least by economists, frequently overlook. Trade outcomes are heavily influenced by national and multilateral rules, for example, rules of origin, rules of local content, antidumping rules, COCOM rules, government procurement rules, and national rules to regulate telecommunications and financial services. The GATT has little to say about many of these rules and what it does say, as in the case of the GATT antidumping code, is vague and largely unenforceable. Governments actively attempt to manage trade outcomes to realize their trade and industrial policy objectives by unilateral adjustments in such rules.

A managed trade agreement of a "rules-oriented" type can be defined as an agreement that specifies a set of policy rules and guidelines that will be adhered to by the signatories to the agreement for the sectors covered by it. Examples of such agreements include the COCOM restrictions on dual-use technology exports to the Eastern bloc; the U.S.-Canadian auto pact; the recent EC antidumping rules; and parts of the semiconductor agreement. The rules do not specify quantitative

---

Politics and Productivity: The Real Story of Why Japan Works (Ballinger, 1989), pp. 3–38, 59–140.

6. To a lesser extent, the same criticism can be made of Rudiger W. Dornbusch's proposal to set a target for the rate of growth of manufactured exports from the United States to Japan. Although this proposal concentrates on manufactured trade rather than on the overall trade imbalance between the two countries, it does not make any sectoral distinctions within manufacturing. Consequently, it allows the Japanese to determine which manufactured goods to import from the United States and in what quantities to hit the proposed target. For more on the Dornbusch proposal, see his paper.

outcomes for sectoral trade, but they certainly influence such outcomes in profound ways.

Sectoral managed trade agreements can also be "results-oriented." The distinguishing feature of such agreements is the establishment of quantitative trade targets. Most often, such agreements take the form of limits on trade in particular products among the signatories. These limits can be expressed in value or volume terms and in allowable levels or rates of growth. These types of agreements are the ones most often criticized by economists and proponents of free trade. Most managed trade agreements for outcomes are protectionist in spirit and design. They establish quantitative limits on imports of specific products into particular countries to protect domestic producers. Examples include the multifiber agreement and a variety of voluntary export restraint (VER) agreements and orderly marketing agreements (OMA) limiting trade in certain industries or products among particular nations.

In contrast to managed trade agreements that limit imports, the semiconductor agreement is a managed trade arrangement designed in part to expand imports by Japan, one of its signatories. Such an agreement is an example of what Jagdish Bhagwati has called a "voluntary import expansion" (VIE) agreement. In Bhagwati's words, "Whereas VERS restrict imports of specific goods from specific countries by getting those countries to adopt export quotas and restraints, VIEs require imports of specific goods by specific countries by all possible means."[7]

In Bhagwati's view, both the export restraints and the voluntary import expansion agreements are protectionist—the export restraints constitute import-protectionism, while the import expansion agreements constitute export-protectionism. But, there are important differences between the two. The import expansion agreements do not discriminate against imports to the advantage of domestic producers, and they do not directly restrict the volume of trade. Indeed, they are meant to expand the volume of trade by setting a quantitative import floor in markets perceived closed to import competition by policy or structural barriers. To the extent that this perception is warranted, the import expansion agreements are designed to reduce protectionism and to increase competition and the flow of trade. As such, their intent is trade liberalization, not trade restriction.

Moreover, as I discuss later, a managed trade agreement that restricts

7. Jagdish Bhagwati, *Protectionism* (MIT Press, 1988), p. 83.

competition and trade in the short run may increase them in the long run. In dynamic industries the time frame used in evaluating the effects of a managed trade agreement is critical.

Sectoral Managed Trade Arrangements and the Nation's Trade Strategy

To evaluate the wisdom of sectoral managed trade arrangements, it is necessary to be clear about their goals.

First, such arrangements would not be a solution to the overall trade deficit. The deficit reflects not only—and not primarily—market access for U.S. goods abroad and foreign goods at home but also—and much more significantly—patterns of national saving and investment. No form of trade policy, including managed trade arrangements, can substitute for the macroeconomic adjustments in national saving and investment necessary to restore a sustainable U.S. trade balance over the long run.

Second, although sectoral managed trade arrangements may help domestic high-technology producers by breaking down barriers to foreign markets or by establishing rules regulating promotional policies abroad, such arrangements should not substitute for other policy measures to build a strong national base in high-technology industries. For example, if the goal of policy is to promote more R&D spending in such industries, then some form of R&D subsidy is the most effective policy. More generally, the well-known prescription of traditional trade theory continues to apply: if the rationale for policy is the presence of external benefits, such as those that characterize high-technology industries, then trade policy is at most a second-best policy response, whose adverse effects, such as higher import prices, may more than offset anticipated benefits.

There are really two defensible goals for managed trade arrangements in high-technology industries. First, because of widespread policy intervention in these industries by national governments—intervention that is not effectively covered by the GATT and that can have profound effects on trade outcomes—it is critical that there be internationally accepted rules of the game for competition. This suggests a role for sectoral managed trade arrangements to specify and enforce such rules for national governments and producers.

Second, as a strategic move to press for the introduction of such rules, to induce other nations to open their markets, or to deter other nations from closing their markets, managed trade arrangements specifying sectoral outcomes may be defensible.[8] An outcome approach may be essential if barriers to critical foreign markets are causing serious harm to domestic producers in important high-technology industries. A negotiated outcome approach may look especially attractive if the likely political alternative is unilateral, aggressive reciprocity, with the threat of retaliatory beggar-thy-neighbor actions abroad.

Under current economic circumstances, managed trade arrangements in high-technology industries have an important role to play in U.S. trade policy. If the United States is to achieve a balanced current account sometime in the mid-1990s, it needs a turnaround in its trade position of about $120 billion to $200 billion. Since the energy import bill is likely to rise during the next several years—perhaps by as much as $60 billion— and since neither service nor agricultural net exports will be large enough to cover more than a fraction of the required turnaround, the brunt of adjustment must fall on trade in manufactured goods. How this adjustment is realized, however, greatly depends on foreign factors.

If key foreign markets, particularly the Japanese market, remain relatively closed to American producers, if the unification of the European market raises barriers to U.S. exports, and if the newly industrializing countries continue to promote and protect their domestic producers in industries in which U.S. producers have competitive strength, the adjustment of the U.S. trade imbalance will be much more difficult to realize and will require a greater drop in the dollar's value and greater cuts in U.S. imports, both of which imply a greater toll on future U.S. living standards.

A fundamental goal of American policy should be an expansionary adjustment, fueled by U.S. exports and import substitution, not an austerity adjustment accomplished by import contraction and a sharp fall in the dollar's value. To facilitate an expansionary adjustment, the United States needs to secure greater access to world markets for exports of manufactured goods produced in the United States. This effort will require new approaches to trade policy.[9]

8. Of course, as Avinash Dixit suggests in his comments on this paper, the U.S. policy process as it now works is ill suited for using such strategic moves to influence the behavior of other nations. When the administration and Congress differ within themselves and between each other on the appropriate use of policy to influence the behavior of a major trading partner, such as Japan, it is difficult to use strategic threats and promises in a credible way.

9. Because of the dramatic increase in foreign direct investment in the United States, foreign-owned operations are likely to play a significant role in the reindustrialization

Although the United States should continue its commitment to multilateral negotiations to broaden the GATT, the GATT framework is ill suited to deal with trade policy issues for many manufactured goods. The changes in the GATT, at least as currently contemplated, will not be sufficient to secure a meaningful improvement in market access for U.S. exports. In addition, timeliness is important.

It is extremely unlikely that substantial progress in the Uruguay round talks will be realized on such critical issues as intellectual property protection, trade-related investment measures (TRIMs), and telecommunications and other services in the near future. The GATT talks are notoriously slow moving, which is one reason why the GATT has lost its relevance for many national policymakers. Meanwhile, actions taken now by other governments can have important effects on the U.S. trade imbalance and on the future competitiveness of American producers. Temporary market-closing policies abroad can have long-term effects not easily or costlessly reversible, as the experience of the American semiconductor industry sadly demonstrates. And rules of origin, such as the ones recently adopted by the EC for the auto and semiconductor industries, can have long-term effects on patterns of investment, production, and trade.

The United States must follow a fast-track approach to addressing such policies on a bilateral and sectoral basis, even as it continues to support the GATT negotiations to address them with new multilateral rules. The fast-track approach is likely to include bilateral and regional trade arrangements and managed trade arrangements in certain industries judged to be of special importance to U.S. competitiveness. Sectoral managed trade arrangements negotiated by a limited number of countries for new disciplines and safeguards on rules and behaviors not currently covered by the GATT may serve as a model for future changes in the GATT. To reap the gains from having a strong high-technology industrial base and greater market access abroad, the United States should not be

---

of the U.S. economy and the likelihood of an expansionary adjustment of the U.S. trade imbalance. In fact, the impact of foreign direct investment on U.S. trade performance is already obvious. During the 1980s, the trade deficits of foreign affiliates in the United States averaged about 60 percent of the total U.S. trade imbalance. A more aggressive trade policy, such as the one outlined in this paper, should focus on national trade performance, not on company ownership. What matters is domestically based operations, not domestically owned operations. Exports and imports by foreign-based subsidiaries are equivalent to exports and imports by domestic firms operating in the United States for the purpose of reducing the trade deficit.

blocked by a slow-moving GATT process, but instead should move in new sectoral (and regional) ways to overcome the growing tendency toward trade restrictions at home and abroad. Sectoral managed trade arrangements specifying rules—and where necessary outcomes—for trade in high-technology industries can play a role in realizing this objective.

Theoretical Justifications for Managed Trade in High-Technology Industries

Technology-intensive industries clash with the assumptions of free trade theory—and with the largely static economic concepts that are the traditional basis for U.S. trade policy—in several ways. In such industries, costs tend to fall and product quality tends to improve over time, the returns to technological advance tend to spill over into various other activities, and barriers to entry and first-mover advantages tend to result in imperfectly competitive industrial structures. As a result of these characteristics, a nation's comparative advantage in such industries is less a function of its national factor endowments and more a function of strategic interactions between its firms and government and the firms and governments in other nations. In such industries, comparative advantage is created, not endowed by nature.[10]

During the last decade, new developments in trade theory have recognized the special features of high-technology industries and the dilemmas they pose for evaluating policy. The new trade theory literature[11]

10. Sometimes comparative advantage, which results from the actions of governments, is called arbitrary as opposed to created comparative advantage. The use of the term "arbitrary" reflects the notion that comparative advantage is the accidental, unintentional result of policy intervention. In contrast, the use of the term "created" reflects the notion that comparative advantage is the result of purposeful and successful government intervention. Which term one chooses to use depends largely on one's assessment of the wisdom and effectiveness of government policy. As Dixit notes in his comments, even if one accepts the notion that comparative advantage in some industries is in part created by government action, this does not necessarily imply that such action is always warranted—the costs of such action have to be weighed against the benefits in each case.

11. The literature on the new trade theory is large and growing. Several excellent papers are included in Paul R. Krugman, ed., *Strategic Policy and the New International Economics* (MIT Press, 1986). For a recent summary of the major conclusions of the theory, see Krugman, "Is Free Trade Passé?" *Journal of Economic Perspectives,* vol. 1 (Fall 1987), pp. 131–44. For a complete technical treatment of the theory, see Elhanan Helpman and Paul R. Krugman, *Market Structure and Foreign Trade: Increasing*

demonstrates that in industries with increasing returns, technological externalities, and imperfect competition, free trade is not necessarily and automatically the best policy. Government policy to strengthen the competitive position of domestic producers in world markets may generate even higher levels of national welfare than would result from free trade.

The new trade theory rests on the notion that some industries or activities may be of strategic significance to national welfare in one of three distinct, often interrelated, ways. First, because of imperfectly competitive structures, some industries may generate excess profits or quasi rents over time—the resources employed by them earn higher returns than those available in the rest of the economy. Government policies to win larger world market shares for domestic producers in such industries, and hence a larger share of world excess returns, may improve national welfare. As an illustration, if the world computer industry is a high-profit, high-wage industry, then national protectionist and promotional policies that capture a larger share of the world computer industry for domestic producers may improve national economic welfare at the expense of foreign competitors. Such policies, which act to shift the world pool of excess returns from one set of national producers to another, are inherently beggar-thy-neighbor policies.

Particular industries may be strategic for a second reason: they generate spillover benefits for the rest of the economy, and government policies to promote them can improve welfare by fostering these benefits. The proposition that such policies can improve welfare when an industry generates external economies is part of the conventional theory of trade policy.[12] The new literature has strengthened the case by focusing on externalities from the R&D activities of high-technology industries and by linking the analysis of externalities to the analysis of the imperfectly competitive market conditions inherently characteristic of such industries.

Finally, industries may be of strategic significance because they provide inputs to other industries at decreasing cost over time. The result is what Krugman has called linkage externalities—private increasing

Returns, Imperfect Competition, and the International Economy (MIT Press, 1985). For one of the earlier theoretical pieces that focused on high-technology industries, see James Brander and Barbara Spencer, "Export Subsidies and International Market Share Rivalry," *Journal of International Economics*, vol. 18 (February 1985), pp. 83–100.

12. Jagdish Bhagwati, "Is Free Trade Passé After All?" speech on the occasion of the award of the Bernhard Harms Prize at Kiel, Germany, June 1988.

returns in these industries are the basis for social increasing returns throughout the economy.

High-technology industries, such as semiconductors and computers, are excellent candidates for consideration as strategic sectors. Because of high and rising capital and R&D barriers to entry, such industries have imperfectly competitive structures, they are characterized by oligopolistic behavior, and, in the case of microprocessors and computers, they generate higher than normal returns. Because they are R&D and knowledge intensive, they have generated and will continue to generate huge technological externalities.[13] And because they provide inputs to other industries at decreasing cost over time, they generate linkage externalities.[14]

But although economists might agree that if economically strategic industries exist, these high-technology industries are the best examples, there are serious reservations about the policy implications of the new trade theory. The first reservation is about the feasibility of determining whether an industry is strategic or not. Increasing returns, the nature of imperfect competition, the existence of quasi rents, and the extent of technological or linkage externalities are all notoriously difficult to measure.

The second reservation is about how one evaluates whether a proposed policy will do more harm than good. The answer depends on several imponderables including the exact form of the policy, its effects on other industries that may lose resources as a consequence, and the

13. For evidence on the technological spillovers generated by the semiconductor and computer industries, see Michael G. Borrus, *Competing for Control: America's Stake in Microelectronics* (Ballinger Press, 1988); Kenneth Flamm, *Creating the Computer: Government Industry and High Technology* (Brookings, 1988); and Martin Neil Baily and Alok K. Chakrabarti, *Innovation and the Productivity Crisis* (Brookings, 1988).

14. When a high-technology industry, such as the semiconductor industry, provides inputs to other high-technology industries, the merits of a trade policy or other policy that raises the prices of the input industry must be weighed against the costs of such a policy on the user industries. The fact that the antidumping provisions of the semiconductor trade agreement were partly responsible, along with a cyclical upturn in the demand for semiconductors and supply difficulties associated with the introduction of the one-megabit chip, for the sharp increase in the prices of DRAMs in 1987 and 1988 was a serious weakness of the agreement, since the benefits to the semiconductor producers had to be weighed against the costs to the users of semiconductors. For more on the pros and cons of the semiconductor agreement, see Laura D'Andrea Tyson, "Comments on the Semiconductor Trade Agreement: Lessons for Effective Trade Policy for America's High-Technology Industries," prepared for Trade Policy Conference at the Institute of International Economics, Washington, May 1989.

reactions of domestic and foreign firms and foreign governments. In imperfectly competitive industries, such reactions are extremely difficult to predict, since many different kinds of strategic behavior are possible. If, for example, a promotional policy encourages noncooperative behavior and the entry of new domestic firms, then the potential national benefits of such a policy may be dissipated by competition, which drives excess returns to zero and passes the benefits of national policies to foreign consumers in the form of lower prices.

A third reservation revolves around geography. Although certain industries may generate technological or linkage externalities, it does not necessarily follow that to enjoy these externalities, each nation must have domestically owned—or at the very least, domestically based—producers. As long as these externalities are international in scope and move across national borders through trade in goods and technological information, each nation can benefit whether it has domestic producers or not. This perspective reinforces the standard notion that foreign producer subsidies should be treated as a gift not a threat—a gift that brings not only lower prices but also the generation of new technological knowledge free of charge.

These reservations about the effectiveness and wisdom of policies to promote domestic producers in high-technology industries must be taken seriously—they are based on compelling analytic logic and careful modeling. Moreover, most of the empirical studies derived from such modeling support the conclusion that on balance such policies do not improve national economic welfare.[15] For example, a recent survey of such studies by J. David Richardson concludes that trade liberalization rather than policy intervention to promote domestic producers in imperfectly competitive industries leads to gains from trade that may be two to three times larger than those estimated under perfect competition.[16] This survey also concludes that from a national viewpoint, it is necessarily an empirical question whether there are gains from liberalization or losses, gains from active policy intervention, or losses in imperfectly

15. See, for example, Avinash Dixit, "Optimal Trade and Industrial Policies for the U.S. Automobile Industry," and Robert E. Baldwin and Paul R. Krugman, "Market Access and International Competition: A Simulation Study of 16K Random Access Memories," both in Robert C. Feenstra, ed., Empirical Methods for International Trade (MIT Press, 1988), pp. 141–65, 171–97.

16. J. David Richardson, "Empirical Research on Trade Liberalization with Imperfect Competition: A Survey," OECD Economic Studies, no. 12 (Spring 1989), pp. 8–44.

competitive industries. In other words, there is no simple theoretical guide to policy.

Unfortunately, the empirical questions become even more difficult to answer when the dynamic characteristics of high-technology industries are considered, something that has not been done to any great extent in either the theoretical or the empirical literature. The new trade theory is inherently static in orientation. Even the most sophisticated models are of a comparative statics type—they compare the once-and-for-all gains or losses involved in moving from one policy environment to another. Typically, these models show that under certain limiting conditions, a particular type of policy may induce a once-and-for-all improvement in aggregate economic welfare, owing in the last analysis to an improvement in the terms of trade.

Such static modeling approaches are ill suited to understanding the dynamics of competition in many high-technology industries. Such industries are characterized by what W. Brian Arthur calls self-reinforcement mechanisms—increasing returns, cumulative causation, deviation-amplifying mutual causal processes, virtuous and vicious cycles, and threshold effects.[17] In the presence of such mechanisms, an appropriate modeling strategy requires the comparison of alternative dynamic paths, not the comparison of alternative equilibrium positions. A change in policy results not in a once-and-for-all change in equilibrium position but in a permanent change in dynamic trajectory.

To illustrate the point, the closure of the Japanese market to imports and foreign direct investment in semiconductors in the mid-1970s did not just affect the Japanese trade balance, the profits of Japanese producers, and the welfare of Japanese consumers in the 16K DRAM market in 1976, as the empirical analysis of Robert E. Baldwin and Paul Krugman assumes.[18] Temporary closure encouraged learning, economies of scale, and investment behavior that were critical to Japan's later success in other semiconductor products. To evaluate the welfare effects of the closure policy necessitates a full accounting of its dynamic effects over time, not simply its once-and-for-all effects in 1976.

A dynamic approach to modeling the effects of policy on competition and welfare in high-technology industries requires a distinction between what might be called Ricardian efficiency and what might be called

17. W. Brian Arthur, "Positive Feedbacks in the Economy," *Scientific American*, vol. 262 (February 1990), pp. 92–99.
18. Baldwin and Krugman, "Market Access and International Competition."

Schumpeterian efficiency.[19] The allocation of resources among industries in response to current measures of social profitability and under conditions of nonincreasing returns is generally Ricardian efficient, in the sense that it maximizes current economic welfare. In the presence of increasing returns or static technological externalities, there are in principle many possible points of Ricardian efficiency, and which one is realized depends in part on policy choices.

The allocation of resources among industries can be evaluated not only according to its Ricardian efficiency but also according to its Schumpeterian efficiency—its effects on the pace and direction of technological change over time. The concept of Schumpeterian efficiency is based on Schumpeter's insight that the dynamism of capitalism depends largely on competition in new products and processes rather than on price competition—an allocation of resources on the basis of current price signals, while Ricardian efficient, may not be an allocation that encourages the most beneficial pace and direction of technological change over time.

The idea of Schumpeterian efficiency involves two main strands of thought. First, opportunities for future technological advance vary across industries and products. Consequently, if private agents and policymakers choose a pattern of national specialization and resource allocation on the basis of *current* market indicators, they may pick one that generates an inferior future trajectory of technology and growth. A nation may realize today an efficient allocation of resources by specializing in those industries in which tomorrow's opportunities for future technological change are limited.

The loss suffered from such a choice might not be so large if the nation could benefit from the technological innovations generated by other nations who had chosen a pattern of specializing in activities with greater opportunities for technological change. Indeed, this is simply an extension of the classical idea of comparative advantage: nations that have a comparative advantage in technology-intensive goods on the basis of current price indicators export them to other nations that have a comparative disadvantage in such goods. The Ricardian efficient solution works to the benefit of everyone.

This conclusion must be reconsidered, however, once a second Schumpeterian characteristic of the process of technological change is

---

19. The following discussion of Ricardian efficiency and Schumpeterian efficiency draws on Dosi, Tyson, and Zysman, "Trade, Technologies, and Development."

considered. In contrast to the notion of technology in most economic models, technological knowledge is often not information that is generally applicable and available to all producers or that can be bought or sold for a price. Firms cannot produce and use innovations by dipping freely into a general stock or pool of technological knowledge. Instead, technological knowledge is often gained from the act of production itself. As production occurs, specific problem-solving activities foster new technological skills, competence, and organizational forms. The resulting capabilities provide the potential for future technological advance.

The acquisition of such capabilities is an inherently local and path-dependent process. Such capabilities cannot simply be purchased elsewhere.[20] Seen from this perspective, an important part of technological knowledge does not flow easily across national borders. Such technology-advancing knowledge accumulates in firms in the form of skilled workers, proprietary technology, and know-how that is difficult to copy. It accumulates in communities in such diverse forms as suppliers, repair services, and networks of know-how. And it accumulates in nations in the skills and experiences of their labor force and in the institutions that train workers and diffuse technology.

If industries differ in their opportunities for technological change, and if such change is often a joint output of productive activity, then different mixes of national production today mean different technological opportunities and technological capabilities in the future.[21] As a result, the current pattern of a nation's production and trade specialization can have powerful effects on its future technological trajectory. Technological change is a path-dependent process in which the past and current allocation of resources affects the future scope of learning and innova-

20. Of course, not all technological knowledge is local in nature. Some knowledge is embedded in a product and can be reverse-engineered by its users; some knowledge can be obtained by scientific and educational exchange; and some can be obtained for a price by licensing and other purchase arrangements. Technologies differ in the degree of their publicness and universality versus their localness and specificity. As Japan and some of the successful East Asian countries indicate, nations can catch up technologically and even leapfrog to a new technological frontier. It is important to emphasize, however, that where such development processes have been successful, they have been supported by national policies aimed at monitoring foreign technologies, acquiring them at attractive terms for domestic producers, and diffusing their use within protected domestic markets.

21. For a more complete exposition of the new theories of technological change and technological information, see Giovanni Dosi and others, eds., *Technical Change and Economic Theory* (London: Pinter Publishers, 1989).

tion, and by implication the future growth and well-being of a national economy.

But does this imply a necessary conflict between Ricardian efficiency and Schumpeterian efficiency? Why might current market signals fail to provide sufficient information to ensure the appropriate rate of beneficial technological change? There are three distinct but interrelated reasons. First, the well-known issue of appropriability arises—the social returns to technological innovation often exceed the private returns, sometimes by a considerable margin as in the semiconductor and computer industries.[22] Under such circumstances, current market indicators are an insufficient incentive for socially optimal behavior. Second, as Joseph Stiglitz has argued, capital market constraints are likely to limit investment in innovation—often firms must rely on excess profits or must pay premium rates on external funds to finance such investment.[23]

Third, innovation inherently gives rise to imperfect competition. Technological knowledge always involves some form of increasing returns. There are usually significant set-up or sunk costs in the creation of such knowledge, and usually significant learning effects or dynamic economies of scale occur in the use of such knowledge. As a result, the value of such knowledge increases with the scale of production.

In the presence of increasing returns and spillover effects, the market cannot signal to private agents the unintended outcome of their collective behavior. To put it differently, markets cannot deliver information about or discount the possibility of future states of the world whose occurrences are externalities resulting from the interaction of the present decisions of behaviorally unrelated agents. Under such circumstances, there may be trade-offs between Ricardian efficiency and Schumpeterian efficiency.

But even if this argument is theoretically correct, what does it imply about policy? At least markets might signal present efficiencies. Future dynamic gains, precisely because they cannot be signaled and are inherently uncertain, represent a policy gamble. Neither the market nor policymakers, no matter how clever, can definitely determine whether particular industries are likely to give rise to the most beneficial trajectory

22. For a survey of the differences between private and social returns to technological change, see Baily and Chakrabarti, *Innovation and the Productivity Crisis*.

23. See also Joseph Stiglitz,"Technological Change, Sunk Costs, and Competition," in Martin Neil Baily and Clifford Winston, eds., *Brookings Papers on Economic Activity, Microeconomics 3:1987*, pp. 883–947.

of technological change over time. Moreover, even if policymakers, working with private business, scientific, and engineering leaders, could identify the most promising industries and technologies to promote, no guarantee exists that the policies used would be the correct ones. And national promotional policies, when accompanied by beggar-thy-neighbor measures, might very well encourage retaliatory measures abroad.

Not surprisingly, even when economists agree on the special features of high-technology industries that provide a compelling prima facie case for policy intervention, they disagree on the policy implications. As Paul Krugman has argued, four distinctive views on policy can be identified:[24]

—Immediate activism. According to this view, despite uncertainties, the United States should act aggressively to promote its high-technology industries and should use trade policy, including managed trade arrangements, to offset foreign policy measures that disadvantage American producers.

—Cautious activism. This view, which I hold, would limit immediate policy action to those industries in which the case for intervention seems the clearest. Likely candidates for such industries are semiconductors, sophisticated telecommunications equipment, computers, and aircraft. This view also implies a change in the philosophy of U.S. trade policy from one of free trade to one of sophisticated intervention. Cautious activism is the tone characteristic of the controversial report issued by the Advisory Committee for Trade Policy and Negotiations (ACTPN) in 1989 and is increasingly the view in American business and policy circles.[25]

—Cautious inactivism. According to this view, the uncertainties of any immediate changes in U.S. trade and other policies to promote particular industries outweigh any expected benefits. At most, one might advocate some general policy measures to promote high-technology industries, such as a permanent R&D tax credit and a relaxation of some antitrust laws, and careful monitoring of the effects of foreign policies on U.S. producers. Overall, the U.S. commitment to free trade would be maintained.

—Strong nonactivism. According to this view, the gains from activist

24. Paul R. Krugman, "Introduction: New Thinking About Trade Policy," in Paul Krugman, ed., *Strategic Trade Policy and the New International Economics* (MIT Press, 1986).

25. Advisory Committee for Trade Policy and Negotiations, "Analysis of the U.S.-Japan Trade Problem," Report to Carla Hills, Washington, February 1989.

policy are small, the appropriate policies are uncertain, the United States is singularly ill equipped to make the correct policy choices, and the risks of failure are high because U.S. action is likely to incite retaliatory measures abroad, with threats to the multilateral trading system. Consequently, free trade is still judged the best policy stance for both the United States and the rest of the world.

On the basis of what economists currently know, no one of these views is patently superior to the others—individual choices are more a matter of faith, pragmatism, and policy experience than a matter of pure theory and empirical evidence.

Interventionist Policies to Support High-Technology Industries

During the last several years, high-technology industries have become a favorite target for trade disputes and interventionist policies by the United States and other governments. This development results in part from increasing demands for trade and other policy support by high-technology industries, and in part from an increasing willingness of governments to promote such industries because of their anticipated benefits for national economic welfare.[26]

In the United States, demands for protection and support by high-technology producers have intensified as their competitive position in world markets has weakened. The evidence is growing that U.S. producers have lost their productivity and technological advantages in

---

26. A critical question that has not been sufficiently addressed by governments is whether the anticipated benefits of high-technology industries can be realized through foreign direct investment. For example, does the United States need a domestically owned semiconductor industry to realize its strategic benefits, or is foreign direct investment by Japanese producers in the United States sufficient? A related, but different, question concerns the strategic benefits of foreign direct investment by domestically owned producers. For example, does the Japanese operation of Texas Instruments contribute strategic benefits to the United States or Japan or both? Such questions are rarely raised in policy circles, and when they are, at least in the United States, the presumption seems to be that domestically owned (but not necessarily domestically operated) firms are necessary to obtain the national strategic benefits of high-technology production. The European approach is different—as their recent rule of origin for semiconductors indicates. Provided foreign producers locate "substantial" parts of their production process in Europe, they are to be accorded European treatment. The Europeans appear to be going for a local content approach—to obtain the anticipated benefits of high-technology production, they are compelling foreign firms to locate high value-added, high-R&D parts of their production process in Europe if they want to be treated as "European" firms.

several high-technology industries. The U.S. trade surpluses in most high-technology products declined sharply during the 1980s (table 1). In several industrial categories, the United States now has a trade deficit. Only in three product lines—guided missiles, commercial aircraft and parts, and plastics—has the net trade position improved.[27]

In some high-technology sectors, most notably the electronics sector, the United States' shares of world production and exports have declined dramatically. In some product lines, such as videocassette recorders and FAXs, where world demand is growing rapidly, the United States has no domestic production capacity, and in others, such as high-definition television, where world demand is projected to grow rapidly in the future, U.S. producers are far behind the mark in technological development.[28] In other product lines, such as semiconductors, the U.S. industry has ceded its dominant position to the Japanese, most notably in DRAMs, and its position in other semiconductor devices, such as application-specific integrated circuits and microprocessors, is threatened. Even in computers and supercomputers, where the United States retains considerable technological strength and a dominant position in world markets, some signs of future competitive difficulty have appeared.[29]

Growing pressure for protection and support by many U.S. high-technology producers signals an important change in the dynamics of trade policymaking. Traditionally, U.S. multinational firms and export-dependent firms have been supporters of free trade. Recently, however, a growing number of such firms, especially in high-technology industries, have publicly pressed for a new approach to trade policy. The new approach is neither a free trade approach nor a protectionist approach, but what might be called a strategic approach of using trade and other policies to offset or eliminate protectionist and promotional policies

27. For the purposes of this paper, high-technology products include those that have the highest embodied R&D spending relative to the value of shipments. Table 1 contains an industrial classification of such products compiled by the Department of Commerce. For more on the definitions and measurements behind this classification, see Victoria L. Hatter, *U.S. High Technology Trade and Competitiveness* (Department of Commerce, 1985).

28. For an evaluation of the U.S. position on high-definition television, see Jeffrey A. Hart and Laura D'Andrea Tyson, "Responding to the Challenge of HDTV," *California Management Review*, vol. 31 (Summer 1989), pp. 132–45.

29. Charles H. Ferguson, "Computers and the Coming of the U.S. Keiretsu," *Harvard Business Review*, vol. 68 (July–August 1990), pp. 55–70; and Marie Anchordoguy, *Computers, Inc.: Japan's Challenge to IBM* (Harvard University Press, 1989).

Table 1. *U.S. Trade in High-Technology Products, 1980–88*
Billions of dollars

Products	1980	1984	1988
High-Technology exports			
(Foreign and domestic, F.A.S.)			
Guided missiles and space vehicles	0.7	1.0	1.1
Communications equipment and electronic components	10.3	14.4	21.5
Aircraft and parts	14.6	13.5	25.1
Office, computing, and accounting equipment	8.6	14.7	24.4
Ordnance	0.6	0.8	0.7
Drugs and medicines	2.0	2.7	4.0
Industrial inorganic chemicals	2.9	3.5	4.1
Professional and scientific instruments	6.5	7.2	12.2
Engines, turbines, and parts	3.6	3.2	3.8
Plastics and synthetic resins	4.8	4.4	7.4
Total	54.7	66.0	104.3
High-Technology imports			
(General C.I.F.)			
Guided missiles and space vehicles	0	0.2	0.1
Communications equipment and electronic components	12.2	28.3	42.0
Aircraft and parts	2.7	3.7	6.3
Office, computing, and accounting equipment	2.6	10.4	21.0
Ordnance	0.1	0.2	0.4
Drugs and medicines	1.0	1.7	3.7
Industrial inorganic chemicals	2.4	3.3	3.8
Professional and scientific instruments	4.8	7.9	14.0
Engines, turbines, and parts	1.7	2.3	4.8
Plastics and synthetic resins	0.6	1.4	2.2
Total	28.0	59.4	98.3
High-Technology trade balance			
Guided missiles and space vehicles	0.7	0.8	1.0
Communications equipment and electronic components	(1.9)	(13.9)	(20.5)
Aircraft and parts	11.9	9.8	18.8
Office, computing, and accounting equipment	6.0	4.3	3.4
Ordnance	0.5	0.6	0.3
Drugs and medicines	1.0	1.0	0.3
Industrial inorganic chemicals	0.5	0.2	0.3
Professional and scientific instruments	1.7	(0.7)	(1.8)
Engines, turbines, and parts	1.9	0.9	(1.0)
Plastics and synthetic resins	4.2	3.0	5.2
Total	26.7	6.0	6.0

Source: Figures supplied to the author by the Department of Commerce. For more on methodology, see note 27 in the text. Columns may not total because of rounding.

abroad.[30] Many of these strategic demands embody requests for reciprocity in particular industries and are clearly at odds with the general reciprocity of the GATT's most-favored-nation clause.

The strategic approach underlies the report of the Advisory Committee for Trade Policy and Negotiations.[31] Surprisingly, in this report, a group including business leaders traditionally supportive of free trade called for a sector-specific, results-oriented approach for managing trade with Japan. As the report makes clear, serious concerns about the health of America's high-technology industries motivated this recommendation.

The special features of high-technology producers make their growing demands for strategic trade approaches understandable.[32] As just noted, such producers are often characterized by large economies of scale and steep learning curves. Under these circumstances, access to foreign markets and the behavior of foreign firms and governments can directly affect the profitability of domestic producers. In industries in which the U.S. market is open and large foreign markets are closed, foreign competitors may be able to achieve more efficient scale and learning advantages as a result of increased volume in domestic and overseas markets, while domestic competitors are squeezed into a portion of the domestic market.

And, because of capital market barriers to financing R&D, as the

30. This use of the term strategic is adopted by Helen Milner and David Yoffie, "Between Free Trade and Protectionism: Strategic Trade Policy and A Theory of Corporate Trade Demands," *International Organization,* vol. 43 (Spring 1989), pp. 239–72.

31. The U.S. trade system has developed antiprotectionist counterweights over time. The private sector advisory committees to the president are a key element in this system. These committees are managed by the Office of the U.S. Trade Representative in cooperation with the Departments of Agriculture, Commerce, and Defense. The Advisory Committee for Trade Policy and Negotiations is the oversight or horizontal committee for several sectoral committees, and it is charged with helping to shape the U.S. agenda for the Uruguay round of GATT talks. Under the Super 301 provision of the 1988 trade bill, the advisory committee is also responsible for advising the president on foreign trade practices. The advisory committee report of February 1989 grew out of this provision.

32. A recent study by Milner and Yoffie presents compelling evidence of such demands in three U.S. high-technology industries—semiconductors, telecommunications equipment, and commercial aircraft. They present an insightful discussion of the reasons why high-technology industries are demanding a strategic approach to trade policy in the United States. Their arguments are summarized in the text. See Milner and Yoffie, "Between Free Trade and Protectionism." The following discussion draws on their analysis.

profits of domestic producers are squeezed, they may be forced to cut back on R&D spending, quickly losing out in the race for next-generation technologies. Moreover, because of scale and learning effects, the option of investing abroad to circumvent barriers to foreign markets may be an unattractive one, and often one that is precluded or delayed by formal or informal impediments to foreign direct investment by foreign governments. Under these circumstances, direct access to foreign markets through exports may be a critical determinant of long-run competitive success.

Demands by high-technology producers for strategic trade approaches, even when they embody results-oriented managed trade agreements, are more likely to be treated favorably by the U.S. government than demands for unconditional protectionism by producers in traditional industries for two reasons. First, such demands play into America's sense of fair play. Second, and more important, government officials at home and abroad are increasingly convinced that high-technology industries are of special importance to national economic growth and living standards. Consequently, both the demand for and the supply of managed trade arrangements and other sector-specific policies to promote domestic producers are large and growing at home and abroad. An increase in such arrangements seems inevitable. The real question is how to design them to work effectively and to promote more, not less, competition and trade over time. From a policymaking perspective, the appropriate standard for judging the wisdom of such arrangements is not the standard of free trade. Nor, for the reasons just given, is the free trade standard the appropriate one from a theoretical perspective.

Governments use a variety of policies to create advantage for domestic producers in high-technology industries. Although these policies are not primarily trade policies, their effects on trade can be profound and long term. The most common forms of direct government support for high-technology industries include subsidies for investment or research, restrictions on access to the domestic market by similar goods from foreign producers, restrictions on foreign direct investment in the domestic market by foreign firms, and procurement policies that favor domestic producers.[33]

_____

33. For more on trade policy toward high-technology industries, see David C. Mowery and Nathan Rosenberg, "New Developments in U.S. Technology Policy:

The policy instruments used to promote high-technology domestic producers extend far beyond the border measures that have traditionally been the focus of trade policy. Even—or, perhaps more correctly, especially—antitrust policies can be an important nontariff determinant of trade in high-technology industries. The prevalence and diversity of policies affecting such trade make bilateral and multilateral negotiations for policy guidelines simultaneously more urgent and more difficult.

Also as a result of the special characteristics of high-technology industries, temporary government policies can have long-term effects. As the semiconductor case demonstrates, in the presence of increasing returns to scale, learning curve effects, and technological learning, restrictions on access to a growing foreign market may enable its producers to keep out other competitors and to invade the export markets of these competitors even after formal protection and other government assistance have been terminated.[34] In the words of David Mowery and Nathan Rosenberg, "The combination of trade-distorting policies and strong dynamic effects means that the performance of a firm in such an industry may be influenced by government policies and industry structure in earlier periods. This reality is very difficult to accommodate within a U.S. trade policy enforcement mechanism that focuses primarily on costs, pricing, and subsidies in a static, single-period framework."[35]

Prescriptions for Managed Trade Arrangements in High-Technology Industries

As the preceding discussion suggests, nations employ various policies to promote their high-technology producers. These policies are not primarily trade policies, nor are their objectives primarily trade objectives. The goal of intervention is not simply to improve the trade balance

---

Implications for Competitiveness and International Trade Policy," *California Management Review*, vol. 32 (Fall 1989), pp. 107–24.

34. Tyson and Zysman argue that Japan is characterized by a "moving band of protection." During their developmental stage, industries targeted by the Japanese government are actively protected and promoted by policy. Once they have become internationally competitive—often after substantial overinvestment in capacity for the domestic market, which results in a flood of exports from Japan in search of foreign markets—active protectionist and promotional policies are removed. This pattern can be observed in several Japanese industries that are now world-class competitors. Tyson and Zysman, "Developmental Strategy and Production Innovation in Japan."

35. See Mowery and Rosenberg, "New Developments," p. 113.

or to address external barriers abroad, but to secure a share of world production and employment in such industries with the local knowledge, skills, and other spillover benefits that they are perceived to generate. Both the forms and the goals of policies for high-technology industries in the United States and elsewhere have implications for how the nation should think about managed trade arrangements.

Managed Trade Arrangements for Rules in High-Technology Industries

High-technology industries should adhere to internationally accepted rules of the game for competition at two levels.[36] First, greater uniformity about what is and what is not acceptable government practice should characterize national policy. Because government practice extends far beyond the border measures traditionally covered by the GATT, this aim implies either a broadening of the GATT or new codes of government behavior outside of the GATT. Given the realities of the GATT process and the need for timeliness in the development of new rules, bilateral or limited multilateral negotiations outside of the GATT may be a sensible strategy.

For the firm, international rules of the game are necessary to regulate imperfect competition. Ideally, this aim implies the uniform national rules for antitrust regulation in high-technology industries. In practice, something less encompassing is probably the best that can be hoped for. For example, some of the cooperative arrangements that characterize the integrated Japanese producer groups and that disadvantage United States and other foreign producers in Japan's market would clearly be disallowed under U.S. antitrust law.[37] One approach to this problem would be to negotiate a uniform set of antitrust regulations for the United

36. The following discussion draws on arguments made by William R. Cline in "Reciprocity: A New Approach to World Trade Policy," in William R. Cline, *Trade Policy in the 1980s* (Washington: Institute for International Economics, 1983), pp. 121–58.

37. For more on the nature of cooperative relations among Japanese producers, see Kozo Yamamura, "Caveat Emptor: The Industrial Policy of Japan," in Krugman, *Strategic Trade Policy and the New International Economics*; Daniel Okimoto, "Outsider Trading: Coping with Japanese Industrial Organization," in Kenneth B. Pyle, ed., *The Trade Crisis: How Will Japan Respond?* (New York: Society for Japanese Studies, 1987); Ronald Dore, *Flexible Rigidities* (Stanford University Press, 1986); and Michael Gerlach, "Keiretsu Organization in the Japanese Economy: Analysis and Trade Implications," in Johnson, Tyson, and Zysman, *Politics and Productivity*.

States and Japan. But this approach, while theoretically appealing, is politically unrealistic at least for the foreseeable future. A less ambitious approach, and one that is behind the structural impediments initiative of the Bush administration, would be to identify particular behavioral or structural features of Japanese industry that impede foreign competition and negotiate for their removal.[38] I would call this a managed trade approach specifying allowable rules for firm behavior. In this case, the approach is a bilateral one, although a multilateral one is also possible. Once again, it seems unlikely that the GATT would be an effective forum for negotiating such rules, at least in the immediate future.

Because of the global nature of high-technology industries, managed trade arrangements for rules should be multilateral whenever possible. It is not enough to specify allowable rules of behavior (or outcomes) in particular countries. Both producers and sellers can and do move their transactions to third-country markets to avoid restrictions on their behavior. A deal that specifies rules for allowable behavior by Japanese and American firms in Japanese and U.S. markets can be undermined by their behavior elsewhere. This third-country problem bedeviled the negotiation of the Semiconductor Trade Agreement between Japan and the United States, since any agreement to terminate alleged dumping by Japanese firms in the U.S. market could be easily negated by continued dumping in other markets around the world. Thus, the agreement called for a cessation of dumping by Japanese producers wherever they sold.[39]

Even if managed trade arrangements for rules must be multilateral in scope to be effective, they may not always be multilaterally negotiated. Ideally, the United States should work within the GATT framework to develop multilateral rules for government and firm behavior in high-technology industries, and such rules should be applied and enforced in a nondiscriminatory way. The United States has pressed for GATT negotiations in high-technology areas but has made no progress. From a practical point of view, the alternative to GATT negotiations is multilateral or bilateral negotiations among the principal supplying nations or regions, which for the foreseeable future include the United States, Japan, and Europe.

38. Japanese business practices that are believed to impede foreign access to the Japanese market are a principal focus of the ongoing bilateral trade talks on the structural impediments initiative between the United States and Japan.

39. Not surprisingly, this part of the agreement proved exceptionally difficult to enforce and was a major reason for the formation of a production cartel in Japan.

As both the U.S.-Canada trade agreement and the new provisions for Europe 1992 indicate, surprising progress can be realized on specifying rules for government and firm behavior when the number of countries negotiating is small and when they are strongly linked by trade and investment interests.

As part of a more active trade and industrial policy for its high-technology industries, the United States should work to initiate multilateral negotiations on new policy codes for government and firm behavior among the supplier countries.[40] These negotiations should be sectoral in focus—concentrating on policy codes as they apply to specific industries or groups of industries. The new codes, unlike free trade agreements, would not apply to all trade among the participating countries nor would they be limited to tariff and other border policy issues. Rather, the objective would be at the same time more limited and much more complex: trying to construct a single global market by harmonizing rules for government and firm behavior in certain industries.

As a first step, the United States should call for multilateral negotiations for rules in the semiconductor industry. This industry is now the focus of trade policy and other promotional policy measures around the world, including a new EC rule of origin for integrated circuits that defines a product's origin not as the place where the last substantial process or operation that is economically justified was performed but as the place where the most substantial process was performed.[41] In practice, this stipulation means that to be accorded national treatment within the EC, semiconductor devices must be fabricated there— assembly is no longer enough. This ruling has profound implications for the locational strategies of both Japanese and American semiconductor producers who want to serve the European market.

In addition, the term of the Semiconductor Trade Agreement between the United States and Japan is more than half over, and pressures are growing for its termination or modification. In light of the spillover effects of this agreement on other suppliers and users in the EC—effects that led the EC to lodge complaints against the agreement with the

---

40. Since the principal supplier countries are members of the G7 and regularly negotiate with one another to coordinate macroeconomic policy, sectoral negotiations are a logical extension, especially in global industries.

41. Sylvia Ostry, *Governments and Corporations in a Shrinking World: Trade and Innovation Policies in the United States, Europe, and Japan* (New York: Council on Foreign Relations, 1990).

GATT, to work out its own bilateral deals with Japan, and to introduce more restrictive rules of origin for semiconductors—multilateral negotiations are preferable to unilateral or bilateral actions to modify the semiconductor agreement when it expires.

Opposition to bilateral or limited multilateral negotiations for rules-oriented managed trade agreements is based on the view that such negotiations will violate nondiscrimination, which is the linchpin of the GATT system, weaken the national commitment to an open trading system, and gradually result in the formation of like-minded regional trading blocs. But none of these undesirable consequences is preordained.

New disciplines and safeguards on rules and behaviors not currently covered by the GATT could be negotiated by a limited number of countries and extended on a conditional or participatory most-favored-nation basis—that is, the benefits of the new rules would be accorded to additional countries who agree to adhere to them at a later date. In addition, more completely elaborated rules adopted by a limited number of countries in certain industries may serve as a model for necessary changes in the GATT. As it is now, many GATT rules, although nondiscriminatory, are vague, irrelevant, or nonexistent as they relate to high-technology industries. This is one reason why trade policy among the principal supplying countries in these industries is increasingly the focus of bilateral negotiations and decisions that are often at odds with the GATT provisions. Finally, even in the worst-case scenario—that bilateral and limited multilateral negotiations outside of the GATT continue to undermine its strength—from a national point of view there seems to be little alternative. U.S. producers in high-technology industries have been and will continue to be affected by the behavior of governments and firms in other supplying countries. So a realistic trade policy approach implies negotiating with these countries on rules, and when necessary, on outcomes.

Managed Trade Rules and Antidumping Regulations

Although many kinds of rules affect high-technology industries, including rules on subsidies, trade-related investment rules such as the rule of origin for semiconductors just noted, intellectual property rules, rules of the Coordinating Committee on Multilateral Export Controls, and rules for foreign participation in national research consortia, dumping rules have become most significant in recent years. Indeed, it is probably not an overstatement to say that antidumping procedures became the trade policy instrument of choice in the 1980s, at least in the United States and the European Community.[42] Between 1979 and 1980 these jurisdictions processed more than 1,800 antidumping cases.[43] Moreover, whereas antidumping procedures were traditionally concentrated in industries producing standardized products such as chemicals and steel, they have been increasingly applied in high-technology industries.

Under the GATT, members can use duties to offset dumping by foreign producers if it can be shown that such behavior is causing actual or threatened material injury to domestic producers. According to the GATT definition, dumping is understood as the sale of products for export at a price less than "normal value." Until recently, normal value was usually interpreted as roughly the price for which products were sold by foreign producers on their "home market." Behind this notion was the idea of price discrimination—dumping occurred when foreign producers priced their exports differently from their domestic sales.

Increasingly, however, dumping has been interpreted in the United States and the EC as pricing exports below cost, and most often cost has been interpreted as customary or full cost rather than marginal cost. Indeed, selling below cost is now often regarded as dumping even if sales below cost are occurring in the firm's domestic market as well. This interpretation of dumping underpinned the Semiconductor Trade Agreement and recent amendments in the EC antidumping regulations. It is an interpretation allowable under the GATT's imprecise definition of dumping.

Most economists are united in their skepticism about dumping and the wisdom of antidumping procedures. Even if there is dumping of the

---

42. For a detailed discussion of antidumping procedures in the United States and Europe in recent years, see Ostry, *Political Economy of Policymaking*.

43. The impact of antidumping measures on world trade has been substantial. See Patrick A. Messerlin, "Antidumping," paper presented at the Conference on Trade Policy, Institute for International Economics, Washington, June 1990. During the last two years, however, the number of antidumping and countervail cases in the United States has declined and the current U.S. International Trade Commission caseload is relatively light.

price discrimination variety, the importing country usually benefits unambiguously if it receives access to imported goods at a lower price than it would in the absence of dumping. True, firms and workers in import-competing industries may be hurt, but the benefits to consumers exceed these costs, so in principle it is possible to tax the gainers, compensate the losers, and leave everyone better off. In reality, this redistribution of the net benefits of dumping never occurs.

When dumping takes the form of pricing below cost, the economic arguments are more complex, but the conclusion is generally the same. The precise theoretical arguments depend on whether pricing is below average or marginal cost, on whether short-run or long-run costs and prices are considered, and on the behavior imputed to foreign producers, for example, sales-maximization versus profit-maximization.[44] Under most circumstances, the gains to consumers from dumping outweigh the costs to competing domestic producers, so that on a net basis dumping is beneficial from a national point of view.

The only real exception occurs when dumping is part of a predatory strategy. Predatory pricing is an aggressive pricing strategy in which foreign producers price below cost, perhaps below marginal cost and perhaps supported by subsidies, to drive domestic firms out of business, leaving foreign producers with effective market power. Once this market power is realized, a nation might end up paying more for the product than it would have if it had applied antidumping duties to defend domestic producers before they went out of business. From this perspective, such duties are a form of cartel insurance for the future. Most economists discount the likelihood of a predatory strategy in global industries that usually include many producers.

Increasingly, antidumping measures or the threat of them are being used in the United States and Europe to protect national producers in high-technology industries from low-price, high-quality imports, usually from Japan. This approach is hard to defend from an economic perspective for the reasons just noted. If the objective of policy is to promote national producers, then antidumping measures are not the only, and certainly not the best, method available. Such measures almost always

---

44. For a more complete summary of the economic literature on the effects of dumping on an average and marginal cost basis, see Alan V. Deardorff, "Economic Perspectives on Dumping Law," in John H. Jackson and Edwin A. Vermulst, eds., *Antidumping Law and Practice: A Comparative Study* (University of Michigan Press, 1990), pp. 23–39.

result in higher prices for domestic consumers of the product in question, so that support for the producers comes out of the hide of the consumers. When the consumers are other high-technology industries, an antidumping policy to support one industry may result in harm to an even more important industry. Nor is it clear that the support paid for by the consumers of the product in question will have the desired effect. Nothing guarantees that the higher prices and profits resulting from such measures will be used to improve the underlying competitiveness of domestic producers.

All of these arguments can be leveled against the antidumping provisions of the Semiconductor Trade Agreement and the recent EC antidumping regulations. In evaluating such measures, however, consider two more arguments: the Schumpeterian argument and the predation argument.

The Schumpeterian argument is about capital-market constraints. Opposition to antidumping measures is based on the argument that they disadvantage consumers through higher prices. In high-technology industries, the static argument that says that lower prices are always best must be reassessed to consider the effect of current prices on future innovative activity. Higher prices and profits today may be necessary as an incentive and as a means to finance innovation and technological knowledge for tomorrow. In principle, the net gains to the nation from dumping could be mobilized to support continued R&D by domestic producers threatened by dumping. In practice, this result does not occur, since the injury caused by dumping draws capital resources away from these producers. In principle, also, the loss in profits caused by dumping could be offset by government subsidies or loans to allow domestic producers to match foreign prices, while continuing to finance the big R&D investment required for future competitiveness. In practice, it is also impossible to imagine such a policy response, at least in a timely fashion in the United States given its current budgetary situation. In the absence of such a response, temporary dumping by foreign producers can drive out domestic producers whose innovative activities generate beneficial spillovers for the rest of the economy. These returns, especially those that are local in nature, will be lost and must be considered when assessing the costs and benefits of lower prices caused by foreign dumping.

The predation argument may also have great importance in high-technology industries for another reason. Such industries tend to be imperfectly competitive, with much potential for the exercise of market power. Moreover, because of sunk costs, in the form of R&D investments and specialized capital goods with high depreciation rates and limited applications to other products, the market power of producers in these industries may not be effectively contestable. Under such circumstances, a predatory pricing strategy cannot be dismissed on general theoretical grounds—knowledge about the changing structure of the industry is necessary.

This condition is especially true when the strategy in question is attributed to Japanese producers who operate in a distinctive institutional setting where firm behavior inconsistent with U.S. antitrust notions is standard, where repeated violations of Japanese antitrust law have occurred with impunity, and where cooperative business and government relations pose serious impediments to foreign producers. In business circles in the United States and Europe, the perception prevails that dumping by Japanese firms is part of an overall business strategy, complemented by preferential and protectionist policies and cooperative business arrangements to dominate certain high-technology activities such as semiconductors and computers. Such a strategy means using market access barriers at home and predatory pricing tactics abroad to drive foreign competitors out of business.

To be detrimental to U.S. interests and the interests of other nations in the long run, this strategy would not have to involve predation in the traditional sense, that is, once Japanese producers gain notable market power, they need not use it to extract higher prices. Indeed, no evidence suggests this use of market power by Japanese producers, except in the semiconductor industry where the terms of the semiconductor agreement made it inevitable. Rather, market power can be used in other ways, such as limiting foreign access to new technologies to give Japanese competitors an edge in other product markets. As an illustration, during 1987 and 1988, when worldwide semiconductor markets were extremely tight, several U.S. users experienced delays in obtaining new DRAM supplies from Japanese suppliers. New Japanese DRAMs now appear in Japanese systems products six to twelve months before they become available on the open market. And some U.S. systems producers have been subject to pressure to license their designs to Japanese competition in order to ensure adequate supplies of components.[45] And even if Japanese producers do not use their market power in detrimental ways,

45. For evidence of such behavior by Japanese producers, see Borrus, *Competing for Control*; and Ferguson, "Computers and the Coming of the U.S. Keiretsu."

if they succeed in weakening or eliminating high-technology producers in other countries, many of the strategic national benefits associated with these producers may be lost.[46]

The possibility of meaningful predatory behavior in high-technology industries, especially those in which a few, large, integrated Japanese producers hold or threaten to hold a commanding market share, means that antidumping measures should not be ruled out. A preferred policy approach would be to negotiate new international rules to regulate such behavior and the institutional characteristics encouraging it.[47] But such negotiations will clearly take time. The United States negotiated with the Japanese for improved market access in semiconductors for more than ten years before the semiconductor agreement was concluded. A second-best approach would be a safeguards approach in which the United States responds to evidence of dumping by the Japanese by offsetting subsidies for domestic producers. Under current institutional and budgetary conditions in the United States, such an approach is pure fantasy.[48] As a third-best approach to prevent the exit of domestic producers, a temporary antidumping response may be both politically inevitable and economically defensible. In addition, such a response may have a long-term beneficial effect if it changes the predatory strategy of Japanese producers in other markets in the future.

The United States should press for multilateral managed trade agreements to regulate antidumping procedures. The objective of such agree-

46. Unless, of course, Japanese producers decide to locate some of their high-technology operations in other countries, and these operations provide the strategic national benefits that would have been provided by domestically owned operations. These are possibilities that have not been addressed by most policymakers and that are not addressed here, not because they are unimportant but because to address them adequately would require another paper. It is interesting to note, however, that at least one recent study suggests that the foreign subsidiaries of Japanese firms exhibit distinctive behavior that may limit their strategic benefits for the host countries where they set up operations. See Mordechai E. Kreinin, "How Closed Is Japan's Market? Additional Evidence," *World Economy*, vol. 11 (December 1988), pp. 529–42.

47. To a certain extent, this is the approach taken by the United States in Super 301, the Market-Opening, Sector-Specific talks, the market access part of the Semiconductor Trade Agreement, and the structural impediments initiative talks. Since the possible predatory behavior of Japanese producers disadvantages other national producers as well, a multilateral negotiating approach is preferable to a bilateral one whenever possible.

48. Sematech is an example of this kind of policy response, but the amount of government support was too small and the timing of such support was too late to prevent the exit of significant U.S. production capacity.

ments should be the adoption of more precise and uniform procedures. These negotiations should address questions about the definition and measurement of dumping and injury and should specify allowable responses when both dumping and injury are demonstrated.

Critical questions concern the measurement of cost in high-technology industries. If dumping is to be assessed on the basis of price-cost comparisons, then there should be some agreement on what cost measure to use. Under current practice, the United States and Europe have a tendency to move toward a full average cost standard—dumping is interpreted to occur when price falls below average cost, broadly defined to include both variable and fixed costs and a profit judged high enough to attract investment capital. But even this approach is vague and allows ample variability in its application across products and countries. And it also leaves out important unaddressed questions about the relevant time period for measuring costs and prices and for assessing transportation and other charges that might cause differences in pricing strategies in different national markets.

Other questions concerns relate to the problem of injury. First, there is a definitional problem: what evidence suggests actual or threatened injury in in high-technology industries? Second, timeliness of action is critical. As noted earlier, it may be especially important to determine injury expeditiously and to allow for retroactive assessment of duties in high-technology industries, when dumping is demonstrated. Any agreement on rules should include procedures for regular monitoring of prices and costs.

These concerns highlight the questions about procedures. Because the GATT antidumping code is vague and unenforceable, great national differences occur in antidumping procedures. In the United States, the administration of antidumping is divided between two agencies—the International Trade Commission (ITC), which determines whether there is material injury, and the Department of Commerce, which determines the dumping margin. The system requires judicial review by the ITC and allows for the disclosure of detailed information to exporters and importers. In contrast, Europe has no system of information disclosure, no separation of responsibilities for dumping and injury determination, and only limited judicial review, so the system is largely administrative and bureaucratic. Both systems share the obvious defect that national producers appeal to national bodies for a determination of dumping, and it is unreasonable to presume that such bodies are impartial judges when it comes to choosing between the interests of domestic and foreign firms. A primary objective of new multilateral codes for antidumping in high-technology industries should be the standardization of national procedures allowing for greater transparency, greater access to information, and greater opportunity for judicial review.

Finally, a managed trade agreement for antidumping rules should establish a permanent multilateral commission to supervise its enforcement.[49] At the least, such a commission should have the right to monitor prices and costs to set up a multilateral early warning signal for dumping[50] and to review the national antidumping practices of the countries participating in the agreement to monitor their conformance with it. More ambitiously, the agreement might call for binding arbitration in the event of a dispute, and the commission might serve as part of a dispute settlement mechanism, designed along the lines of the compulsory dispute settlement mechanism in the U.S.-Canada trade agreement.

Managed Trade Arrangements for Outcomes

An alternative to a rules-oriented managed trade approach is a results-oriented managed trade approach. For example, if rules for firm behavior cannot be agreed on or enforced, then a negotiated agreement specifying

49. Although the desirability of a surveillance commission and a dispute settlement mechanism is argued here for an international agreement on antidumping rules, the argument applies for managed trade agreements for other kinds of rules on government and firm behavior.

50. One of the strengths of the Semiconductor Trade Agreement was the establishment of a procedure for regular monitoring of Japanese cost and price behavior in a wide variety of semiconductor devices, including devices, such as microprocessors, in which there was no evidence of dumping at the time the agreement was signed. This procedure allows for early warning of dumping behavior, so that offsetting action by the industry or the government can be taken before substantial injury. One of the reasons why the antidumping provisions of the semiconductor agreement in DRAMs caused dramatic price increases was their timing—by the time the provisions were put into effect, much of the DRAM capacity in the United States had been lost, and the Japanese producers with the overwhelming share of the world market had the potential for great market power, which was realized under the administrative guidance of the Ministry of International Trade and Industry (MITI). In EPROMs, where the United States still had a big share of the market, the antidumping provisions of the agreement did not result in dramatically higher prices by Japanese producers. For more on the role of market power and MITI in the DRAM price increases following the Semiconductor Trade Agreement, see Kenneth Flamm, "Policy and Politics in the International Semiconductor Industry," paper presented to the SEMI ISS Seminar, January 1989.

competitive outcomes that would be reasonable to expect in the presence of such rules is a possible alternative. This approach underlies the market access part of the semiconductor agreement, which specified a target of a 20 percent import share of the Japanese semiconductor market by 1991.[51]

Economists routinely attack managed trade arrangements that specify outcomes. Opposition is equally strong to both voluntary export restraints and voluntary import expansion restraints. Export restraints are attacked because they amount to quantitative limits on the imports of one country from one or several other countries. Such arrangements are clearly protectionist in nature and design. In addition, because they are country specific, they violate the basic nondiscrimination principle of the GATT.

The empirical literature on export restraints is extensive, generally concluding that they have many negative effects including higher prices for both domestic and foreign goods, frequently accompanied by higher wages and salaries of protected domestic producers; higher profits for foreign producers and incentives for them to move to other locations or to higher value-added products to escape the quantitative limits of the agreement; a reduction in competitive forces and the distortion of market incentives for industry rationalization and productive international specialization; the creation of vested interest groups and rent-seeking behavior; and spillover effects on other countries and producers not included in the agreement.[52]

---

51. Formally, the semiconductor agreement did not contain an explicit numerical target for the foreign market share of the Japanese market by the end of the agreement. Instead, the agreement recognized the problem of market access in Japan and called for increased market access. However, the American negotiators believed that Japan had agreed to a steady increase to 20 percent foreign market share by 1991 (or a rough doubling of the existing U.S. market share), and this target was explicitly specified in an intergovernmental side-letter to the agreement. The target of 20 percent was for sales by all foreign-capital affiliated firms, not just U.S. firms. It was based on an estimate of what share U.S. producers would have in the absence of market barriers. This estimate, in turn, was based on the U.S. share in other foreign markets.

52. A dynamic effect of the export restraints, which have been given insufficient attention, is their effect on foreign direct investment decisions. In televisions and automobiles, there is mounting evidence that the export restraints between the United States and Japan motivated considerable Japanese foreign direct investment in the United States. Today, most production of televisions in the United States is foreign owned, and a growing fraction of auto production is foreign owned. For discussion of the empirical literature on the export restraints in steel, textiles, and automobiles, see Cline, *Trade Policy in the 1980s*, pt. 3.

Politically, export restraints are an understandable stop-gap response to the threats to domestic producers caused by imports. They are, however, hard to defend economically. And they are poorly designed to realize their objectives, since the higher profits they generate for foreign suppliers work to their advantage in future rounds of competition. In addition, such restraints are rarely accompanied by programs to rationalize and strengthen the protected domestic industry for such competition. The protected producers are left to decide how to use the higher prices and profits resulting from the restraints. But the protection afforded by export restraints blunts the incentives to use higher returns wisely.

Economically, temporary tariffs or quota auctions are preferable to export restraints as a tactic to safeguard domestic producers. Quota auctions allow foreign producers to compete with one another for shares of an overall import quota. In theory, the low-cost producers will be able to offer the highest bids. This will limit the anticompetitive effects of the quota and will hold down its price effects. Moreover, both the tariff and the auction approach mean that at least part of the higher revenues resulting from protection will go to the government imposing the protectionist measures. These revenues can then be used to support a restructuring program for domestic producers.

Although it is hard to defend voluntary export restraints from an economic perspective, the economic case against the voluntary import expansion restraints is weaker and less well documented. Under the import expansion restraints, a foreign country is induced, by incentives or penalties, to agree to a quantitative import target of specific products from specific trading partners. To date, there are few managed trade agreements that embody import expansion restraints. The semiconductor agreement is a notable exception. But import expansion restraints are likely to become more important in the future in high- technology industries as part of new attention to issues of "fair" market access and reciprocity.

Opposition to the import expansion restraints rests on three grounds: they will result in the cartelization of world markets in specific products; by limiting competition, they will result in higher prices for these products; and because they violate the nondiscrimination principle of the GATT, they further undermine the liberalization of the world trading system. All three of these arguments are subject to qualification.

First, the establishment of a minimum import target by a particular country from one or more of its trading partners is a far cry from an industry cartel. Indeed, if the target applies to a country and an industry in which there is ample evidence of market closure—as is surely true for Japan in the semiconductor industry—and if the target applies broadly to imports from all foreign suppliers or the most important foreign suppliers rather than imports from a specific supplier—as is true in the semiconductor agreement—then the import expansion restraints may enhance competition rather than cartelize world markets. From a static perspective, the target may look like nothing more than a buyer's cartel or a tax on the importing country. But from a dynamic perspective, the target sets in motion changes in supply and demand behavior that can increase competition in both the importing country and the world market.[53]

Consider changes in the semiconductor industry since the signing of the semiconductor agreement. On the supply side, American producers anticipating at least a minimum share of the lucrative Japanese market have increased their investments in sales, distribution, and technical support facilities in Japan. On the demand side, Japanese users of semiconductors in the electronics and automobile industries are beginning to design in features of their products based on U.S. semiconductor devices. Since the import target was stated broadly for devices, covering not only DRAMs but microprocessors in which U.S. producers still have competitive advantages, the opening of the Japanese market can work to the benefit of such producers.[54] In dynamic terms, the appropriate

53. It is too early to tell whether enforcement of the market access provision of the semiconductor agreement will result in a more open market in Japan or will simply result in a buyers' cartel. A recent paper by Kenneth Flamm suggests that MITI has played an important role in the enforcement of the agreement. But there is also evidence that some Japanese auto and consumer electronics producers have signed deals or expressed interest in purchasing U.S. chips since U.S. chip producers have invested more in sales, testing, and design facilities in Japan. And the Electronics Industry Association of Japan, a private industry association, has been active in exploring ways to increase the sales of foreign chips to Japanese users. Further research is necessary to determine whether effective enforcement of the agreement will make the Japanese market for semiconductors genuinely contestable by foreign suppliers, other than foreign suppliers, such as Texas Instruments, which produce in Japan for the Japanese market. For more on MITI's role in the enforcement of the semiconductor agreement, see Flamm, "Policy and Politics and the International Semiconductor Industry."

54. According to Michael Borrus, since U.S. producers have little position in either DRAM or consumer chips in Japan, a 20 percent foreign share of the Japanese market

metaphor for the target may not be a buyer's cartel but a beachhead. And as Richard Baldwin has argued, beachheads by foreign producers in protected domestic markets can have lasting effects on competition.[55]

Because of the potential for greater competition resulting from the import expansion restraints, their effects on prices are uncertain. Indeed, if an import restraint encourages more competition among suppliers and more choice for demanders, prices may fall rather than increase, at least in the long run. The importance of distinguishing between the short-run and long-run price effects of an import expansion agreement is evident in assessing the semiconductor agreement. Compelling evidence suggests that the Japanese government encouraged the formation of an investment and production cartel among Japanese producers of DRAMs to enforce the agreement in 1987 and 1988.[56] Cartelization was possible because of the market power of the Japanese producers. By 1986, six integrated Japanese companies accounted for about 80 percent of world production for 256K and higher DRAMs[57]—and because of the tradition of cooperative relations among these producers and between them and the Japanese government.[58] The production cartel restricted competition among Japanese producers and was one of several factors behind a sharp increase in DRAM prices in world markets.[59] In addition, however, higher DRAM prices, along with the Japanese promise to double the foreign share in its domestic semiconductor market by 1991, has gradually encouraged new entry in DRAM production capacity by some U.S. and foreign producers.[60] The entry of new capacity will increase com-

---

implies thorough foreign dominance of some market segments in Japan, most notably in microprocessors and peripherals. For more on the Semiconductor Trade Agreement, see Borrus, *Competing for Control.*

55. Richard Baldwin, "Hysteresis in Import Prices: The Beachhead Effect," Working Paper 2545 (Cambridge, Mass.: National Bureau of Economic Research, March 1988), and "Some Empirical Evidence on Hysteresis in Aggregate U.S. Import Prices," Working Paper 2483 (Cambridge, Mass.: National Bureau of Economic Research, January 1988).

56. Flamm, "Policy and Politics in the International Semiconductor Industry."

57. David Yoffie, "The Global Semiconductor Industry, 1987," Harvard University, Business School Case 388-052, 1987.

58. For evidence of earlier collusive and cooperative behavior by these Japanese integrated producers in the television market, see Yamamura, "Caveat Emptor: The Industrial Policy of Japan."

59. There were at least two other factors contributing to the increases in DRAM prices in 1987 and 1988: a cyclical expansion of demand, which traditionally brings higher prices in the industry; and technical difficulties in supply resulting from the move from 256K DRAM production to one-megabit DRAM production.

60. Initially, the entry of new DRAM production capacity following the conclusion

petition in the global semiconductor market over time and will reduce the market power of the Japanese producers. In this sense, although the semiconductor agreement clearly reduced competition in the short run, it may ultimately result in a more competitive structure that serves as "cartel insurance" in the long run.

Finally, even though import expansion restraints may be sector specific and country specific, they may be liberalizing over time. In the case of the semiconductor agreement, the target for market access in Japan covers "all foreign-capital affiliated firms." Contrary to popular misconception, it is not a target for sales of American companies only. Rather, it is a target for a minimum opening of the Japanese market in semiconductors—in this sense, it is meant to liberalize the Japanese import regime.[61]

In high-technology industries, where government promotional and protectionist policies are strong, and where even temporary exclusion from foreign markets can have long-term dynamic effects, import expansion restraints setting quantitative targets for market access by excluded foreign producers cannot be discounted as a reasonable policy response. Given the long lags involved in negotiating managed trade arrangements for rules in these industries, managed trade arrangements for outcomes may be a wise short-term measure with unexpected benefits for long-term competition.

---

of the Semiconductor Trade Agreement was disappointing. In recent months, there have been announcements of new plans to add to DRAM capacity both at home and abroad by several U.S. producers and announcements by several Japanese producers to set up DRAM fabrication facilities in the United States and Japan.

61. The semiconductor agreement calls for a 20 percent share of the Japanese market for foreign-owned companies rather than for foreign-based companies, thereby ruling out the possibility of the target being satisfied by Japanese imports from Japanese-owned production facilities in the United States. In addition, sales by Texas Instruments from its Japanese production facilities count toward the 20 percent share. In these two ways, the agreement seems to reflect a U.S. corporate perspective rather than a U.S. national perspective. If the United States can realize the external benefits associated with semiconductor production from foreign-owned production facilities in the United States, including Japanese facilities, then the appropriate target for voluntary import expansion restraints would specify a share of the Japanese market for foreign-based companies rather than foreign-owned companies. In addition, if such external benefits for the nation are not realized by the foreign operations of domestically owned companies, such as the Japanese operations of Texas Instruments, then the appropriate target for import expansion restraints would exclude sales from such operations. Whether the domestic operations of foreign-owned companies or the foreign operations of domestically owned companies can provide the national external benefits from high-technology industries is a question that requires further research.

Policy Conclusions

Given the magnitude of the trade adjustment required by the United States during the next several years and the competitive pressure on U.S. high-technology producers from interventionist policies abroad, the United States needs to act on several trade policy fronts at once. Certainly, the United States should continue support for the Uruguay round of the GATT talks to extend the GATT's coverage and improve its functioning. The treatment of intellectual property under the GATT is an especially important issue for high-technology industries. At the same time, the United States should continue to press for greater liberalization in bilateral trade relations, especially with Japan. Japan is the principal source of competition for American high-technology industries, and despite formal liberalizing measures, structural impediments to the Japanese market, particularly in these industries, remain strong.[62]

Europe, however, should not be overlooked. The European Community is also committed to promoting certain high-technology industries and has already taken actions that will disadvantage the competitive position of foreign producers who do not locate the technologically significant parts of their production process within the Community.

Under these circumstances, it is wise for the United States to negotiate with the other advanced industrial countries to develop managed trade agreements specifying allowable rules of behavior in certain high-technology industries. The basic objective of such agreements would be greater coordination and standardization of behavior in specific industries that are increasingly global in nature but in which the United States, Europe, and Japan have strong national interests. Seen in this light, such agreements are a logical extension of macroeconomic policy coordination among these countries. Like macroeconomic coordination, the underlying motivation for such agreements is economic interdependence. The fate of each nation's high-technology industries is increasingly linked to government and firm behavior in other nations.

As an alternative to managed trade arrangements for rules, managed trade arrangements specifying outcomes may be called for, at least as a short-term measure. If the policy objective is to control imports, managed

---

62. For recent evidence on the continued closure of the Japanese market, see Robert Lawrence, "How Open Is Japan?" paper presented to the National Bureau of Economic Research, "Conference on the United States and Japan: Trade and Investment," National Bureau of Economic Research, October 19–20, 1989, forthcoming in a volume of conference proceedings edited by Paul Krugman.

trade arrangements should take the form of auction quotas or temporary tariffs whose proceeds are used to finance restructuring programs for domestic producers. Such arrangements should be temporary, with a deadline for their elimination or renegotiation. For all of the reasons just noted, voluntary export restraints should be avoided.

If the objective of policy is to increase market access abroad, voluntary import expansion restraints may be a useful policy tool. To maximize their potential liberalizing effects, they should be broadly defined for the products and the exporting countries they include. The goal should be improved market access for all foreign suppliers, not just for a select few.

Although managed trade rules to promote freer trade in high-technology sectors should be given priority, managed trade outcomes as a prod to develop and enforce such rules may be the best one can hope for in several industries. Because Japan, the EC, and many newly industrializing countries have a policy agenda to build or strengthen their domestic industrial base in high-technology industries, and because in pursuit of this agenda, competitive foreign suppliers are disadvantaged relative to domestic suppliers in various ways, it may prove impossible to agree on rules of the game for policy intervention. Are managed trade arrangements establishing a minimum share of national markets for imports of certain high-technology goods really as anticompetitive as many economists seem to believe? Not if the alternative is a system in which several national markets are preserved for national suppliers or foreign suppliers willing to locate a big fraction of their production facilities to these markets, especially if the other foreign suppliers disadvantaged by this system are low-cost, high-quality producers. These are the real alternatives against which the wisdom of managed trade arrangements for outcomes must be assessed.

Discussion by Avinash K. Dixit

Laura D'Andrea Tyson describes herself as a "cautious activist" in trade policy. She believes that immediate U.S. policy action to manage trade in high-technology industries is justified, and she offers some suggestions to this end. I am closer to being a "cautious inactivist" on trade policy. I agree with many of her arguments criticizing the orthodox free trade dogma and have participated in research that has led to the new thinking on trade policy. Our differences are often ones of emphases and nuances, but they build up to very different judgments about the overall U.S. trade policy.

Let me begin with a wholehearted agreement. Irrespective of any theoretical merits or demerits, free trade is not a relevant alternative; political realities dictate otherwise. But I do ask that proposals for managed trade should be judged by the same standards as Tyson urges in her criticism of free trade. I will argue that Tyson's proposals are seriously flawed when judged in the light of political realities.

Now a general point of disagreement. Tyson claims that "there are no simple theoretical guidelines for making trade policy in today's world" and that managed trade arrangements should be discussed as practical, factual questions, not as questions of theory or general principles." But facts are never used, and indeed are not usable, without some organizing principles. I shall therefore begin by stating four such basic principles. This will help to evaluate Tyson's review of the facts and the theories and set the stage for my assessment of her policy proposals.

—*Targeting*. The best way to treat a market failure is at its source; therefore trade policy is an inferior response to domestic distortions. Many of the ills with the U.S. economy identified by Tyson call for domestic policy measures, some macroeconomic and some microeconomic, not for managed trade. Tyson recognizes this fact but immediately goes on to defend the use of trade policy in such situations because others do it too, and the United States should join them in evolving a negotiated system of managed trade rules or outcomes. Although in the world of the second best, two wrongs can sometimes make a half right, each such claim needs proof, and none is offered. Reliance on internationally accepted rules of the game is not enough.

Tyson claims that the deterioration of the U.S. net export position in several sectors is the fundamental real factor behind the U.S. trade deficit. But as she states elsewhere, "the overall trade position of a nation is mainly a consequence of macroeconomic forces." Improving productivity in high-technology sectors will raise the average standard of living in the United States but will not reduce the aggregate trade deficit. That needs policies to raise aggregate net national saving. And subsidies to U.S. producers to promote research and development or to compensate them for injury might be first-best policies, but she dismisses them as "pure fantasy" in the current budgetary conditions and argues for trade restrictions such as antidumping duties in these circumstances. These restrictions raise the prices received by U.S. producers and paid by U.S. consumers—exactly as if the producers were subsidized by taxing the consumers. The fantasy has become a reality, only the revenue to pay the subsidy is raised in a way for which there is usually neither an efficiency nor an equity rationale, for example, a tax on U.S. computer manufacturers who use DRAMs to subsidize U.S. firms that produce them. Of course the whole operation is kept off the budget and that is the political reason for this approach. But economists owe it to society to expose such costly charades wherever they are found and not accept them without protest as "second-best constraints."

—*Recognition that creating comparative advantage has costs as well as benefits.* The mere fact that comparative advantage can be created in some industries does not mean that it should be. For example, Richard Baldwin and Paul Krugman found that Japan's closure of the DRAM market enabled them to dominate this market but at too high a cost: the losses of Japanese users of DRAMs more than outweighed the gains of the makers. Tyson counters this by asserting vague benefits of a Schumpeterian dynamic kind, but she offers no empirical evidence of the magnitude of such effects. This argument, coming from someone who believes in the superiority of facts over theory, is very strange.

It is not true that dynamic considerations will always strengthen the case for policy intervention. First, entry is likely to be freer in the long run, so short-run, profit-shifting arguments are likely to become weaker or nonexistent. Second, even when persistent profits are to be had, proper dynamics should take into account the costly activities including rent seeking that will be undertaken in anticipation of these profits. Finally, detailed models of the dynamics of research and development in a trading economy do not support simple policies of trade restriction or even subsidies. The two market failures inherent with research and development—spillovers and monopoly profits—interact, and policies that correct the first problem can easily worsen the second by a greater amount.[63]

—*Prerequisites for strategic behavior.* Japan's support of its export industries can help the United States by improving terms of trade but can also hurt the United States if Japan forecloses profit opportunities for U.S. firms or reduces the scale of U.S. production in sectors with beneficial domestic spillovers. In such cases, the United States can in

---

63. Gene M. Grossman and Elhanan Helpman, "Growth and Welfare in a Small Open Economy," Working Paper 2970 (Cambridge, Mass.: National Bureau of Economic Research, May 1989).

principle use strategic policies, basically threats of actions that will harm Japan, to influence its actions. But successful threats must meet certain preconditions: the threat must be in place before Japan takes its actions; the threat must be credible; and it must be equally credible that the United States will not take the hurtful action anyway even if Japan complies with U.S. wishes. Sadly, the U.S. policy process fails to fulfill any of these conditions. Given U.S. concern for due process, and the existence of many special interest groups with delaying powers, the United States cannot often move quickly or firmly. Even worse, once the nation erects trade barriers as a threat, they take on their own life, and the United States cannot credibly promise not to use them outside the context that generates the threat.[64]

—*Recognition that management can lead to cartelization.* This Stiglerian claim is well supported by the theory of industrial organization and borne out by reality. First, agencies that are supposed to regulate an industry often turn into the industry's allies in sustaining high prices; the U.S. airline industry of the 1970s was a prime example of this result. Second, management requires communication, which facilitates establishment and monitoring of collusive agreements. Often the simplest way to manage is to carve up the markets among the sellers; that monopolizes all the markets at once.

In trade policy, the U.S. auto and steel markets provide clear examples of the operation of this principle. Voluntary export restraints have enabled foreign firms and countries to achieve mutually credible output restrictions, and U.S. firms have been able to raise prices under the umbrella of the exporters' cartel.

Tyson claims that voluntary import expansion agreements are different and that the Semiconductor Trade Agreement has led to increased competition because the number of U.S. producers has increased. But there is no general, simple connection between numbers and competition in industrial organization. In this context, if A and B agree to have fixed shares of each other's market, that is not competition. For competition, A needs to fear that if he raises his price, B will win over some of A's customers. The share agreement precludes this possibility. A pair of markets with agreed mutual export shares is just as much a monopoly as

---

64. For more details on this point, see Avinash Dixit, "How Should the United States Respond to Other Countries' Trade Policies?" in *U.S. Trade Policies in a Changing World Economy*, Robert M. Stern, ed. (MIT Press, 1987), pp. 245–82; and Avinash Dixit and Barry Nalebuff, *Thinking Strategically* (W. W. Norton, forthcoming), chap. 6.

a pair of carved-up markets. Once again, management does imply cartelization. The clinching evidence in the semiconductor agreement case is the price of DRAMs, which has increased substantially and stayed far above the path it was on before the agreement.

Tyson recommends multilateral or bilateral negotiations to manage trade as well as industrial policies for high-technology industries in three respects: antitrust, antidumping, and voluntary import expansion. Let me begin with the obvious question: how are high-technology industries to be identified? Tyson emphasizes two relevant characteristics, namely, the high sunk costs of research and development, which lead to an imperfectly competitive market structure, and beneficial spillovers to the rest of the economy. Both are extremely difficult to identify in advance, that is, in time for the policy decision. Research and development is inherently highly uncertain, and spillovers by nature leave no objective trail of economic transactions. Therefore both will come to be judged by political criteria, and policies will be formulated using political procedures. For example, within a few weeks of the first claim of successful cold fusion, very large federal funding for it was being discussed in congressional hearings, rather than at the National Science Foundation. Hot fusion has successfully appropriated much larger support for more than thirty years, and its promises always keep receding into the future. Finally, to generate enough political support, the industries will scatter their activities over as many states as possible, thus dissipating the beneficial effects of agglomeration—the Route 128 or Silicon Valley phenomena—that are thought to be so important in research and development. These realities of U.S. politics make me skeptical of the results of Tyson's favored policies.

Let me turn from these general points to the trade policies Tyson proposes.

—*Antitrust policies.* The premises underlying Tyson's recommendations seem to be that the purpose of negotiations should be to get Japan to adopt policies similar to those of the United States. Of course the industry-government alliance in Japan is happy with Japan's present antitrust policies (an oxymoron?). The United States must either coerce Japan or offer it something else in return. The United States probably still has the power to coerce, but I argued earlier that the policy process cannot wield this power with the necessary speed or credibility. And can the United States hope to come to a domestic agreement about a quid pro quo?

Furthermore, Japan is not the whole of the rest of the world. A stronger and more united Europe will not let the United States and Japan dominate the high-technology industries. And some emerging industrial countries such as South Korea, India, and maybe Brazil are staking out their claims, too. But there are enough high-technology industries to go round. Once negotiations for a managed regime start, the likeliest outcome is a carve-up, an agreement for each country or bloc to monopolize a sphere of interest of appropriate size. Such a collection of monopolies will not be conducive to aggregate economic welfare anywhere.

—*Antidumping duties*. Tyson basically justifies these duties by claiming that the predation argument is more serious in high-technology industries with their large sunk costs. But sunk costs are an exit barrier as much as an entry barrier. If Japan tries predatory dumping, the U.S. firms, having already sunk their costs, should remain active. If they do not, the reasons are to be found in capital markets, and the appropriately targeted remedies lie there.

The sharp rise in antidumping cases across most industries in recent years is the result of the fall of the dollar from its 1985 height. When exchange rates are volatile, it makes perfectly good sense for foreign firms to tolerate a phase of prices at below-average or even at marginal costs, because the tangible or intangible capital they have invested to sell in the United States has an option value.[65] This result has no predatory intent or consequence, and antidumping duties are economically unjustified. The proper action is to achieve more stable exchange rates by pursuing better domestic monetary and fiscal policies.

—*Voluntary import expansion*. Tyson claims that agreements to expand imports, or more specifically, to reduce existing barriers, can be a beneficial move. I argued earlier that they will not increase competition. Furthermore, such agreements are voluntary in name only. Why would Japan agree to import more semiconductors?[66] Either Japan would give in to U.S. threats, or it would get something in return. My arguments on these points in connection with antitrust policies apply equally. U.S. threats are likely to be either ineffective or damagingly heavy handed; there is little that the U.S. policy process can offer in return.

---

65. See Avinash Dixit, "Hysteresis, Import Penetration, and Exchange Rate Passthrough," *Quarterly Journal of Economics*, vol. 104 (May 1989), pp. 205–28.

66. Removing their trade barriers will help its consumers, but Japan's political and administrative process seems to care even less about its consumers than the U.S. process cares about U.S. consumers.

Perhaps the difference between a cautious activist and a cautious inactivist is best captured in their different judgments about where the burden of proof should be placed. A cautious activist regards government intervention as the norm but can be persuaded by evidence that some policies will do more harm than good. A cautious inactivist regards free markets as the norm but can be persuaded by evidence of market failure and by arguments about the efficacy of specific policies. I remain unconvinced by Tyson's proposals, but feel I owe the reader a brief statement of the alternatives that a cautious inactivist has to offer. I believe the United States should focus its search for better policies on the domestic arena where most of the problems originate. The nation must make genuine efforts to reduce the federal budget deficit that is the root cause of the aggregate trade imbalance and exchange rate misalignment. The nation should recognize that its antitrust policies were designed in an era when trade competition was much less important. Serious changes are needed to deal with new realities.[67]

I recognize two important, potential roles for strategic trade policy: to induce other countries to open their markets where the United States has a genuine potential export opportunity (for example, rice, but not autos, in Japan); and to deter other countries from closing their markets to U.S. exports (for example, aircraft in Japan, and a fortress Europe after 1992). But the United States must modify its domestic policy process before it can wield threats with skill and success—the nation must learn to act quickly, unambiguously, and credibly.

General Discussion

Anne Krueger said that simply applying protection would foster inefficient industries. She argued that the positive dynamics resulting from competition are at least as important as those from protection. In contrast to most U.S. protectionist proposals, she pointed out that Japan's targeted protection was coupled with an insistence that firms become world-class exporters.

(Robert Blecker emphasized that the optimal degree of intervention for promoting innovation was essentially an empirical question.)

Krueger also argued that the principle of comparative advantage

---

67. Markets such as steel and autos, where imports are restricted by quantity constraints, are effectively closed at the margin, and antitrust liberalization in such industries is not justified on grounds of trade competition.

remains valid regardless of what determines comparative advantage. She stressed that the gains from trade result from differences in comparative costs, and these gains are present even where comparative advantage is not based on resource endowments.

Fred Bergsten questioned what was meant by "managed trade" when the definition encompassed both rules and outcomes. He suggested one criterion for managed trade was that the rules (or outcomes) be sector specific—a point with which Tyson agreed. I. M. Destler felt that the concept of managed trade should be more closely identified with the use of trade policy as a component of industrial policy.

Paula Stern, citing U.S. measures in steel and semiconductors, commented that Tyson seemed to be advocating almost precisely the policies currently practiced by the United States. Stern suggested that the semiconductor arrangement had done little to deal with the industry's problems. Michael Mussa recalled that, ultimately, the first-mover advantage in semiconductor DRAMs, which had rested with the United States, did not prove decisive. Processing, vital to competitiveness in DRAMs, appears to be a Japanese strength. Mussa noted, however, this was not a stage in which traditionally large profits were made. He felt a high-productivity labor force was more important than the promotion of specific sectors. But Tyson defended the semiconductor agreement. She blamed economists for refusing to recognize problems that were evident in the case of semiconductors in the 1970s. Although she acknowledged the agreement had been implemented too late for DRAMS and resulted in high prices, she emphasized the agreement was written for all semiconductor devices and pointed to benefits in EPROMS, microprocessors, and AISICs.

Tyson said that the current policy situation was unsatisfactory and chaotic. At home, U.S. industries use political pressures and the trade laws to obtain assistance. Abroad, other countries apply different rules and policies. It would be much better, Tyson argued, to obtain an agreement on the rules for high-technology industries. She felt that the United States would have a strong presence in these industries if U.S. producers were not discriminated against in Europe and Japan and if antitrust and antidumping regulations were brought into conformity throughout the world market. Since such an agreement is unlikely because of the agendas in Europe and Japan, the best the United States can hope for today is an agreement on outcomes.

Robert Kuttner supported Tyson's view that the United States needed to respond in sectors such as semiconductors where the United States lost markets that it should not have lost under some idealized set of free trade rules. He also argued that the United States should not stand by and treat dumping or the subsidies that accrue from a closed market as a gift. Kuttner felt Tyson's approach was valuable because it moved beyond the pretense that free trade exists toward the messy problem of finding sets of rules. But Jeffrey Schott felt the GATT could actually deal with the problems Tyson had laid out, both through new agreements and through dispute settlement. He also stressed trade laws were being circumvented rather than used, citing the proliferation of voluntary export restraint agreements.

Gary Hufbauer asked to what degree Tyson's policies were justified on their own grounds and to what degree they were justified simply as a response to Europe and Japan. In a similar vein, Robert Reich observed that because the GATT was not working effectively, Tyson advocated managed trade as a short-run tactic to achieve a system of rules. But he noted she also made a second argument that stressed dynamic learning effects that result in a zero-sum game between countries. Reich noted this rationale was not readily reconciled with a system of rules. It suggested managed trade might be a long-run solution. Tyson agreed these conflicting elements were present.

Brian Turner asked why so many participants were pessimistic about industrial policies when they were applied so broadly in other countries. He suggested the United States would not be able to reverse the fortunes of key industries without such policies. Tyson agreed and stressed that managed trade by itself was not sufficient to deal with the problems facing high-technology industries. She felt additional policies to stimulate the U.S. semiconductor industry were necessary.

Kenneth Flamm questioned why Tyson advocates an antidumping code when she herself has pointed to the problems in the current antidumping rules that outlaw marginal cost pricing. Flamm noted that, even if constrained in export markets by such a code, firms could use marginal cost pricing at home. Since high-technology products are often intermediate inputs, this reality would create problems downstream.

Paula Stern and Gary Hufbauer asked how the strategic sectors requiring managed trade should be chosen. Hufbauer noted that not too long ago, steel was considered a crucial strategic sector. Charles L. Schultze stressed that applying selective policies in the United States is politically difficult because a basic dictum for the government is, 'never be seen as doing harm.' Gary Hufbauer suggested that to some people, political capture was a virtue rather than a vice. He also pointed to the problem of whether U.S. firms or U.S.-based economic activity should be favored. Thomas Mann stressed that more thinking had to be done about how choices might be structured so that politicians would favor longer-term, broader interests.

Stern and Schultze emphasized the importance of taking account of how strategic sectors interact. When protection is conferred on a producing sector, such as semiconductors, using sectors, such as computers, are hurt. Schultze pointed out that because many high-technology sectors produce intermediate inputs rather than final products, many dynamic externalities occur in using rather than producing industries. He also noted that, given Japanese spending patterns, voluntary import expansions would eventually raise Japanese exports and could have a negative impact on the competing sectors in U.S. high-technology industries. Thus, although mandating U.S. exports to Japan might improve the U.S. terms of trade, it would not necessarily provide aggregate dynamic effects that were positive.

Michael Mussa said the rejection of managed trade by many was based on experiences such as the Multifiber Arrangement and agricultural trade rather than ideological or doctrinal grounds. These experiences suggested the public interest simply was not served. But Destler mentioned agriculture as an area in which U.S. sectoral policy had successfully encouraged technological developments. Mussa endorsed the Dixit position of being a cautious inactivist. Pleas for trade actions did not have to be stimulated artificially. The presumption should be against sector-specific intervention, particularly through trade policy.

Reich asked that if the U.S. government could be immune from political pressures, what should its strategic trade policy look like? Dixit replied the top priority should be to adopt a forward-looking approach that preserved areas in which the United States currently leads. Once the position has eroded, he said, it will be too late. The United States should drive a better bargain when allowing foreigners to use its technology. Dixit also said the United States should use its political power to enhance its exports. He also mentioned the attraction of lowering U.S. protection in textiles and banking to obtain less protection abroad.

Commentary

Robert E. Baldwin, I. M. Destler, and Robert B. Reich

Each author has provided comments on the papers presented in this book.

Robert E. Baldwin

One of the many merits of the three papers presented in this book is that they clearly set forth two quite different trade strategies for the United States. Anne O. Krueger presents the case for free trade. The increasingly complex structure of industry, she argues, strengthens the need for liberal trade policies. In contrast, Rudiger W. Dornbusch and Laura D'Andrea Tyson spell out the case for managed trade. Both authors propose adopting a results-oriented or performance-oriented approach to opening export markets in the face of perceived unfair practices by foreign countries. Dornbusch, for example, says the United States should establish a target growth rate for Japanese imports of U.S. manufactures of 15 percent a year for ten years, with a sanction mechanism automatically restricting Japanese manufacturing imports into the United States if the target is not reached. Tyson supports, at least for the short run, voluntary import agreements such as the semiconductor agreement between the United States and Japan. She also urges the development of an international code regulating trade and governmental promotion of high-technology industries, and if agreement on such a code cannot be reached, she favors various unilateral actions by the United States.

The Definition of Managed Trade

Before commenting on specific points in the papers, I should like to consider the meaning of the term *managed trade,* which has been used frequently in the papers. In defining managed trade as trade that is controlled, directed, or administered by government policies, Tyson points out that much of current trade policy is already managed in one form or another. Indeed, the notion of an international trading order or regime implies, as Stephen D. Krasner points out, "implicit or explicit principles, norms, rules, and decision-making procedures around which actors' expectations converge in a given area of international relations."[1] These conditions apply whether the trade regime is a liberal one in which efforts are made to keep government intervention to a minimum or one in which the state determines the volume and composition of trade. Thus, the term managed trade is not very useful for distinguishing trade-policy positions, when defined in the broad manner proposed by Tyson.

What does distinguish advocates of different trade policies is simply whether they favor more or less government intervention to make exports larger and imports smaller than they would be in the absence of such intervention. Krueger obviously favors less intervention than now exists. Dornbusch supports the liberalization of U.S. import policies but wants active government intervention on the export side to correct for perceived unfair trade practices of foreign countries. Tyson argues for selective government intervention on both the export and the import side.

Growth Rates and Managed Trade

I have few comments to make about Krueger's paper, since, like her, I favor a liberal trade policy characterized by efforts to reduce existing tariff and nontariff controls over international trade. The great lesson of economic development history during the last forty-five years, whether it be in the developing countries, the communist countries of Europe and Asia, or the advanced capitalistic industrial countries, is that, when the theoretical case for widespread government intervention is implemented in the real world, the result is nearly always a slowing of a country's development pace and a decline in its international competitive ability. The very real adjustment difficulties faced by workers and capitalists under a market-oriented trading system should be eased not

1. Stephen D. Krasner, "Structural Causes and Regime Consequences: Regimes as Intervening Variables," in "International Regimes," Stephen D. Krasner, ed., special issue of *International Organization*, vol. 36 (Spring 1982), p. 185.

by trade interventions to prevent the necessity of adjustment but, as Krueger argues, by appropriate, temporary social policies.

Managed Trade and Fiscal Policy Changes

Initially, I was surprised at the magnitude of the change in the international trade regime that Tyson and Dornbusch propose in relation to the significance of the problems they are concerned about. Both authors recognize, for example, that the trade policies they advocate are not a means of solving the problem that has stimulated the increased interest in a more aggressive U.S. trade policy, namely, the U.S. trade deficit. As Dornbusch points out, under present full-employment conditions, a sudden, great increase in market access might, but need not, improve the U.S. balance of trade.

Their argument for forcing open foreign markets is not that it will help solve the deficit problem, but that it will ease the adjustment in real income required to solve the problem. They argue that the increase in demand for U.S. exports brought about by the opening of foreign markets will help reduce the need for a deterioration in the country's terms of trade that otherwise will be necessary. Certainly, it is helpful to a country that has lived beyond its income for many years to be favored by an increase in demand for its exports just when it is beginning to face the need to accept a real income reduction to balance its accounts. But in the absence of evidence that its principal trading partners are seriously restricting access to their markets, such a development can hardly be regarded as the country's right or even one that will help prevent future spending excesses.

Neither author presents any estimates of how much export demand would increase as a result of trying to overcome perceived unfair foreign trade practices through agreements that require import increases. Nor do they say how the result would compare with the terms-of-trade decline otherwise needed. In recommending that Japan be required to increase imports of manufactured goods from the United States by 15 percent a year during the next decade (a fourfold rise over the period), Dornbusch presumably believes this percentage indicates the amount by which Japan now discriminates against U.S. goods. He rejects the argument that Japan's relatively scarce supplies of natural resources may account for the country's low import ratio of manufactured goods on the grounds that the level of intraindustry trade should still be high despite the country's poor resource endowment.

However, in separate studies, Marcus Noland, Robert Z. Lawrence, and Gary R. Saxonhouse explicitly model intraindustry trade. Their results on whether Japan is an "outlier" among the other industrial countries in its total volume of exports and imports are mixed.[2] Japan's trading pattern is not out of the ordinary, say Noland and Saxenhouse, while Lawrence finds it is. Lawrence believes Japan's imports of manufactured goods would rise by a little more than 40 percent if all unusual trade barriers to Japanese trade were removed. But the dollar magnitude of this increase would be modest, and America's share of the increase more modest still. Moreover, Japan's exports would also rise. In the end, Lawrence writes, the import-liberalizing actions would have reduced Japan's worldwide surplus in manufactured trade in 1980 by only $9.4 billion or 10 percent, and the U.S. $20 billion deficit with Japan in manufactured goods in that year would have been cut by only about $2 billion.

Furthermore, since Dornbusch advocates trade liberalization on the import side at the same time that the United States tries to pry open foreign markets, the increase in import demand resulting from dismantling U.S. import barriers could offset the favorable terms-of-trade effect from this modest increase in export demand. Tyson advocates import substitution along with the opening up of foreign markets. In this case the loss in real income linked with increased protectionism could offset the real income gain linked with the expected increase in export demand. No one knows how these various trade-offs are likely to work out in practice, but those who propose them have the burden of proof to show that the effects of such interventions have the "right" sign and are significant in magnitude.

The Special Characteristics
of High-Technology Industries

For Tyson, the argument for managed trade goes well beyond its claimed beneficial effect on the terms of trade. She argues that trade

---

2. See Marcus Noland, "An Econometric Model of the Volume of International Trade" (Washington: Institute for International Economics, 1987); Robert Z. Lawrence, "Imports in Japan: Closed Markets or Minds?" *Brookings Papers on Economic Activity, 2:1987,* pp. 537–38; and Gary R. Saxonhouse, "Differentiated Products, Economies of Scale and Access to the Japanese Market," paper presented to the tenth annual Middlebury Conference on Economic Issues, 1988.

management is one aspect of a broader industrial strategy to deal with the special characteristics of high-technology industries, such as their favorable technological spillover effects on the rest of the economy and what she terms the dynamic Schumpeterian efficiency effects associated with the establishment of such industries. She states that such domestic policies as research and development subsidies are the best way to deal with these special features rather than trade policy. However, she argues that managed trade arrangements can also be defended on two grounds. First, there are widespread policy interventions in such industries by one's trading partner—interventions that Tyson says are not covered by the GATT. Second, trade interventions can be used as a tactical device to force the GATT to draw up rules covering these interventions.

There is no question about the theoretical validity of the technological externality argument that Tyson uses, that is, if such externalities are an important element of modern economic growth, a deliberate strategy of promoting such industries, including the use of trade intervention, might well be warranted. The real issue however is an empirical one. How significant are such spillover effects in the real world? As Tyson points out, most studies of industries in which government subsidies have been justified on these grounds conclude that the subsidization has on balance *reduced* the country's economic welfare. It seems, therefore—and I shall so argue in more detail later on—that modifications in the GATT subsidies code, coupled with improved monitoring and dispute-settlement processes, can deal adequately with those limited cases in which government intervention can be justified.

Managed Trade and Improving U.S. Competitivenes

It seems to me that the proposal of Dornbusch and Tyson for a results-oriented approach to the opening of U.S. export markets is not likely to accomplish the goal they seek, namely, an increase in U.S. international competitiveness as a means of increasing the real rate of U.S. economic growth. On the contrary, acceptance of their proposals could result in the United States becoming a slow-growth nation. Both of their proposals promote a divided world economy that undermines stable and peaceful international relations and forces nations to spend larger sums to protect their national interests. Finally, the legitimate concerns they raise can be handled successfully by actions consistent with the existing international economic order.

Dornbusch and Tyson seem unaware of the lessons the United States has learned from long experience with the political aspects of trade policy. To imagine, for instance, that one could gain domestic political agreement to dismantle import controls on such products as textiles and apparel, steel, and automobiles, and, at the same time, negotiate agreements binding foreign countries to import certain amounts of U.S. goods comes close to wishful thinking. Because of the importance of intraindustry trade, many of the groups that lobby for import controls also lobby for the use of governmental pressure to gain assured access to foreign markets. Both measures tend to raise profits in the affected industries and, to the extent these pressure groups have the political clout to obtain assured export markets, they also have the clout to retain import controls.

It is equally unrealistic politically to think a policy assuring fixed export amounts for domestic producers can be put into effect temporarily and then dismantled in favor of a liberal trade policy once the desired reforms by foreign countries are achieved. The history of U.S. import controls on sugar and textiles shows that once interventionist policies get started, they develop momentum and become very difficult to reverse. The nation is likely to get export agreements that are as hard to eliminate as the current import controls.

Furthermore, to believe that somehow the United States can practice discriminatory policies that increase its exports without other countries following suit ignores an abundance of experience. The United States would only be encouraging others to adopt beggar-thy-neighbor policies that will undermine any gains the nation may temporarily receive. The consequences of such foreign retaliation as well as the entrenchment of the new export and old import measures are likely to result in a weakening of American competitiveness and a reduction in U.S. growth rates.

More basically, the managed trade and bloc-building policies being advocated would divide the world into economic and political groups who would come to view international economic relations as a zero-sum gain in which each unit must strive to increase its power at the expense of other blocs. For example, strong forces in Europe wanted to convert the Europe 1992 movement into a "fortress Europe." Insistence by the United States on a multilateral approach has been critical in helping to offset these views. But inward-looking views are likely to gain dominance in Europe if the United States adopts the managed trade approach suggested by Dornbusch and Tyson.

The Eastern Pacific Rim should be the greatest foreign policy concern for the United States. The situation there is potentially unstable under existing conditions. Countries such as Japan, Korea, and Taiwan are highly dependent for their continued prosperity on imports of raw materials and exports of manufactured goods. They rely mainly on the developing countries of Southeast Asia for their raw materials and on the United States for their exports of manufactured goods. As the developing countries of this area become increasingly industrialized, pressures will increase in these countries to limit their exports of raw materials to Japan and the resource poor newly industrializing countries of the North. Limiting access to essential raw materials is a more serious economic blow than limiting exports, and pressures will build in the resource-poor industrial countries to try to prevent such an outcome. If, at the same time, the United States further threatens their standards of living by curtailing U.S. imports of their manufactured goods, pressures for destabilizing intervention could rise to a dangerous point, threatening U.S. national security interests in the region.

Problems in the Present Trading Framework

Adjusting to the fiscal changes required in this country, dealing with the spillover benefits from high-technology industries, and reducing external and internal trade-distorting measures are problems that the present international economic regime can handle satisfactorily. The advocates of aggressive bilaterialism and managed trade seem to have accepted as true the simple slogans imputing irrelevancy to the present regime based on the GATT. But the GATT has proved a surprisingly effective forum for reducing trade barriers, both fair and unfair, through negotiations. This effectiveness is emerging in the Uruguay round discussions about agriculture, textiles, services, and intellectual property rights. And, of course, over the years the GATT has been instrumental in greatly reducing tariffs. The GATT has had difficulties in significantly changing entrenched political arrangements, such as those covering agriculture and textiles. Because some countries would probably be harmed by such changes, any new agreements covering these sectors may be weak and contradictory. But the recent progress in agricultural and textile negotiations demonstrates that even great changes in existing trade practices can be made when the United States works closely with other like-thinking countries and exerts leadership.

The drawbacks of the GATT have encouraged the greater use of bilateral, plurilateral, and unilateral approaches by large countries and blocs, such as the United States and the European Community, to achieve desired changes in trade-policy behavior. And the GATT allows for the use of these approaches. It explicitly allows for the formation of free trade areas, for example, if they apply to substantially all trade between the partners and do not raise barriers against third countries. As Jeffrey J. Schott points out, the presumption that they be more trade creating than trade diverting has also been incorporated in GATT working-party reviews of notifications of free trade area agreements.[3] Thus, although I generally favor the multilateral approach over the trading bloc approach for achieving trade liberalization, I welcome such arrangements as the U.S.-Canada Free Trade Agreement when it seems clear that their trade-creation effects will outweigh their trade-diversionary impact. But, in concluding such agreements, the United States should make clear that the final objective is liberalization by all trading nations. The inclusion of any additional members in such agreements should promote this objective.

Bilateral negotiations are also not inconsistent with the GATT; the articles of agreement call for such negotiations in many places as a means of resolving disputes. What would be inconsistent with the existing international trading regime, however, are bilateral agreements that include performance requirements for bilateral trade balances or that are not subject to GATT review and rules.

The Conditional versus Unconditional Most-Favored-Nation Principle

The merits of the unconditional most-favored-nation principle, which is set forth in the first article of the GATT, are also a subject of concern. Although the founders of the GATT regarded this principle as one of the cornerstones of the agreement, they did allow exceptions. Permitting customs unions and free trade areas is not inconsistent with this principle, for example. Providing tariff preferences to the developing countries and allowing countries to enjoy the benefits of some of the Tokyo round nontariff codes only if they accept the responsibilities of these codes illustrate subsequent derogations from this principle.

3. Jeffrey J. Schott, "More Free Trade Areas?" in Schott, ed., *Free Trade Areas and U.S. Trade Policy* (Washington: Institute for International Economics, 1989), p. 24.

It is not only the advocates of managed trade who believe the United States should change to a conditional most-favored-nation principle; some economists, such as Gary C. Hufbauer, who are strong supporters of a liberal trading regime, also support this change.[4] The problem with reducing trade barriers on an unconditional basis is that some countries may attempt to free ride on the reductions made by others without making any, or only modest, cuts themselves. This response, in turn, may cause those who are willing to reduce their trade barriers to cut back on their own offers in order to achieve reciprocity. The final outcome could be one of much less trade liberalization than most countries want.

On the basis of this logic, one would expect that the extent of tariff cuts achieved over the years through multilateral negotiations would have been modest. However, such has not been the case. Since the end of the Second World War, average tariff levels for manufactured goods in the chief industrial countries have been cut from around 45 percent to less than 5 percent. The principal group of trading nations that has been unwilling to make serious duty reductions is the developing countries, and these countries have been excluded from the responsibility of making reciprocal tariff cuts in GATT-sponsored multilateral negotiations. However, the developed countries have responded to this behavior by not reducing duty levels significantly on products of special export interest to the developing countries, namely, labor-intensive goods such as textiles, apparel, and footwear.

Since, historically, free riding has not proved a serious problem to multilateral negotiations about tariff reductions, one might expect it not to be a problem in negotiations to reduce nontariff trade distortions. But, in fact, negotiators have been concerned about free riding in this area and have sometimes adopted a conditional most-favored-nation approach. For example, under the government procurement code negotiated in the Tokyo round, national treatment and nondiscrimination in awarding government contracts applies only to countries that sign the agreement and specify the agencies covered under the agreement.[5] The basis for this decision was the fear that countries believing it was

---

4. Gary C. Hufbauer, "The Unconditional Most-Favored-Nation Principle: Should It Be Revised, Retired, or Recast?" paper presented at the conference on International Trade Problems and Policies, Monash University, Melbourne, Australia, 1984.

5. The code is open ended, however, in the sense that additional countries could become signatories by also agreeing to liberalizing government purchasing policies for comparable agencies.

politically impossible for them to open up their procurement markets to foreign suppliers would take advantage of others doing so and flood these markets with exports.

Had the agreement specified the liberalization of government markets for particular commodities rather than for all purchases of particular government agencies, the fear of free riding might have proved unfounded for the same reasons as in the tariff-cutting negotiations. However, in the case of procurement, free riders and active participants may not be divided neatly by commodity groups. Thus, there could be validity in the argument that it was a choice between no liberalization or some liberalization under the conditional most-favored-nation principle.

One should realize, however, that the output response of producers to liberalization is likely to be weaker under conditional most-favored nation than under unconditional most-favored nation. Under the conditional most-favored-nation principle in the government procurement code, producers in a signatory country face the risk that, after expanding their capacity to take advantage of the new opportunities to meet the procurement demands of foreign governments, they will be forced into an unprofitable position because another country in which there are producers with lower costs later signs the agreement. Consequently, producers in countries that are among the initial signatories to such agreements are likely to be cautious about increasing their capacities and, at the same time, to lobby against the admission of new signatories.

When additional countries sign such codes, the initial signatories may also want to renegotiate the list of agencies covered, since the balance of concessions is changed by the new members of the agreement. This problem of the government having to keep renegotiating agreements shortly after they were made was an important consideration in the U.S. government's abandonment of the conditional most-favored-nation principle in 1923. The renegotiation process impeded the country's efforts to expand trade.

Although the unconditional most-favored-nation principle best promotes world welfare by ensuring that traded goods are produced by the lowest cost suppliers, sometimes insistence on this principle will slow the process of trade liberalization. In deciding whether the conditional most-favored-nation principle should be followed, situations in which these conditions seem to apply should be judged in much the same way that new free areas should be. If trade creation is likely to dominate trade diversion and if there is good reason to believe that the agreement will be a step toward liberalization on a multilateral basis, such agreements are consistent with a liberal international trading regime. But the United States must guard against the outcome that such agreements divide the world into politically destabilizing trading blocs.

Reducing Trade-Distorting Subsidies and Other Nontariff Measures

The GATT multilateral negotiating framework already provides an adequate basis for exerting the pressures to achieve the kind of changes needed in such areas as subsidization, dumping, trade-related performance requirements, intellectual property rights, and other nontariff measures. However, in my view the potential for achieving these changes within this framework has not been fully utilized. Comprehensive negotiations on such nontariff measures aimed both at formulating rules more consistent with modern production and trading conditions and at reducing existing trade-distorting measures inconsistent with these rules are needed. For example, comprehensive negotiation about subsidies could be conducted in a manner similar to the old item-by-item tariff negotiations.[6] The objective would be to phase out particular subsidies gradually, to bind their levels for periods of time, or perhaps to introduce export taxes (where permitted) to offset the export-subsidizing element in domestic subsidies. The incentives for another country to engage in such negotiations would not only be the possibility of reducing one's own subsidy budget but the threat of other countries' carrying out countervailing duty actions permitted under the GATT rules.

Each country would undertake a comprehensive evaluation of the subsidizing practices of other countries that it believes are causing material injury to one or more of its domestic industries, seriously prejudicing its interests, or nullifying or impairing its GATT benefits. A country would then make requests of other countries concerning the reduction or offset of injury-causing subsidies. At the same time, the country would announce the countervailing duty actions it was prepared to initiate domestically if bilateral or multilateral negotiations were not successful. If experience is any guide, most countries would be willing to enter into serious negotiations aimed at preventing the imposition of

---

6. Robert E. Baldwin, "GATT Reform: Selected Issues," in Henryk Kierzkowski, ed., *Protection and Competition in International Trade: Essays in Honor of W. M. Corden* (Basil Blackwell, 1987), pp. 204–14.

countervailing duties against their exports. Countries that believe their subsidies do not violate the GATT rules could announce that they will request the formation of GATT panels of experts to make decisions on their contentions or to specify the retaliatory action that would be allowable if countervailing duties are imposed. With a large number of panels, great progress could be made in establishing precedents and procedures in the panel decisionmaking process.

This approach, which could be described as aggressive multilateralism, is consistent with the behavior the United States has often followed in the GATT. For example, in the Kennedy round the threat by the United States to walk out of the negotiations finally led to the acceptance by the European Community of a linear approach to tariff reductions in contrast to the harmonization approach they favored. Similarly, at the insistence of the United States, new codes of behavior for nontariff measures were negotiated in the Tokyo round. And, as already noted, such issues as agriculture, trade in services, and intellectual property rights would not be on the agenda of the Uruguay round but for the pressures exerted by the United States. Working to modify rather than completely change the present GATT framework has the advantage of not risking the destruction of an international trading regime that has served the United States well in the past and, despite its flaws, is still serving the nation reasonably well. The GATT is also likely to prove more effective in achieving overall results than the time-consuming series of bilateral negotiations now being used to gain U.S. trade policy objectives with respect to several nontariff measures.

Restrictive Business Practices

One issue raised by Dornbusch cannot be handled in the present GATT framework. That is his contention that Japanese private producers favor other private Japanese firms over foreign firms in purchasing needed production inputs and capital equipment. Present GATT rules do not cover this type of discrimination by private firms. A code on restrictive business practices, such as in the charter for an International Trade Organization (ITO) that was proposed, but not accepted, just after the Second World War is needed to deal with such situations. Limiting access to markets by discriminating against enterprises is mentioned in the ITO charter as a private business practice that should be prevented.[7]

7. See United Nations Conference on Trade and Employment, ''Final Act and

As the United States learns that eliminating distortionary government practices is not enough to open markets, it may be time to examine whether a GATT code dealing with restrictive business is needed, and if needed is feasible.

I. M. Destler

Much of the political commentary in this book has been thin and one-sided, offered to buttress particular policy arguments rather than to illuminate the larger workings of the system. Discussion has also tended toward the negative—seeing politics as an adversary of good trade policy, a threat that must be contained if it cannot be eradicated.

This perspective on trade politics is not wrong. But it is incomplete. It ignores what I wish to emphasize: that liberal-leaning U.S. trade policy has been a product of constructive political management. And its key component has been to shift the focus from imports—what certain U.S. producers might lose—to exports—what other U.S. producers might gain. Persistent resort to this strategem by both executive branch and congressional trade leaders helped bring about both the decades of barrier reduction since the 1930s and the aggressive bilateralism and Super 301 of the 1980s.

In my comments I will develop this point. But let me first acknowledge that the negative perspective is not without basis. An excellent practitioner of trade politics in the Nixon administration, William Pearce, labeled support of liberal policies an "unnatural act" for politicians, since it requires holding back on favors that would clearly benefit specific petitioners for the sake of more thinly spread, hard-to-see, present and future gains.[8] Hence the "slippery slope" type of argument advanced by Anne O. Krueger: once the United States grants protection for one industry how can it withhold protection from another? To recognize that this argument can be valid one need only recall Smoot-Hawley, log-rolling protectionism gone wild. This legacy explains why ever since

Related Documents," Havana Charter for an International Trade Organization, Article 46 (New York, 1948).

8. "Outline for Remarks by William R. Pearce," before the Committee on Foreign Relations," Des Moines, Iowa, December 11, 1974. As deputy special representative for trade negotiations, Pearce was responsible for winning House approval for what became the Trade Act of 1974.

that time Congress has been reluctant to grant new statutory protection, even for textiles. And one reason Congress has been able to avoid doing so is the spread of free trade ideology, to which Krueger rightly points as an important political counterweight.[9]

But the slope does not always prove slippery. Political movement is not always toward further protection once some is granted. That has been the pattern for textiles, but not for autos, certainly not for shoes, and not always for steel.[10] Nor can ideology operate on its own. U.S. policy decisions are taken by politicians and bureaucrats working within a particular institutional framework. Strikingly little has been said about that framework, about the evolving American system for managing trade policy.[11]

Although his policy prescription differs radically from Krueger's, Rudiger Dornbusch agrees with her that sector-specific restrictions are undesirable. For Japan, he would replace such restrictions with "across-the-board tariff surcharges on Japanese imports, triggered automatically and proportionate" to the failure of Japan's import growth to meet targets determined by the United States. Besides being questionable policy, this suggestion strikes me as impractical politically. The central fact in the lives of trade policy practitioners is pressure from particular industries. How that pressure is managed—with resistance here, limited concession there—determines the overall shape of the U.S. trade regime. One thing officials cannot do is avoid product-specific matters. (However, Dornbusch's characterization of U.S. trade policy to date as a massive foreign aid program strikes me as *politically* on the mark. It mirrors the sentiments of the least-informed rhetoricians on Capitol

---

9. On the impact of ideas, see John S. Odell, *U.S. International Monetary Policy: Markets, Power, and Ideas as Sources of Change* (Princeton University Press, 1982). For emphasis on the impact of liberal ideology on trade policy, see Judith L. Goldstein, "A Reexamination of American Trade Policy: An Inquiry into the Causes of Protectionism," Ph.D. dissertation, University of California at Los Angeles, 1983.

10. Gary Clyde Hufbauer and Howard F. Rosen, *Trade Policy for Troubled Industries*, Policy Analyses in International Economics, no. 15 (Washington: Institute for International Economics, 1986), esp. chap. 2; and Gary Clyde Hufbauer, Diane T. Berliner, and Kimberly Ann Elliott, *Trade Protection in the United States: 31 Case Studies* (Washington: Institute for International Economics, 1986).

11. Baldwin and Pastor are among those who have written extensively and wisely about it. See Robert E. Baldwin, *The Political Economy of U.S. Import Policy* (MIT Press, 1985); and Robert Pastor, *Congress and the Politics of U.S. Foreign Economic Policy, 1929–1976* (University of California Press, 1980).

Hill. The foreigners are playing us for suckers; if we would just get tougher. . . .)

Laura D'Andrea Tyson's paper shows somewhat more political sophistication, not surprisingly for one who has been mapping the twists and turns of the struggle over semiconductors. She states correctly the old political principle that the first best can be the enemy of the good, so we need to explore alternatives. But her argument is also thin.

The missing element in all of the papers, and in most of the discussion, is a sense of the positive role of politics and of the necessity of building and maintaining a strong political foundation for a positive and open trade policy. The discussion overlooks the ways that U.S. leaders have gone about this constructive task since the 1930s and how the approach they have taken relates to the troubles U.S. trade policy is facing today.

Executive branch officials and trade-minded members of Congress are activists in what Robert Kuttner rightly calls a political business: trade policy. Contrary to the ideal prescriptions of economic theory, trade-policy leaders must respond to pressures from producers. And their task is not just damage limitation, though blocking and limiting outrageous proposals is an important part of it. But U.S. leaders must also build up and maintain constituencies in support of open policies in a world that is still, on balance, moving in this direction—notwithstanding widespread perceptions to the contrary.

The real anomaly of American trade politics in the post Smoot-Hawley era is that on balance political action has been constructive, pressure managing, and actively liberalizing. How could a system responsive to specific pressures manage to bring about a series of big *reductions* in trade barriers? How did U.S. trade-policy leaders pull off such a success? Understanding the answer to this question will help explain how the United States arrived at Super 301, aggressive bilateralism, and pressures for managed trade in high-technology products. For as I shall try to show, one of the principal techniques for managing trade politics in the past half century has led logically and naturally, if not too happily, to Super 301.

This technique, of course, was the emphasis on opening export markets. The genius of the Reciprocal Trade Agreements Act of 1934 was to shift the locus of action, to some extent, from U.S. to foreign markets, from U.S. trade barriers to foreign ones, from the import to the export arena. The United States would reduce its tariffs, but only as part of a process in which other nations reduced theirs. This stratagem brought export, pro-trade interests into the political game, not displacing or even equaling protectionist, antitrade interests, but providing a partial political offset, a source of counterpressure that executive branch leaders could draw on and reinforce.

The arena for mutual tariff reduction was bilateral negotiations in the 1930s, multilateral from the 1940s onward. The stress on export politics continued into the Tokyo round, where the prime target shifted to nontariff barriers and continues into the Uruguay round today. It has also been applied to bilateral negotiations, especially with Japan. In the late 1970s, for example, the main political pressure on trade came from import-affected industries such as color television, steel, and later, automobiles. Carter administration officials, led by Special Trade Representative Robert Strauss, made some accommodation to these industries, but the *initiatives* they took were trade-expanding, export-promoting ones. They pushed negotiations to open markets abroad for beef and citrus and telecommunications and tobacco. And unlike the situation in steel and autos, on the export issues government officials got the action started and invited the private interests to join in.[12]

Internationalist, export, and investment-minded producers were a key support group for practitioners of liberal trade policy. Multinational corporations were central to this coalition. For most of the postwar period, the stakes of these producers in any trade policy action were typically modest, but they favored an open, liberal economic order and could be summoned, in time of need, to resist protectionist pressures and support legislation authorizing serious new trade negotiations. In 1967, for example, Lyndon B. Johnson more or less invented the Emergency Committee for American Trade. Responding to a new drive for quotas, he got on the phone with business leaders, and a new, pro-trade organization emerged.[13] Producers of high-technology goods were

12. When I made this point several years ago at a Washington trade policy forum, and an official in the Office of the U.S. Trade Representative contested it, a Commerce aide approached me and whispered, "Ask him whether the tobacco people came to Washington or whether they [the officials] flew to North Carolina!"

For fuller development of this argument, see I. M. Destler, *American Trade Politics: System under Stress* (Washington: Institute for International Economics and New York: Twentieth Century Fund, 1986), esp. pp. 15–16, 93–94. For how the politics played out in bilateral talks with Japan, see I. M. Destler and Hideo Sato, eds., *Coping with U.S.-Japanese Economic Conflicts* (Lexington Books, 1982).

13. See I. M. Destler and John S. Odell, *Anti-Protection: Changing Forces in United States Trade Politics*, Policy Analyses in International Economics, no. 21 (Washington: Institute for International Economics, 1987), chap. 6.

a chief component of the supporting coalition, and not without reason, for their output has been a central, and until recently, growing source of comparative advantage for the United States.[14] So successful were these export-oriented trade politics that many American unions were among the supporters of negotiations to liberalize trade.

Insofar as this export push mostly meant the dismantling or reduction of foreign trade barriers on a most-favored-nation basis, it posed no problems for economists or liberal trade adherents. They could cheer wholeheartedly, since such negotiating efforts, if successful, would (by their analyses) increase both national and global welfare. The fact that, outside of agriculture, private sector export advocates tended not to take the initiative, but rather to be on call for Johnson and others, only added to the flexibility of policy leaders and hence to their capacity to tilt U.S. trade politics in a market-expanding direction.

This emphasis on exports belies the "soft" label characteristically stuck on U.S. negotiators. For in practice the negotiators were leaning against the political winds. The path of least resistance in regard to Japan, for example, would almost always have been to negotiate voluntary restraint agreements. Such agreements responded to pressures on Washington and were far easier politically in Tokyo than easing or removing beef and citrus quotas. U.S. officials did of course resort to the agreements from time to time but preferred to push for trade-expanding measures. By tilting toward export market negotiations and away from import management, they took the tougher road.

But for the approach to retain its basically liberal character, it had to depend on continued support of open trade from export-minded industries. And this, in turn, depended on these industries' market experience. One could hardly expect them to give priority to liberal economic doctrine if their bottom lines were shrinking or even changing color, and if trade competition, particularly "unfair" competition, seemed to be to blame. Hence the move documented by Helen Milner and David Yoffie: industries like semiconductors and telecommunications have shifted from general to conditional supporters of free trade, the condition being reciprocal access to foreign markets.[15]

---

14. See, for example Robert Z. Lawrence, *Can America Compete?* (Brookings, 1984).

15. Helen V. Milner and David B. Yoffie, "Between Free Trade and Protectionism: Strategic Trade Policy and a Theory of Corporate Trade Demands," *International Organization,* vol. 43 (Spring 1989), pp. 239–72.

It was natural, and to some extent politically necessary, for executive branch trade brokers to respond to this shift, to edge toward sectoral reciprocity arrangements. Hence the semiconductor agreement and sanctions discussed in Tyson's paper. A logical outgrowth of the growing trade frustration of leading U.S. industries is also the 1989 report of the U.S. Trade Representative advisory committee calling for a "results-oriented trade policy" to open Japanese markets, negotiating sectoral Japanese import targets, and invoking prompt sanctions if the targets are not met.[16]

Political dependence on opportunities for export expansion can also drive officials toward bilateralism. It is hardly surprising that U.S. Trade Representative (1981–85) William Brock's interest in bilateral free trade arrangements increased after the GATT Ministerial Conference of 1982 ended in sharp and public disagreement. He needed some running room, a credible avenue to future trade expansion, in order to ward off those on the protectionist side. If the Europeans were reluctant to provide it, perhaps the Canadians would, and this possibility would help him in keeping the trade-expansion game going.

Pressure to press export expansion in ways that might conflict with GATT doctrine could only be increased, of course, by the emergence of twelve-digit trade deficits. For these have, as everyone knows, cast an enormous political shadow over trade policy in Washington. The expert consensus, endorsed by all three papers, is one I certainly share: the United States is primarily responsible for creating, and, I hope, eliminating, its trade imbalance, and this task is one for macroeconomic policy, not trade policy. At most, successful export bargaining can play a facilitative role. It can improve the composition of U.S. adjustment, allowing production expansion in areas of comparative advantage and reducing the amount of dollar depreciation that is required.

But the persistent U.S. trade deficit puts U.S. negotiators on the political defensive in Washington. It increases distrust in Congress and the resulting propensity to curtail executive discretion. Consequently, more than ever, executive leaders feel a need to show toughness toward trading partners. They must identify with the interests of trade-minded U.S. producers in order to maintain political support and policy leeway.

If one adds to this potent brew a healthy dose of techno-nationalism— anxieties about Japan taking the lead; the limitations of everybody's

16. Advisory Committee for Trade Policy and Negotiations, "Analysis of the U.S.-Japan Trade Problem," Report to Carla Hills, Washington, February 1989.

doctrines in explaining Japan's remarkable economic success; the productivity slowdown and middle-class squeeze in the United States—it is hardly surprising that liberal trade ideology lacks the overwhelming elite support that it enjoyed a generation ago. It is remarkable, perhaps, that it retains as much allegiance as it does.

Given these circumstances, one could hardly expect U.S. trade policy leaders to screen export action opportunities through a fine liberal sieve, to eschew those that might bring trade-distorting as well as trade-creating effects. One could hardly expect officials to close their ears and their doors to vocal, internationally minded industries when these interests slide from allegiance to openness per se to advocacy of managed and conditional openness. Governmental practitioners' ability to resist trade-restrictive pressures has depended on the existence of a credible, ongoing process of export expansion. It is hard to retain credibility if officials refuse to consider the concerns of the Semiconductor Industry Association, for example, when its members are seeking access to Japan's market and can argue with some plausibility that their products face informal but effective import barriers.

And once officials do decide to press such a case and pursue sector-specific negotiations, it is hard not to use access to the U.S. market as a bargaining chip. After all, the integrated Japanese electronics firms, Hitachi, Fujitsu, Nippon Electric, and others, have a stake in selling chips (or telecommunications equipment) in the United States. The prospect of reduced sales abroad might make them more amenable to market-opening steps at home. It is also hard to resist such devices as quantitative export targets, with sanctions for noncompliance. For if the barriers are invisible, the only way to be sure they have been eased is to hear the cash registers ring.

Thus the emphasis on export bargaining that was, for Cordell Hull and his successors, a politically astute means of expanding two-way trade, risks becoming in today's environment an end in itself. The United States used to say it would reduce its tariffs in return for other countries cutting theirs. Now, in some instances, the United States says it will increase tariffs if others do not open their markets. "Reciprocity" used to refer to the balance of concessions in a specific negotiation. Now, it increasingly refers to the balance of market conditions.

Will current U.S. superaggressiveness on exports prove transitory, a short-term means of coping with an unusual imbalance in trade and trade politics? Or does it signal a transition to a very different sort of U.S. trade policy?

If the answer to the first question proves affirmative, then specific reciprocity, Super 301, and so on can be viewed as modest tactical responses to the current situation of extraordinary trade imbalances: responses less protectionist than plausible alternatives, and likely to be relaxed once the United States gets its economic house in better order and international imbalances are reduced.

But the United States could be in transition to a different trade policy, one with a clearly mercantilist emphasis, making the relative commercial advantage for U.S. firms the overriding goal, and perhaps integrating trade policy with a broader U.S. microeconomic strategy.

Whether such a shift is desirable is the question around which this book was organized. Thus far I have dodged it by focusing on understanding the dynamics of U.S. trade politics. The evolution of such politics has led to the conclusion that some shift in the direction prescribed by Dornbusch or Tyson was politically inevitable, and perhaps even desirable to save the basic, liberal orientation of policy. But the ultimate substantive question remains the one put forth by Jeffrey Schott during discussion—whether alternative policies promise the nation, at the margin, better outcomes than traditional liberal policies do.

The burden of critics goes beyond establishing the presence of economic sin. It goes to showing how, in real situations, actions taken pursuant to liberal principles harm the nation and how alternatives would help. Arguments for liberal policies are not weakened by the obvious point that the world is rife with violations of the GATT (or Economics 101) principles. No one claims that other governments, in their trade interventions, act as reliable maximizers of collective national welfare. And although invoking Jospeh Schumpeter may be useful in underscoring the limits of David Ricardo, or the broader limits of the liberal approach in addressing changes in comparative advantage over time, it tends to raise as many questions as it answers. Even if, for example, one concludes that technology is a key and that firms systematically under-invest in it, that does not prove that trade intervention is the appropriate response.

Hence one can accept Tyson's assertion that the second best may be the best substantive policy that is politically achievable, and one can still reject the argument that a variant of managed trade would be better for U.S. welfare than the course that Krueger continues to champion. One can also find Krueger's political analysis insufficient without rejecting her basic, substantive position.

Robert B. Reich

In trade policy, as in most other areas of public policymaking, the way choices are posed and goals tacitly accepted can make all the difference. The three papers and discussions of them have been interesting and useful, but they have not sufficiently clarified the policy options the United States now faces in international trade, nor have they explicitly defined the goals that the options are designed to serve.

What Is Free Trade?

Surely the choice is not between free trade and managed trade. Anne O. Krueger's thoughtful defense of the neoclassical ideal of free trade notwithstanding, this ideal is no option in today's world in which formal tariffs and quotas are being superseded by a wide range of what are euphemistically called nontariff barriers.

Formal tariffs and quotas clearly block trade; their purposes and effects are indisputable. But what is one to make of a recent ruling by the Federal Communications Commission, for example, that Japan's technical standard for high-definition television will not be acceptable in the United States because it will render obsolete television sets now in
· use? The effect of this ruling is to block, or seriously impede, Japanese manufacturers of high-definition televisions from selling their products in the United States. But that is not the ruling's purpose, or at least not its avowed purpose. Similar examples could be found for a wide range of government policies, here and abroad, whose explicit purposes affect public health and safety, the environment, national defense, public procurement, publicly supported research and development, antitrust, intellectual property, standards of compatibility, and so on, but whose effects are to burden foreign manufacturers who wish to sell their wares in other countries.

A definition of nontariff barrier that turned on whether the policy in question burdened foreign producers wishing to sell in the domestic market presumably would include every instance in which the citizens of the importing nation preferred a higher degree of safety, environmental cleanliness, compatibility with older appliances, or whatever, than citizens of most other nations. Obviously, such a definition is unworkable. If one nation's citizens wish to pay more for products that are safe or do less damage to the environment or are more compatible with older appliances than the products that foreign producers are offering, and such citizens collectively decide, perhaps because of perceived externalities, that they do not want the option of purchasing the cheaper product, that decision should not be classified as a nontariff barrier.

Even if one tries to draw the circle a bit tighter by defining nontariff barrier as any policy that imposes a higher burden on foreign producers than on domestic producers, one soon discovers many of the same difficulties. Domestic producers inevitably will have somewhat different attributes than foreign producers, in access to raw materials, level of technological development, labor costs, or any number of special assets. Thus, a government policy that was absolutely neutral on its face, which imposed exactly the same requirements on domestic and foreign producers, might well have the effect of favoring domestic producers over foreign ones if domestic producers, by virtue of their unique attributes, could meet the requirements at a lower cost than the foreign producers. Japan's complex system of product distribution, for example, applies to all producers, domestic and foreign alike, but clearly favors Japanese producers who have far more experience and other specialized assets appropriate to circumnavigating the complex system than do foreign producers. America's policy of barring lobsters smaller than a specified size clearly favors American lobstermen who have special equipment and access to certain coastal waters ideal for catching larger lobsters.

Indeed, virtually any domestic policy that is incompatible with policies of the foreign producer's home actions can be discriminatory, in the sense that it can prevent the foreign producer from gaining certain economies of scale at home that can then be applied to the export market. To be sure, such incompatibility puts the domestic manufacturer in precisely the same boat, with regard to potential sales in the foreign market. But the incompatibility might impose a special handicap on the foreign producer if it prevents him from gaining a scale efficiency in some aspect of production or sales in which he otherwise would have a particular advantage over domestic producers. Incompatibility would also impose a special burden on the foreign producer if the domestic market is large and lucrative relative to incompatible markets in which the foreign producer already has made marketing investments and established a leading position.

It is no answer to suggest that one look to the underlying purpose of the domestic policy and ask whether—regardless of justification—it is motivated by a desire to block (or otherwise burden) imports. Given that most legislation and most regulations emerge from a confluence of motives rather than from a single rationale, such an inquiry is almost always inconclusive. It could not function as a standard of international trade.

In sum, formal tariffs and quotas are easily recognizable, and their elimination or reduction is a step toward free trade. But nations are moving into a world of nontariff barriers that reflect national preferences for all sorts of things unrelated to trade. Because one cannot separate legitimate from illegitimate barriers, one has no a priori standard for determining what is "free." Thus, the free trade ideal no longer has an operational meaning, short of international agreement about how it is to be defined.

What Is Managed Trade?

The term "managed trade" conjures up all sorts of government restrictions and intrusions on what is an otherwise free trading system. But once one accepts the proposition that free trade has no meaning apart from international agreement about how it is to be defined, then the distinction between free trade and managed trade collapses. The international agreement itself is a form of management.

The real policy choices concern how trade is to be managed—what is to be the area of potential agreement, who is to be party to it, and how it is to be enforced. Laura D'Andrea Tyson and Rudiger W. Dornbusch presented several alternative ways of viewing the matter, but it may be useful to set out four variables:

—*Rule oriented or outcome oriented.* Agreements may emphasize rules or outcomes. The GATT, for example, is a system of rules; the steel agreements negotiated between the United States and most foreign steel producers constitute a system of outcomes. The two categories are not airtight, however. Rules may be designed with certain outcomes in mind. Likewise, an agreement on outcomes may, in practice, evolve into a system of rules designed to achieve certain outcomes.

—*Sectoral or uniform.* Agreements may or may not be limited to specific technologies, industries, or sectors. Here again, however, the choice is not absolute. Even the GATT excludes certain industries (like agriculture) and sectors (services).

—*Aggressive or passive.* Agreements may be enforced aggressively, by the implicit or tacit threat to close the domestic market (and effectively withdraw from the agreement); or they may be enforced passively, through previously agreed-on procedures for handling such disputes and penalizing wrongdoers. Once again, the choice is often more subtle than this dichotomy suggests, since tacit threats of market withdrawal may guide the creation (or alteration) of agreements about how to handle future disputes.

—*Bilateral or multilateral.* Agreements may be multilateral in which any signator gains the same access and must grant the same access as that enjoyed by any other signator; or they may be more limited. But again, the choice is less stark than meets the eye. Even broad, multilateral agreements, like the GATT, comprise only a limited number of countries; many agreements that are regarded as bilateral evolve into broader agreements. To the extent that Europe, East Asia, and the Americas develop into specialized trading blocs, they may be characterized both multilaterally and bilaterally—multilateral agreements within the bloc, coupled with bilateral agreements among the blocs.

Each choice, in other words, is a matter of degree. And since there are at least these four categories of choice, there are many combinations through which trade might be managed. Is a particular trade agreement or trade policy outcome oriented, sectoral, aggressive, bilateralist? Is it rule oriented, uniform, passive, multilateralist? Or is it something in between?

Goals

The choice of a desirable trade strategy from this four-by-two matrix depends on the goals one seeks to accomplish through trade, and on one's faith in the capacity of government to implement such a strategy.

None of the papers discussed goals explicitly, but they are not in agreement about what the goals should be. Here again, it might be useful to list the alternatives:

—*More trade.* Both Krueger and Dornbusch suggest that the chief goal is to increase the amount (quantity and value) of goods that is traded among nations. For Krueger, free trade seems to be synonymous with more trade. I find Dornbusch's analysis more subtle, but his objective seems to be the same: the major point to be made is that bilateralism is a productive strategy for freeing trade. Nowhere do they explain exactly why more trade is an appropriate policy objective, apart from Krueger's restatement of the argument for comparative advantage, which of course assumes that in a free market more trade would not occur unless it improved the welfare of both trading partners. Dornbusch, however, seems willing to concede that more trade, as he defines it, may not be good for both partners but will be good for the United States—a point that leads to the next possible set of goals.

—*Zero-sum gains or positive-sum gains.* Dornbusch holds that U.S. trade strategy should seek to improve the standard of living of Americans, even at the possible expense of a reduced standard of living for foreign citizens. Aggressive, outcome-oriented bilateralism, for example, might be necessary, as Dornbusch suggests, to force Japan to accept more American goods, even if, as a consequence, Japan imports fewer goods from other nations that have less bargaining clout with Japan—and thus reduces the welfare of such third-party nations. Aggressive, outcome-oriented bilateralism might also be necessary to force Japan to simplify its distribution system so that American producers can enter more easily, even if the Japanese people prefer the distribution system they now have, and such a change would make them feel worse off.

There are several problems with such an approach, however. First, it may not be sustainable over time. A zero-sum trade policy may work in the short term, but it may breed political resentment in other nations, which eventually erodes their willingness to cooperate in devising and enforcing a broader system of trade relationships. Such an approach may also jeopardize other foreign-policy objectives, such as cooperation on defense or the environment. Finally, one may legitimately ask whether such a position is morally tenable in a world growing ever more interdependent, in which national boundaries are becoming less and less significant.

Although it is theoretically possible for one nation to behave strategically in such a way as to improve the welfare of its citizens at the expense of another nation's welfare, that is no argument for why the first nation should try to do so. For more than forty years the United States has been willing, in effect, to sacrifice short-term economic advantage for the sake of long-term gains to be enjoyed jointly by itself and other trading nations. The benefits of such an approach, both economic and noneconomic, have been evident. Even if a strong case could be made that Japan is now free riding upon the United States—playing a strategic game instead of assuming its appropriate responsibilities within this multilateral trading system—that is insufficient reason for why the United States should abdicate its role.

—*Relative wealth.* Some advocates of zero-sum strategic trade policy emphasize relative, as opposed to absolute, wealth. That is, they want a trade policy that leaves the United States relatively wealthier than other trading partners, even if, by consequence, everyone grows more slowly. The distinction can be observed in the following choice, which I sometimes pose to my students: suppose that with trade policy A, the U.S. economy will grow 10 percent over the next four years and the Japanese economy will grow 20 percent; with trade policy B, the U.S. economy will grow just 5 percent and the Japanese economy will grow 8 percent. Which will you choose? Most of my students choose policy A. But a large minority of students choose B. Why? Because they do not like the idea of Japan gaining in relative wealth. They imagine that they will feel poorer. Or they worry about the implications of such a relative gap for American power and influence in the world.

None of the discussants took this position, at least explicitly. But my survey of managed trade should take it into account. Policymakers, and those whom they represent, think in relative terms as well as absolute terms, and this point of view is well represented in current debates.

—*Profits for American corporations.* None of the discussants suggested that the goals should be to improve the profitability of American-owned corporations, but much of the discussion one hears about American trade policy in Washington these days assumes that this should be the goal. By this view, one should seek to improve the profitability of American-owned corporations, even if many of their employees happen to be non-Americans. By the same token, one should give no advantage to foreign-owned corporations, even if most of their employees are Americans living and working in the United States. In sectors where American corporations have a technological lead but lack scale economies, for example, the best strategy, according to this view, might be to help them penetrate large potential markets from production facilities located anywhere around the world—by means of aggressive, bilateral, sectoral negotiations. (The United States has pursued precisely this strategy, incidentally, with regard to opening the Japanese market to Motorola cellular telephones, many of which are made outside the United States.)

But such a goal may not improve the standard of living of Americans nearly to the extent that living standards would be improved if companies (both American owned and foreign owned) undertook high value-added production in the United States. Returns to financial capital are limited by how much Americans save and how wisely they invest, here and abroad. Returns to human capital have no such limits: they depend instead on how much Americans learn, including their cumulative experience on the job.

I raise this issue, not only because it is one of increasing confusion and importance, as American-owned corporations undertake more and more of their production outside the United States and as foreign-owned companies undertake an ever greater portion of their production in the United States, but also because it puts in rather stark relief the question of created comparative advantage of the sort that Tyson discusses in her paper, and which I offer as the last of the possible goals for trade policy.

—*Work force learning.* Dynamic learning effects can, over time, create a national comparative advantage in knowledge-intensive industries. But because new knowledge easily leaks out beyond the corporation—creating, for example, a Silicon Valley—investments in employee learning often are not appropriable by investors. Government subsidies might potentially overcome this problem if made available to corporations (of whatever nationality) that undertook complex production within the United States, thus providing Americans with valuable on-the-job training. Foreign nations, meanwhile, would be discouraged from blocking the resulting high value-added products. Toward this end, as Tyson suggests, the goal of trade and industrial policy is "not simply to improve the trade balance or to address external barriers abroad, but to secure a share of world production and employment in such industries with the local knowledge, skills, and other spillover benefits that they are perceived to generate."

But is this goal to be zero sum or positive sum? (Tyson is far from clear on this point, and apparently she has not made up her mind.) A zero-sum strategy might favor, for example, domestic content rules for the sale of certain high technologies in the United States, coupled with aggressive, bilateral, outcome-oriented efforts to prevent foreign nations from implementing precisely the same sort of domestic content rules in their own nation. A positive-sum approach might instead favor multilateral, rule-oriented negotiations designed to limit the total amount of such subsidies and to create a process through which nations could decide how much of that amount each of them would be allowed to utilize.

Of all these possible goals, I find most compelling a positive-sum approach to work-force learning. Others may feel differently, but it should be apparent that any discussion of trade strategy or managed trade in which such goals are not explicitly debated runs the risk that participants will be speaking past one another. In reviewing this discussion, I fear that insidious danger has prevailed.

The Capacity of Government

Whichever goal or combination of goals is favored, one might conclude in principle that, at least on occasion, an outcome-oriented, sectoral, aggressive, and/or bilateral approach to trade could better achieve it than can a more rule-oriented, uniform, passive, or multilateral approach. To take an example, the goal that I favor (a positive-sum approach that focuses on work-force learning) would seem well served by a rule-oriented, passive, multilateral strategy (more likely to have positive-sum results) geared to particular sectors characterized by significant learning effects (for example, high technologies).

And yet, one might still be reluctant to embark on such a finely tuned strategy. Why? The view is often expressed that government simply is incapable of undertaking trade strategy of this sort. Krueger is concerned, for example, that unless government were to develop appropriate procedures or mechanisms that might be used to identify potentially strategic technologies or sectors, every industry will assert the existence of important externalities—opening up a Pandora's box of special pleadings. And even with appropriate procedures, it is likely, she says, that political pressures will arise to expand the scope of policy beyond that intended and devised under the criteria and procedures. "It is in the nature of the political process that pressures will arise for extending favorable treatment to ever larger groups than those initially intended for eligibility."

When considering the capacity of government to implement policy, economists who otherwise are careful to ground their conclusions in detailed studies of prices and markets often fall back on the loosest form of anecdotal evidence, mixed with strong assertions based on "public-choice" economic doctrine. To be sure, those who seek it can find ample evidence of government's inability to form and implement microeconomic policy without succumbing to the pleasing of the loudest and best-connected constituencies.

But is one talking about all governments or just the U.S. government? Although Japan is not immune to special industry pleadings, most would agree that Japan has proved capable of undertaking a strategic trade policy, at least a policy more strategic than that employed by the United States. Some participants in the seminar agreed that while other governments, notably Japan, may be able to marshal the necessary authority and gain the requisite competence, the American government as constituted does not stand a chance.

There have been times and occasions, however, at which even the U.S. government has been quite strategic about international trade. One obvious piece of evidence is the central role played by the United States in establishing the GATT, the International Monetary Fund, the World Bank, Bretton Woods, and related mechanisms—no small accomplishment in the face of demand by particular industries and sectors for favorable treatment. Another source of evidence is found in the many industrial-development programs undertaken by the United States in the postwar era. Interestingly, those American industries that are now among the most productive and competitive—aerospace, aircraft, telecommunications, agriculture, pharmaceuticals, and biotechnology—are also the industries in which the U.S. government has been most actively involved, through public procurement, publicly funded research and development, and regulation.

As to competence in American government, it is worth noting that certain government agencies have enjoyed a high degree of competence and public trust over many years, despite their important effects on American business. I would include in such a list the Antitrust Division of the Justice Department, the Securities and Exchange Commission, the Office of Management and Budget (at least, until the second Reagan administration), the Congressional Budget Office, the Defense Advanced Research Projects Administration in the Department of Defense, and even, dare I say it, the Council of Economic Advisers. Each of these agencies has been able to attract a high-caliber professional staff. Each has proved capable of fashioning policy with the interests of the American economy as a whole in mind, rather than the interests of the loudest business constituencies. Each, moreover, has fashioned policies that, at least on occasion, have imposed special burdens on particular industries and firms—thus violating Charles L. Schultze's first rule of governance, "do no harm."

In any event, to argue that a certain course of public policy is desirable but cannot be implemented is hardly to end the conversation. If other nations are being more strategic about their trade policies than the United States is, to U.S. detriment, then it is entirely reasonable to conclude that the United States must change its ways. If this means that the way public policy is executed must change, then let the nation at least attempt to do so. An attitude of resignation about the capacities of the U.S. government to implement good or effective policy is no more justifiable than resignation over the substance of policy itself.

Contributors

ROBERT E. BALDWIN
Professor of Economics
University of Wisconsin-Madison

I. M. DESTLER
Professor, School of Public Affairs
Director, Graduate Program on Public
* Policy and Private Enterprise*
University of Maryland

AVINASH K. DIXIT
John J. F. Sherrerd 1952 University
* Professor*
Princeton University

RUDIGER W. DORNBUSCH
Ford International Professor of Economics
Massachusetts Institute of Technology
Research Associate
National Bureau of Economic Research

ANNE O. KRUEGER
Arts and Sciences Professor of Economics
Duke University

ROBERT KUTTNER
Economics Editor
New Republic

ROBERT Z. LAWRENCE
Senior Fellow
Brookings Institution

ROBERT B. REICH
Lecturer on Public Policy
John F. Kennedy School of Government
Harvard University

CHARLES L. SCHULTZE
Director, Economic Studies
Brookings Institution

LAURA D'ANDREA TYSON
Professor of Economics
University of California at Berkeley

Index